LIBRARY OF HEBREW BIBLE/
OLD TESTAMENT STUDIES

701

Formerly Journal for the Study of the Old Testament Supplement Series

Editors
Claudia V. Camp, Texas Christian University, USA
Andrew Mein, Durham University, UK

Founding Editors
David J. A. Clines, Philip R. Davies and David M. Gunn

Editorial Board
Alan Cooper, Susan Gillingham, John Goldingay,
Norman K. Gottwald, James E. Harding, John Jarick, Carol Meyers,
Daniel L. Smith-Christopher, Francesca Stavrakopoulou,
James W. Watts

PROVERBS 1–9 AS AN INTRODUCTION TO THE BOOK OF PROVERBS

Arthur Jan Keefer

t&tclark

LONDON • NEW YORK • OXFORD • NEW DELHI • SYDNEY

T&T CLARK
Bloomsbury Publishing Plc
50 Bedford Square, London, WC1B 3DP, UK
1385 Broadway, New York, NY 10018, USA
29 Earlsfort Terrace, Dublin 2, Ireland

BLOOMSBURY, T&T CLARK and the T&T Clark logo
are trademarks of Bloomsbury Publishing Plc

First published in Great Britain 2020
This paperback edition published in 2022

Copyright © Arthur Jan Keefer, 2020

Arthur Jan Keefer has asserted his right under the Copyright, Designs and Patents Act, 1988, to be identified as Author of this work.

For legal purposes the Acknowledgements on p. vii constitute an extension of this copyright page.

All rights reserved. No part of this publication may be reproduced or transmitted in any form or by any means, electronic or mechanical, including photocopying, recording, or any information storage or retrieval system, without prior permission in writing from the publishers.

Bloomsbury Publishing Plc does not have any control over, or responsibility for, any third-party websites referred to or in this book. All internet addresses given in this book were correct at the time of going to press. The author and publisher regret any inconvenience caused if addresses have changed or sites have ceased to exist, but can accept no responsibility for any such changes.

A catalogue record for this book is available from the British Library.
A catalog record for this book is available from the Library of Congress.

ISBN: HB: 978-0-5676-9334-1
PB: 978-0-5676-9690-8
ePDF: 978-0-5676-9335-8

Series: Library of Hebrew Bible/Old Testament Studies, ISSN 2513-8758, volume 701

Typeset by: Forthcoming Publications Ltd

To find out more about our authors and books visit www.bloomsbury.com and sign up for our newsletters.

Contents

Acknowledgements   vii
List of Abbreviations   ix

Chapter 1
INTRODUCTION   1
    1.1. Proverbs 1.1-7 and the Didactic Function of Proverbs 1–9   4
    1.2. Prologues in Biblical Wisdom and in Ancient Near Eastern Texts   7
    1.3. Early Interpretations of Proverbs 1–9 as an 'Introduction'   15
    1.4. Current Interpretations of Proverbs 1–9 as an 'Introduction'   17
       1.4.1. Proverbs 1–9 as an Introduction   17
       1.4.2. Proverbs 1–9 as an Independent Section   21
    1.5. Conclusions on Context   27
    1.6. Methodology: A Macro-Redactional Approach   28
    1.7. Two Methodological Avenues to Proverbs   35
    1.8. Outline of Chapters   38

Chapter 2
CHARACTER TYPES   46
    2.1. The Identity of Character Types   51
       2.1.1. Character Types in Proverbs 10.1-5   51
       2.1.2. Character Types in Proverbs 1–9   55
       2.1.3. Character Types Outside of the Book of Proverbs   64
       2.1.4. The Function of Proverbs 1–9 for Proverbs 10.1-5   67
       2.1.5. Conclusion   72
    2.2. The Rhetoric of Character Types   72
       2.2.1. Character Types in Proverbs 10.1–22.16   76
       2.2.2. Character Types in Proverbs 1–9   79
       2.2.3. The Function of Proverbs 1–9 for 15.2 and 18.2   82
       2.2.4. The Function of Proverbs 1–9 for 29.11   87
       2.2.5. Conclusion   90

Chapter 3
EDUCATIONAL GOALS 93
 3.1. The Aims and Values of Proverbs 94
  3.1.1. Educational Goals in Proverbs 10.1–22.16 94
  3.1.2. Educational Goals in Proverbs 1–9 100
  3.1.3. The Function of Proverbs 1–9 for Proverbs 22.1 111
  3.1.4. Proverbs 30 116
  3.1.5. Conclusion 126
 3.2. Discerning Moral Ambiguity 128
  3.2.1. Moral Ambiguity in Proverbs 1–9 129
  3.2.2. Moral Ambiguity in Proverbs 10–29 132
  3.2.3. The Function of Proverbs 1–9 for Proverbs 18.8 and 14.12 139
  3.2.4. Conclusion and Implications 140

Chapter 4
THEOLOGICAL CONTEXT 143
 4.1. Human Postures towards the Lord 145
  4.1.1. Human Postures towards the Lord in Proverbs 16.3 145
  4.1.2. Human Postures towards the Lord in Proverbs 1–9 148
 4.2. The Supremacy of the Lord's Wisdom and Sovereignty 151
  4.2.1. Wisdom and Sovereignty in Proverbs 16.9 151
  4.2.2. Wisdom and Sovereignty in Proverbs 1–9 154
  4.2.3. The Function of Proverbs 1–9 for 16.9 158
  4.2.4. Summary of Proverbs 16.3 and 16.9 160
  4.2.5. The Function of Proverbs 1–9 for Human Postures
   and the Lord's Supremacy in Proverbs 22.17-21 161
  4.2.6. Conclusion 167
 4.3. The Lord's Affection and Assessment 167
  4.3.1. The Lord's Affection and Assessment in Proverbs 16.2 168
  4.3.2. The Lord's Affection and Assessment in Proverbs 1–9 171
  4.3.3. The Function of Proverbs 1–9 for 16.2 177
  4.3.4. The Qualifications and Context of Proverbs 1–9
   as an Introduction 179
  4.3.5. Conclusion 180

Bibliography 184
Index of References 192
Index of Authors 203

Acknowledgements

The longer I worked on this project, the clearer its complexity and importance became. Clearer too was my understanding of why no one had yet addressed the status of Proverbs 1–9 as an introduction at a book's length. Thankfully, there have been several people who made my attempt possible and, perhaps, plausible, including Professor C. John ('Jack') Collins, who inspired the idea, and Dr. Katharine Dell, who accepted a bare form of this proposal and supervised it at the University of Cambridge, encouraging me at the right times and cautioning me in those moments when humility and prudence were most needed. Dr. Nathan MacDonald also read a bulk of this work in its dissertation form, all of which was examined by Dr. Alison Gray and Professor Stuart Weeks, whose formidable appraisal made the work publishable. Two reviewers for LHBOTS and Claudia Camp gave charitable feedback on the manuscript, and Duncan Burns was a great help during the production stage. Any errors or shortcomings are certainly my own. Clare College, Cambridge provided a space where the results of this study, prior to being in print, could benefit students and also supplied a generous scholarship during two years of my research. I am indebted to the resources of Tyndale House library and grateful for the professional and personal direction of friends like David Illman, Dr. Richard Oosterhoff, the Rev. Dr. James Hawkey, and many colleagues unnamed here.

My parents have always supported my studies, not least financially, and continue to see the value of biblical studies for the church and world. My brother, Forrest, checked in on the process more than anyone else, from the start of this book to its conclusion, and Emem, my wife, though no expert in Hebrew or the norms of biblical research, is expert in asking the right questions and encouraging me in the right way. Her love and friendship have shaped, more than anything, my character, and for her I am immensely grateful.

List of Abbreviations

AB	Anchor Bible
AEL	Miriam Lichtheim, *Ancient Egyptian Literature: A Book of Readings*, 3 Vols. Berkeley: University of California Press, 1973–80
ANE	Ancient Near East(ern)
ANET	James B. Pritchard, *Ancient Near Eastern Texts Relating to the Old Testament.* Princeton: Princeton University Press, 1950
AOTC	Apollos Old Testament Commentary
BBR	*Bulletin for Biblical Research*
BKAT	Biblischer Kommentar Altes Testement
BZAW	Beihefte zur Zeitschrift für die alttestamentliche Wissenschaft
CAD	*The Assyrian Dictionary of the Oriental Institute of the University of Chicago.* Chicago: Oriental Institute, 1956–
CBQ	*Catholic Biblical Quarterly*
CBQMS	Catholic Biblical Quarterly Monograph Series
CBR	*Currents in Biblical Research*
BCOT	Baker Commentary on the Old Testament
ESV	English Standard Version
FAT	Forschung zum Alten Testament
GKC	*Gensenius' Hebrew Grammar*, edited and enlarged by E. Kautzsch, trans. A. E. Cowley, 2nd ed. Oxford: Clarendon, 1910; repr. with corrections, 1966
HCOT	Historical Commentary on the Old Testament
IBHS	Bruce K. Waltke and M. O'Connor, *Introduction to Biblical Hebrew Syntax*. Winona Lake, IN: Eisenbrauns, 1990
ICC	International Critical Commentary
JBL	*Journal of Biblical Literature*
JETS	*Journal of the Evangelical Theological Society*
JHS	*Journal of Hebrew Scriptures*
JM	Paul Joüon and T. Muraoka, *A Grammar of Biblical Hebrew*. 2nd ed. Subsidia Biblica 27. Rome: Gregorian and Biblical Press, 2011
JNSL	*Journal of Northwest Semitic Languages*
JSCE	*Journal of the Society of Christian Ethics*
JSJSupp	Supplements to the Journal for the Study of Judaism
JSOT	*Journal for the Study of the Old Testament*
JTI	*Journal of Theological Interpretation*
LHBOTS	The Library of Hebrew Bible/Old Testament Studies
LXX	Septuagint

MS(S)	manuscript(s)
MT	Masoretic Text
NASB	New American Standard Bible
NIB	*The New Interpreter's Bible: General Articles & Introduction, Commentary, & Reflections for Each Book of the Bible, Including the Apocryphal/Deuterocanonical Books*, ed. Richard Clifford, vol. 5. Nashville: Abingdon Press, 1994
NICOT	The New International Commentary on the Old Testament
NIDOTTE	*New International Dictionary of Old Testament Theology and Exegesis*, ed. William A. VanGemeren, 5 vols. Grand Rapids: Zondervan, 1997
NIV	New International Version
NRSV	New Revised Standard Version
OBO	Orbis Biblicus et Orientalis
OT	Old Testament
OTE	*Old Testament Essays*
OTL	Old Testament Library
SOTS	Society for Old Testament Study
Syr	Syriac
TDOT	*Theological Dictionary of the Old Testament*, ed. G. J. Botterweck et al., trans. D. E. Green et al., 15 vols. Grand Rapids: Eerdmans, 1974–2015
TOTC	Tyndale Old Testament Commentaries
TWOT	Bruce K. Waltke, R. Laird Harris, and Gleason Archer, *Theological Wordbook of the Old Testament*. Chicago: Moody, 1980
VT	*Vetus Testamentum*
VTSup	Supplements to Vetus Testamentum
WBC	Word Bible Commentary
ZAW	*Zeitschrift für die Alttestamentliche Wissenschaft*

1

INTRODUCTION

The first nine chapters of the book of Proverbs are often labelled an 'introduction' or 'prologue' for the remainder of the book, and in this monograph that claim is put to question. The root of the issue is not what exactly is or could be meant by 'introduction'; it is instead an issue of function. How does Proverbs 1–9 function within the book as a whole? Few studies have properly articulated the function of Proverbs 1–9, and no study, beyond suggesting a couple of examples, has clearly demonstrated in depth how it operates, especially as it precedes and juxtaposes with Prov. 10.1–22.16.[1] This latter portion of text, being a collection of proverbs with pithy literary forms, contrasts with the initial chapters of the book, Proverbs 1–9, which contains lengthy poems, developed and storied scenarios, and predominately second- rather than third-person address.[2] For a section of biblical material that has been referred to as an 'introduction' for so long, it is surprising that so little has been shown regarding its introductory nature, not least how it may inform the meaning of the proverbs that follow it. The present work aims to determine and demonstrate how Proverbs 1–9 operates for the rest of Proverbs, providing the justification and guidelines for those who wish to treat 1–9 as an 'introduction'.

The argument revolves around two aspects of Proverbs, namely, the interpretive challenges posed by Proverbs 10–29 and the interpretive promises made in Prov. 1.1-7. The proverbs within chapters 10–29 pose challenges for at least two interrelated reasons: first, their assumptions and second, their brevity. By assumptions, I mean the information or mental faculties that the proverbs require for interpretation, information

1. See the discussion below.
2. Proverbs 1–9 might be viewed as a 'collection' of poems and instructions. Though preferring standard chapter and verse references, I adopt the accepted language of 'Collection I' for Proverbs 1–9 and 'Collection II' for Prov. 10.1–22.16.

that is often latent within proverbial sayings due to their pithy nature. For example, Prov. 16.3 baldly commands the reader to 'Commit your work to the Lord', implying that the Lord is worthy of trust.[3] To questions like, 'why should I trust the Lord?', Prov. 10.1–22.16 provides a limited set of answers: if you trust the Lord then 'your plans will be established' (16.3b), or trust the Lord because he is wise and in control (16.1, 9); trust him because he dispenses hatred, favour and punishment to humans (16.5; 12.2; 21.3). These texts establish a notably affective and transcendent God and yet, outside of his bald power and recompense, they offer little incentive to trust him and most importantly make little explicit connection between human trust in God and a justification for it. While not true of every proverb, many of them, like 16.3, deliver intriguing hermeneutical challenges. Some leave obvious questions unanswered while others call for additional insight, each inviting the reader to seek a fuller sense of meaning.[4]

This is the point in the interpretive quest at which a reader might turn to Prov. 1.1-7 for guidance. For it promises the acquisition of interpretive skill in order that its audience might 'understand words of insight…a proverb and a saying, the words of the wise and their riddles' (1.2b, 6). As explained in full below, this inaugural promise accounts for the difficulties of Proverbs 10–29 by telling the audience that they will be able to comprehend its enigmatic material, denoted here as 'proverbs' and 'sayings' (1.6) which, I will argue, refer to the content of Proverbs 10–29 and corroborate its challenging nature. Proverbs 1.1-7 indicates

---

3. Throughout this study, I use 'God' and 'the Lord' to refer respectively to אלהים and יהוה, and 'wisdom' and 'Wisdom' to distinguish between the concept of wisdom and the personified, female figure, often called Lady Wisdom.

4. Other proverbs and pithy literary forms from the ancient Near East exhibited difficulties for their interpreters. Certain Sumerian proverbs were supplemented with 'explanatory additions', and pithy, metaphor-loaded sentences within omen texts of Mesopotamia received explanatory comments. For instance, 'Mesopotamian scholars often felt a need to provide "factual" information on omen protases, either because they were too unspecific, too cryptic, or so unrealistic that a re-interpretation was necessary to make them applicable' (Eckart Frahm, *Babylonian and Assyrian Text Commentaries: Origins of Interpretation*, Guides to the Mesopotamian Textual Record 5 [Münster: Ugarit Verlag, 2011], 79; see also 69, 80–5, 336). Certain mistranslations and misinterpretations of the Mesopotamian texts, though, were due not so much to brevity but to outdated forms of language. For 'explanatory additions' of Sumerian proverbs, see Bendt Alster, *Proverbs of Ancient Sumer: The World's Earliest Proverb Collections* (Bethesda, MD: CDL, 1997), xxviii. Thanks is due to Yoram Cohen for his personal correspondence about this scholarly discussion.

that Proverbs itself will enable the reader to make sense of these materials, that is, 'to understand words of insight…a proverb and a saying, the words of the wise and their riddles' (1.2b, 6).

Both the challenges of Proverbs 10–29 and the promises of 1.1-7 suggest that an interpretive need and its solution reside within the book of Proverbs itself, fortifying the hypothesis that Proverbs 1–9 functions in some discoverable way for much of the book.[5] I argue that Proverbs 1–9 is that very portion of Proverbs which provides insights into the terse sayings and certain perplexities of the book, that it functions didactically by helping its audience to understand the material in Proverbs 10–31. Now, this does not mean that the proverbial material stands before the interpreter as an impenetrable text unless an aid, such as Proverbs 1–9, comes to the rescue. It means that a portion of Proverbs offers insight into material that appears in certain ways challenging largely due to its terse proverbial form and tight, poetic content. My suggestion is that when Proverbs is read as a whole, 1–9 furnishes insights into certain challenges of 10–31, namely those related to character types, educational goals, and references to the Lord, and in this way functions didactically.

Focusing on these three areas, the bulk of my work will articulate and demonstrate the role of Proverbs 1–9 through an extended treatment of examples from Prov. 10.1–22.16, since it provides a larger and formally more consistent section than 22.17–31.31. However, I include selected examples from the remaining material for each topic, incorporating the character types of Prov. 29.1, the educational goals of 30.1-9, and the theology of 22.19, to extend the hermeneutical reach of Proverbs 1–9 to passages representative of the entire book. In addition to the text of Proverbs itself, two things prompt a study into the function of Proverbs 1–9: first, the long-voiced proposals from interpreters about the nature of this section and second, a cross-comparison of Proverbs 1–9 with its ancient Near Eastern counterparts. This chapter accounts for each of

---

5. Briefly examining the relationship between Proverbs 1–9 and 10–22, Richard Clifford ('Reading Proverbs 10–22', *Interpretation* 63 [2009]: 244, also 245–6) moves in this direction but in much less detail than I do. Beginning with Proverbs 10–22, he says that 'Reading through such a collection is like wandering into a tool shed and wondering what all the instruments hanging on the wall are meant to do'. According to Clifford, Proverbs 10–22 seems to lack a context – perhaps more precisely, an explanatory framework – and thus poses a particular challenge to the interpreter. Clifford argues that Proverbs 1–9 provides just such a context for the sentence literature, and that it does so in three ways: it establishes the narrative context of the book; it clarifies the divine origins of the proverbs; and it reminds the reader of the importance of memory and learning.

these, taking stock of the book's opening comments (1.1-7), assessing the relationship of Proverbs 1–9 to examples from the wider ancient Near Eastern world, and tracing the history of labelling 1–9 as a prologue. It then lays out a methodology and a summary of my argument.

1.1. *Proverbs 1.1-7 and the Didactic Function of Proverbs 1–9*

I mentioned that Prov. 1.2 and 1.6 account for the interpretive challenges of Proverbs 10–29 by telling the audience that they will be able to interpret the book's enigmatic material. Riddled with diachronic debates, the redactional history of these passages and Proverbs as a whole requires attention and is addressed later. At this point, a closer look at the language of 1.1-7 will both validate and clarify the possible function of 1–9 and the best point of entry into Proverbs. As the opening verses of the book, 1.1-7 itemizes the goals and key concepts of Proverbs, claiming that the audience will know wisdom and instruction (1.2) and receive training in justice and equity (1.3). To these activities, 1.6 adds that the book offers expertise in literary interpretation: 'to understand/explicate a proverb and a saying, the words of the wise and their riddles' (להבין משל ומליצה דברי חכמים וחידתם). What I have translated 'to understand/explicate' comes from the *hiphil* בין that occurs here, as it does also in 1.2, and yet it carries a distinct sense in each verse. The *hiphil* בין can resemble the *qal*, meaning 'learn', 'understand', and especially 'discern' (1 Kgs 3.9, 11; Prov. 8.5; 14.8; 28.11), which, involving more than heeding or grasping cognitively, elsewhere refers to capturing the true sense of information that is prone to being misunderstood (Prov. 8.9; Neh. 8.2-3; Dan. 8.23, 27; cf. Ps. 119.34). This sense of the *qal* fits with the *hiphil* occurrence in Prov. 1.2, as the interpreter will 'understand' learned sayings. However, *hiphil* בין sometimes carries a causative nuance of 'teach' or 'explicate', as in Nehemiah when the priests 'explicate' the law to the people (Neh. 8.7, 9; cf. 8.8), and in the book of Job when Job asks the Lord to teach and to 'make him understand' how he erred (Job 6.24; see also Ps. 119.130, 144, 169; Isa. 28.9). This sense of 'explicate' – that is, 'interpret' in the sense of 'explain the meaning of' – suits Prov. 1.6, as readers may 'explicate a proverb and an epigram, the words of the wise and their riddles'.[6]

---

6. These general senses of the *qal* and *hiphil* are often affirmed, but when interpreting Prov. 1.6 the *hiphil* occurrence is recognized as 'understand' without comment (see, e.g., Helmer Ringgren, 'בִּין *bîn*', *TDOT* 2:102–3). As an exception, J. A. Loader (*Proverbs 1–9*, HCOT [Leuven: Peeters, 2014], 61–2) defends the meaning of 'explicate' here.

In addition to the verbs of 1.2 and 1.6, the literary lexemes of 1.6 in the context of the opening verses of Proverbs suggest that the book aims to inculcate interpretive competence. The lexeme משל ('proverb') refers at least to the pithy sayings of Collection II (10.1, משלי שלמה), while דברי חכמים ('words of the wise') reappears in 22.17, referring to the text of Proverbs itself: 'Incline your ear and hear *the words of the wise*; apply your heart to my knowledge'. While 'proverbs' and 'words of the wise' clearly refer to material within Proverbs, the more enigmatic lexemes of 1.6 – מליצה ('[dark] saying') and חידת ('riddles') – have produced more contention with regard to their meaning.[7] For מליצה appears only once outside of Prov. 1.6 (Hab. 2.6) and there it parallels חידות and משל. The lexeme חידה appears more frequently than מליצה and often refers to something that requires interpretation (Judg. 14.12-19; Num. 12.8; Dan. 8.23) and even challenges understanding (1 Kgs 10.1; 2 Chron. 9.1).[8]

Aside from the precise meaning of these lexemes and the literary form or content to which they might refer, they all signify enigmatic material that requires interpretation and, taken together, call for hermeneutical application.[9] Timothy Sandoval has hypothesized about the significance of these lexemes for Prov. 10.1–22.16 when he writes that they 'alert the reader to the interpretive efforts one will need to undertake as one continues reading the book.... The one who reads past the prologue should expect to encounter a complex piece of literature and a challenging interpretive process'.[10] In short, משל, דברי חכמים, מליצה and חידת refer to the literature of Proverbs itself, enigmatic material that Prov. 1.6 claims the reader will be able to unravel.

---

7. See William McKane, 'Functions of Language and Objectives of Discourse according to Proverbs 10–30', in *La Sagesse de l'Ancien Testament*, ed. Maurice Gilbert (Leuven: Leuven University Press, 1979), 166–85; A. S. Herbert, 'The "Parable" (MĀŠĀL) in the Old Testament', *SJT* 7 (1954): 180–96.

8. Stuart Weeks (*Instruction and Imagery in Proverbs 1–9* [Oxford: Oxford University Press, 2007], 41 n. 17) attributes the least enigmatic meaning to these 'riddles' (חידה) when he writes that, in Ps. 78.2, the term 'is used to refer to the recitation of quite unmysterious events in history'. However, he still acknowledges that Prov. 1.6 indicates 'a recognition that wisdom literature may be obscure and require interpretation'. See also Michael V. Fox, *Proverbs 1–9: A New Translation with Introduction and Commentary*, AB 18A (New York: Doubleday, 2000), 63–7; cf. W. T. Davison, *The Wisdom-Literature of the Old Testament* (London: Charles H. Kelly, 1900), 124.

9. Bruce K. Waltke, *The Book of Proverbs: Chapters 1–15*, NICOT (Grand Rapids, MI: Eerdmans, 2004), 180.

10. Timothy Sandoval, 'Revisiting the Prologue of Proverbs', *JBL* 126 (2007): 469, 471.

It seems that Prov. 1.6 simply reiterates a point already made in 1.2, which promises the audience that they will understand the wisdom of Proverbs. However, Prov. 1.6 does not simply reaffirm this, claiming the reader will understand the enigmatic material, but rather adds a notion of 'explicate'. This concept coheres with other statements in 1.1-7, particularly the promise that the interpreter will teach 'simpletons' and 'youth[s]' (1.4) and acquire educational competencies (1.5).[11] Expecting to teach such people and acquire competency, readers will not only discover the meaning of the sayings for themselves (1.2) but will interpret their meaning for others too (1.6). The Egyptian term *wh'* was used in instructional texts, where the student would 'untie' or 'explain' learned writings, as *Amenemope* says, 'Fill yourself with them, put them in your heart / And become a man who *explains* them / One who *explains* as a teacher' (XXVII.13-15).[12] Likewise, Prov. 1.1-6 indicates that its audience will be able to interpret its material in both senses of the word: to understand (1.2) and to explicate (1.6) its contents. In other words, Proverbs suggests that it proffers didactic faculties for interpreting the book itself. By 'didactic', I mean that the book intends to teach, and by 'interpret', I mean 'understand', which stands as a necessary prerequisite for the activity of 'explicating', both of which are instated by 1.2, 6.[13] Proverbs instils its readers with faculties that enable them to explicate the material within the book itself.

Proverbs 1.1-7, according to Fox, 'regards the sayings in Proverbs as *text* that must be studied and interpreted, not just heard and obeyed…[it] regards the interpretation of proverbs and enigmas as a goal in itself or views proverbs as an object of explication…wisdom as a text that requires interpretation and that trains the reader in hermeneutical skills'.[14] Fox, it seems, would agree with the train of thought given so far: that Proverbs trains the interpreter, functioning didactically to help those who approach

---

11. See Arthur Keefer, 'A Shift in Perspective: The Intended Audience and a Coherent Reading of Proverbs 1:1-7', *JBL* 136 (2017): 103–16.

12. Nili Shupak, *Where Can Wisdom Be Found? The Sage's Language in the Bible and in Ancient Egyptian Literature*, OBO 130 (Fribourg: Academic Press Fribourg, 1993), 63–5. See also Fox (*Proverbs 1–9*, 76–8), who claims that the *hiphil* בין in 1.6 is not causative, though he overlooks occurrences of the term (listed above) and his later comments support my position.

13. These definitions correspond to the *Oxford English Dictionary*'s first two entries for 'interpret': '1.a. To expound the meaning of (something abstruse or mysterious); to render (words, writings, an author, etc.) clear or explicit; to elucidate; to explain. 1.b. To make out the meaning of.'

14. Fox, *Proverbs 1–9*, 76.

its enigmatic material. However, Fox remarks that nothing in Proverbs 'actually tells *how* to penetrate and interpret the writings', as if a promise is made in Proverbs but the hermeneutical guidance is missing.[15] I contend that it is Prov. 1.2 and 1.6 that tell us how to do this, giving reason to look for a means of interpretive training within the book of Proverbs itself, and I propose that this preparatory instruction occurs in Proverbs 1–9, as it functions didactically. This function will be elucidated by showing that 1–9 supplements the interpretation of 10–31, and that it does so by complementing other sources of interpretive insight, such as historical context, OT topoi, and surrounding proverbs, but also by surpassing those sources, in cases where they do not resolve questions of meaning. I therefore demonstrate the significance, and in certain respects the interpretive authority, of Collection I for understanding and illuminating hermeneutical difficulties within the remainder of Proverbs.

1.2. *Prologues in Biblical Wisdom and in Ancient Near Eastern Texts*

Prologues in Ecclesiastes, Job, and some non-biblical ancient Near Eastern texts support the hypothesis that Proverbs 1–9 functions as a didactic guide for 10–29. A 'prologue' (1.1-11) and an 'epilogue' (12.9-14) frame Ecclesiastes, illuminating the remaining enigmatic content of the book itself.[16] Fox has given much attention to the function of these passages in Ecclesiastes and concludes that an 'Awareness of the frame-narrative gives us a fundamental insight into the proper reading of the book as a whole'.[17] According to Fox, the bookends function in stages, establishing the reality of Qohelet's character type and the interpreter's attitude towards him to create a dialogic ambiguity. The ambiguity arises from the 'unorthodox book' that is then paired with 'orthodox affirmations' found particularly in 12.9-14. The text's opening verses (1.1-2) introduce readers to Qohelet in the third person, who then speaks in the first person starting at 1.12, while the remainder of the prologue (1.3-11) includes a thesis (v. 3) and poetic reflection (vv. 4-11) that prefigure much of the book's message. Aside from issues of date, editorial process, nuances of genre, and how much

---

15. Fox, *Proverbs 1–9*, 78.
16. Craig G. Bartholomew, *Ecclesiastes*, BCOT (Grand Rapids: Baker Academic, 2009), 110.
17. Michael V. Fox, 'Frame-Narrative and Composition in the Book of Qohelet', *HUCA* 48 (1977): 105. See also Fox, *Ecclesiastes: The Traditional Hebrew Text with the New JPS Translation* (Philadelphia: Jewish Publication Society, 2004), xiii, xv–xvii.

credence is given to notions of the book's 'orthodoxy', most agree that the bookends are essential for the interpretation of the whole.[18]

The question stated in Eccl. 1.3 for example – 'What is the gain for man in all his toil at which he toils under the sun?' – creates an inquisitive framework that unifies many of the experiences and observations of Qohelet. His introductory monologue about his endeavour, then, can be read as an exposition of this question about 'gain' (יתרון) in toil (1.12-18), and his subsequent quest for pleasure in 2.1-11 explicitly falls under the rubric introduced by 1.3, as he discovers that 'there is no gain under the sun' (v. 11). The question of 1.3 thematically banners much of Ecclesiastes and perhaps invites the reader to contemplate the question itself while assessing Qohelet's answers to it.[19] The passage represents a single example of how Eccl. 1.1-11 functions as a 'prologue' for the book.

The book of Job also employs a narrative frame. Job 1–2 and 42.7-17 stand as passages essential for understanding the sections of material in Job 3.1–42.6, producing theological and hermeneutical tensions that, according to some scholars, actually create the message of the book.[20] Norman Habel has argued that the 'prologue' (Job 1–2) especially integrates with the dialogues (3.1–42.6) and even establishes the literary, rhetorical, and theological contexts of the story.[21] For example, Job 1.1-5 introduces the reader to the man Job, his exceptional character, status, and wealth, in order to provide background information for the narrative of 1.6–2.13 and 42.7-17. Job 2.11-13 then closes this narrative by depicting Job's grief and incorporating the other characters who feature in chapters 3–42, in this way preparing the reader for the dialogues that follow. Job's companions see his suffering and engage on an emotional level (2.11-13),

---

18. Choon-Leong Seow, *Ecclesiastes: A New Translation with Introduction and Commentary*, AB 18C (New York: Doubleday, 1997), 111; Bartholomew, *Ecclesiastes*, 74, 110; Andrew G. Shead, 'Ecclesiastes from the Outside In', *RTR* 55 (1996): 24–37, esp. 31; Daniel Fredericks, *Ecclesiastes & the Song of Songs*, AOTC (Downers Grove, IL: InterVarsity Press, 2010), 68–9; Leo G. Perdue, *Wisdom Literature: A Theological History* (Louisville, KY: Westminster John Knox Press, 2007), 190, 193.

19. Bartholomew, *Ecclesiastes*, 107, 110.

20. Martin A. Shields, 'Malevolent or Mysterious? God's Character in the Prologue of Job', *TynBul* 61 (2010): 255–70; see also Samuel Balentine, *Job* (Macon, GA: Smyth & Helwys, 2006), 14–15; David J. A. Clines, *Job 1–20*, WBC 17 (Dallas, TX: Word Books, 1989), xxxvi–xxxvii; Andrew E. Steinmann, 'The Structure and Message of the Book of Job', *VT* 46 (1996): 85–100.

21. Norman Habel, *The Book of Job: A Commentary*, OTL (London: SCM Press, 1985), 25–35, 80–5.

setting a relational context that frames the theological advice and increasingly heated counsel in the dialogues.[22] Job 1–2, therefore, functions as a sort of introduction by establishing the book's many contexts. In short, Ecclesiastes and Job, different from Proverbs but sharing its interest in wisdom and its 'bookended' form, arguably depend upon introductory and concluding passages to create a framework that aids the interpretation of enigmatic materials in each book.[23] While not further explored here, these connections warrant further study in light of the model set out in what follows for approaching Proverbs.

Other instructional texts from the ancient Near East include such prologue and epilogue sections. It has been argued that the framing passages of the *Instruction of Ptahhotep* connect with each other to establish the setting of the instruction.[24] 'The maxims', observes Richard Parkinson, 'expressing diverse attitudes might seem to be a partly random anthology of sayings for which an assumption of thematic unity is inappropriate'.[25] But with the context cast by the introduction (1-50), the reader understands that these apparently disparate sayings carry an authoritative antiquity and that they aim to mature the obedient student in wisdom and devotion (37-42). A lengthy epilogue expands on these aims and forecasts the success that obedience brings: 'If you listen to my sayings, All your affairs will go forward'.[26] The sayings within the body of *Ptahhotep*, then, acquire an authority and educational purpose thanks to the passages that begin and end the book.

The *Instructions of Amenemope* (III.9–IV.2) arguably reflects the form of Proverbs in its inclusion of a self-referential, interpretive introduction. So according to *Amenemope*'s first chapter (III.9–IV.2),

> Give thy ears, hear what is said,
>   Give thy heart to understand them.
> To put them in thy heart is worth while,
>   (but) it is damaging to him who neglects them.
> Let them rest in the casket of thy belly,
>   That they may be a key in thy heart.

---

22. The 'friends' graduate from explaining Job's situation as divine discipline (5.17) and calling for a humble approach to God (5.8; 6.13-15; 8.3-6, 20), to challenging Job's wisdom and guilt (15.4-6, 9-10), and then to calling him evil (22.5, 21).

23. As to the 'bookended' form of Proverbs, see the discussion below.

24. R. B. Parkinson, *Poetry and Culture in Middle Kingdom Egypt: A Dark Side to Perfection* (London: Continuum, 2002), 258–66.

25. Parkinson, *Poetry*, 260.

26. *AEL* 1:73.

> At a time when there is a whirlwind of words,
>   They shall be a mooring-stake for thy tongue.
> If thou spendest thy time while this is in thy heart,
>   Thou wilt find it a success;
> Thou wilt find my words a treasure of life,
>   And thy body will prosper upon earth.[27]

The first line refers to 'what is said' in *Amenemope's* instruction itself and bids the interpreter to understand it, evincing, in other words, a self-referential introduction. Parts of this passage appear in Prov. 22.17-18, a famous parallel that extends to Prov. 23.10 and fortifies the literary similarities in the first chapters of both texts. Later in this study, I suggest that Prov. 22.17-21 reiterates the didactic function of Proverbs 1–9, but for now it is simply worth noting the conceptual overlap and similar literary location of *Amenemope's* passage and Proverbs 1–9.[28] Although *Ptahhotep* and *Amenemope* contain two of the clearest analogues to Proverbs 1–9, it can be said, based on several instructional texts from the ancient Near East, that introductory and sometimes concluding statements motivate the audience to listen to and enact the contained instructions (*Ani* 7.4), enable interpretation by creating a discourse context (*Ankhsheshonq* §1-4), and show self-awareness by referring to their own text (*Amenemope* III.9–IV.2), all of which are qualities that show striking similarities with Proverbs.[29]

Distinctions between these materials, though, ought to be held in mind. To this end, Proverbs 1–9 has been helpfully differentiated from Egyptian literature, given that the availability of Egyptian texts, aside from *Amenemope*, to Israelite scribes is unclear and cautions textual comparisons.[30] Furthermore, Proverbs 1–9 boasts of a literary complexity

---

27. *ANET*, 421–2.
28. See the discussion in section 4.2.
29. Christopher B. Ansberry, *Be Wise, My Son, and Make My Heart Glad: An Exploration of the Courtly Nature of the Book of Proverbs*, BZAW 422 (Berlin: de Gruyter, 2011), 13–19. Lichtheim (*AEL* 3:160) writes of *Ankhsheshonq*, 'the text has an introductory narrative which purports to describe the circumstances that led to the composition of the maxims, and, like its prototypes, the introduction is a literary device and a fiction' (see *ANET*, 421–5). For further examples, see *Amenemhet* i.2; *Ptahhotep* i.51-60; *The Teaching of a Man for His Son* 1-3; for narrative contexts, *Wisdom of Ahiqar* and *Neferti*; and *Shuruppak* 8-13.
30. E.g. the *Instructions of Hardjedef*, *Ptahhotep* and *Kagemni*. See Weeks, *Instruction*, 4–11, also 12–66. For a helpful overview of scribal culture, see R. N. Whybray, *The Composition of the Book of Proverbs* (Sheffield: Sheffield Academic Press, 1994), 132–41.

not found among other 'instructional' material, as it integrates narrative and teaching (e.g. Prov. 7), speeches within speeches (e.g. Prov. 4), and varies the identity of the teacher (cf. God, Wisdom, grandfather, father).[31] So while these texts share the element of a father instructing his son and thereby constitute 'instruction', the distinctive character of Proverbs 1–9 is not unnoticed. I am not proposing a theory of dependence, in literary or historical terms, but I am suggesting that certain similarities of Proverbs with ancient Near Eastern instructional texts and the biblical books of Job and Ecclesiastes encourage an exploration of how Proverbs 1–9 might function as a 'prologue'.

Lastly, the opening chapters of the extra-biblical book of Ben Sira, a later text clearly dependent on the book of Proverbs, reflect the primary concerns of Proverbs 1–9. Although Ben Sira includes an explanatory, prose prologue more reminiscent of Greek historical works, Sir. 1.1-10 contains a hymn to Wisdom like Prov. 8.22-31, and Sir. 1.11-30 features the fear of the Lord, a passage that, according to James Crenshaw, 'serves as a programmatic statement for the entire book'.[32] Wisdom and the fear of the Lord are worked out in their particularities throughout Sir. 2.1–4.10, chapters punctuated with language ('my son'; 2.1; 3.12; 4.1) and themes (e.g. humility, filial duty, discipline) found in Proverbs 1–9. After another brief praise of Wisdom (4.11-19) the sentence instructions begin at Sir. 4.20, showing structural similarity with Proverbs too. The blatant reflection of the first nine chapters of Proverbs in Ben Sira's first

---

31. Weeks, *Instruction*, 33–66. Berend Gemser ('The Instructions of 'Onchsheshonqy and Biblical Wisdom Literature', in *Studies in Ancient Israelite Wisdom*, ed. James Crenshaw [New York: KTAV, 1976], 142–7) argues, especially in light of *Ankhsheshonq* which resembles Proverbs' atomistic collection of sayings, that the book of Proverbs stands as a more developed form of literature than its ancient counterparts. So Kenneth Kitchen, 'Biblical Instructional Wisdom: The Decisive Voice of the Ancient Near East', in *Boundaries of the Ancient Near Eastern World: A Tribute to Cyrus H. Gordon*, ed. Meir Lubetski, Claire Gottlieb, and Sharon R. Keller (Sheffield: Sheffield Academic Press, 1998), 363. While Kitchen stresses the uniqueness of Proverbs and autonomy of ancient Near Eastern instruction compilers, the similarities, which I account for, should not be overlooked. See Christa Kayatz, *Studien zu Proverbien 1–9* (Neukirchen-Vluyn: Neukirchener Verlag, 1966), 26–75; cf. R. N. Whybray, *Wisdom in Proverbs: The Concept of Wisdom in Proverbs 1–9* (London: SCM Press, 1965), 61–71; Whybray, *Proverbs* (London: Marshall Pickering, 1994), 23–30.

32. James Crenshaw, 'Sirach', *NIB* 5:650, also 642, 647. See also T. J. J. Corley, 'An Intertextual Study of Proverbs and Ben Sira', in *Intertextual Studies in Ben Sira and Tobit: Essays in Honor of Alexander A. Di Lella, O.F.M.*, CBQMS 38 (Washington, D.C.: Catholic Biblical Association of America, 2004), 180–2.

four chapters suggests that the structural distinction of Proverbs was significant. In view of texts that are often considered the nearest relatives of Proverbs, chapters 1–9 stand apart in aspects of form and content, not to mention their nearly unrivalled length when taken collectively as an introduction. But the length and introductory capacity of 1–9 is not entirely unmatched, and there is some precedent for relatively lengthy, interpretively influential material that has been placed onto the front of ancient texts.

Sara Milstein has coined a phenomenon known as 'revision by introduction', a practice whereby scribes supplemented a pre-existing text with introductory material in order to shape the reader's interpretation of what follows.[33] According to Milstein, such revision occurred in biblical and Mesopotamian texts, and is evident in 'hard evidence' – namely, extant textual witnesses that attest to variations in the material – and also in the final form of certain texts, which lack concrete evidence of change but nonetheless contain inconsistencies that make revision by introduction a plausible phenomenon. This 'soft evidence', or inconsistencies within the final form of a text, is a well-known starting point for historical-critical studies of the OT.[34] Changes in genre, shifts in form, and the unity of self-contained textual units within a larger portion of literature all serve to convince some scholars that an extant text had a certain pre-history. Tracing why and how editors may have adjusted the text that we have is further cause for debate, but the idea that introductory material was deliberately added to pre-existing material seems persuasive and is corroborated by several examples, which I would add to those mentioned above: Isaiah 1, Psalm 1 (and 2), Nehemiah 1 and, possibly, longer portions of Deuteronomy and Judges.[35] Milstein considers each of

---

33. Sara Milstein, *Tracking the Master Scribe: Revision Through Introduction in Biblical and Mesopotamian Literature* (New York: Oxford University Press, 2016).

34. I realize that the language of 'historical-critical' is not preferred by all, but it conveniently captures the many methods of critical study to which I refer, whether source, form, redaction or 'literary'. For a current survey of methods of text- and historical-critical study of the OT, see Ville Mäkipelto, *Uncovering Ancient Editing: Documented Evidence of Changes in Joshua 24 and Related Texts*, BZAW 513 (Berlin: de Gruyter, 2018), 1–14.

35. For literature, see Milstein, *Tracking the Master Scribe*, 58–60 nn. 41–9. The additions that she considers in depth sometimes introduced smaller narratives within a text (e.g. Judg. 6–9), and in cases such as the *Epic of Gilgamesh* they fronted the entire story. Milstein makes a convincing case for the introductory function of passages in *Gilgamesh* (124-136) but her biblical examples do not include Job, Ecclesiastes or Proverbs.

these as examples of 'revision by introduction' despite the lack of 'hard evidence', and while these cases are debatable they nevertheless provide some precedent for considering Proverbs 1–9 as a later, deliberate introduction to the book.

More persuasive than the biblical examples is the hard evidence of Mesopotamian literature, those cases that have several versions of a text, some with introductions and some without.[36] The Sumerian King List (SKL), for instance, exists in several forms, and some versions contain an antediluvian section at the text's outset. Other versions contain no antediluvian section, and still other texts show that this antediluvian section circulated on its own, without the traditional SKL included. In short, we have the SKL with prefatory material and without prefatory material, and evidence that prefatory material formed an independent text all its own. Add to this that the introductory portion has notable differences from the SKL, and the notion of revision by introduction becomes quite plausible.

A similar example is the *Instructions of Shuruppak*, which is perhaps worth even more attention given its similarities to Proverbs. Three versions of this text suggest that an introduction was added, namely the two Early Dynastic (ED) versions and single Old Babylonian (OB) version from approximately 700 years later.[37] The ED versions contain several initial lines considered by most to function as a sort of 'introduction'.

> The intelligent one, who knew the (proper) words,
> and was living in Sumer,
>   Suruppak, the...

---

36. It is right to remember the difference in quality of conclusions about biblical redaction based on the MT versus redaction grounded in the attestation of various textual witnesses. For it 'would be a mistake to assume that literary-critical reconstructions are evidence of the same caliber as preserved textual witnesses' (Reinhard Müller, Juha Pakkala and R. B. ter Haar Romeny, *Evidence of Editing: Growth and Change of Texts in the Hebrew Bible* [Atlanta, GA: SBL, 2014], 15).

37. The ED versions are from Adab and Abū Ṣalābīkh, the latter being the clearest and therefore quoted as lines 1-8 above. For discussion and literature, see Milstein's doctoral dissertation ('Reworking Ancient Texts: Revision through Introduction in Biblical and Mesopotamian Literature' [PhD diss., New York University, 2010], 46–8), where she also rightly qualifies the language of 'lines' when speaking about this text. Translations are taken from Bendt Alster, *The Instructions of Suruppak: A Sumerian Proverb Collection*, Mesopotamia: Copenhagen Studies in Assyriology 2 (Copenhagen: Akademisk Forlag, 1974). Interestingly, these introductory lines reappear in lines 78-87 and 148-157, material also missing from certain sources (see Alster, *Instructions*, 69).

> The intelligent one, who knew the (proper) words,
> and was living in Sumer,
>> Suruppak gave instructions to his son:
>> My son, let me give you instructions,
>> May you pay attention to them! (lines 1-8 [Abū Ṣalābīkh])

The OB version adds to this material approximately seven lines that do three things: they further identify Shuruppak and his son (7-8); they accentuate the antiquity of his instructions (1-3); and they further encourage his son to obey them (9-13; additions are in italics):

> *In those days, in those far remote days,*
> *In those nights, in those far-away nights,*
> *In those years, in those far remote years –*
> *In those days,* the intelligent one, *who made the elaborate words,*
>> who knew the (proper) words, and was living in Sumer,
> Suruppak – *the intelligent one, who made the elaborate words,*
>> *who knew the (proper) words, and was living in Sumer –*
> Suruppak gave instructions to his son,
> *Suruppak, son of Ubartutu,*
> gave instructions to his son Ziusudra,
>> My son, let me give you instructions, *may you take my instructions!*
>> *Ziusudra, let me speak a word to you,* may you pay attention to it!
>> *Do not neglect my instructions!*
>> *Do not transgress the word I speak!*
>> *The instructions of an old man are precious, may you submit to them!*
>>> (lines 1-13)

These additions are, in the first place, clearly additions, lines added to a pre-existing text and intended to influence the reader's approach to it. Second, *Shuruppak* has a striking resemblance to Proverbs, especially in its admonitions to 'take my instructions' and 'not neglect' them (lines 9-13), giving further support to the possibility that Proverbs 1–9 was later added to Proverbs 10–29. Proverbs 1–9 is, of course, much longer than the thirteen introductory lines of *Shuruppak*, but that need not deter us from the hypothesis. For in view of all the evidence for revision by introduction, Milstein concludes that the new introductions 'could be substantial in length', though she presents no cases of instructional literature in that regard.[38] She likewise concludes that 'the new introduction could introduce a different genre or format' to the pre-established text and that it could 'anticipate elements in the material that follows'.[39] It is

---

38. Milstein, *Tracking the Master Scribe*, 74.
39. Milstein, *Tracking the Master Scribe*, 74.

these elements that, I would argue, characterize Proverbs 1–9, and it is the collective evidence that Milstein presents for this phenomenon that further justifies the assumption to read Proverbs 1–9 as a later addition to the book of Proverbs. As for what this implies methodologically, that will be taken up below.

In summary, the interpretive challenges of Proverbs 10–29, the readerly promises of 1.1-7, and the significance of comparable literature warrant an investigation into the didactic function of Proverbs 1–9, a function explored, unsurprisingly, by exegetes for more than the last three centuries.

1.3. *Early Interpretations of Proverbs 1–9 as an 'Introduction'*

Proposals about the significance of Proverbs 1–9 for the rest of Proverbs go back to at least the seventeenth century CE. What we might perceive as modern commentary appears as early as 1659, when an English, Anglican theologian, Henry Hammond, claimed that Proverbs 1–9 lays a 'foundation and introduction' to the sentences that follow.[40] Matthew Poole, forty years later, explained that chapters 1–9 'were only a preface or preparation [to Prov. 10.1–22.16], containing a general exhortation to the study and exercise of wisdom, to stir up the minds of men to the greater attention and regard to all its precepts, whereof some here follow'.[41] It is the exhortatory and prefatory role of Proverbs 1–9 that exegetes of the seventeenth and eighteenth centuries, like Hammond and Poole, had in view when they labelled Proverbs 1–9 as an 'introduction'. Their works represent the limited remarks made over the centuries prior to the nineteenth about the function of Proverbs 1–9 and the relationship between 1–9 and 10.1–22.16. During the nineteenth century itself, the situation began to change, as German biblical scholars started to debate and further articulate the idea that Proverbs 1–9 might serve as an introduction.

Early in the nineteenth century, Hermann Muntinghe and Carl Umbreit remarked that the first collection sits as an 'Einleitung' and has a thematic and formal coherence in itself, which led to questions that soon became more acute for Heinrich Ewald and Ernst Bertheau as they debated over

---

40. Henry Hammond, *A Paraphrase and Annotations Upon the Books of the Psalms* (London: Royston, 1659), 455. For interesting but unclear comments on Prov. 1.1-7 by Jewish exegetes in the tenth century CE, see Ilana Sasson, 'The Book of Proverbs between Saadia and Yefet', *Intellectual History of the Islamic World* 1 (2013): 162.

41. Matthew Poole, *Annotations upon the Holy Bible*, 3 vols. (New York: Robert Carter & Brothers, 1696), 2:230; similarly, see Matthew Henry's *Commentary on the Holy Bible*.

the precise nature of the first nine chapters of Proverbs.[42] In 1837, Ewald argued for the coherence of chapters 1–9 and called it a long, detailed introduction ('Einleitung') and preparatory work ('Vorbereitung') for Collection II. In his view, the author had placed Collection I at the outset as a supplement to the older proverbs that follow. Proverbs 1.1, 6 and 10.1 connect the collections by mentioning 'proverbs', and Ewald saw the primary contribution of Collection I as an endorsement of wisdom, calling the audience to cherish it. Bertheau critiqued that position in 1847. While acknowledging Collection I's place as an opening section because it instructs the audience to grasp wisdom, Bertheau denied its coherence and its role as an introduction, arguing that if the author intended Proverbs 1–9 as an introduction then it would explicitly refer to Collection II. Although he acknowledged the introductory role of 1.1-7, Bertheau seemed to overlook the possibility that 1.2 and 1.6 refer to the contents of 10.1–22.16. Ewald noticed this connection and, in doing so, set the trajectory for the theory of a didactic function for Proverbs 1–9.[43]

For over 150 years, commentators from Britain, Germany and the United States continued to label Proverbs 1–9 an 'introduction', 'prologue', or 'Einleitung' for chapters 10 and following, but they rarely elaborated on how it functions as such.[44] Wildeboer, for instance, noted

42. Hermann Muntinghe, *Die Sprüche Salomo's* (Frankfurt: Jäger, 1800), xii; Friedrich Wilhelm Carl Umbreit, *Commentar über die Sprüche Salomo's* (Heidelberg: J. C. B. Mohr, 1826), lxii. Heinrich Ewald, *Die Poetischen Bücher des alten Bundes* (Gottingen: Vandenhoeck & Ruprecht, 1837), 39–40; Ernst Bertheau, *Die Sprüche Salomo's* (Leipzig: Weidmann, 1847), xxi.

43. Ewald also formulated substantial arguments about the redaction of Proverbs, but they do not seem significant for this particular conflict with Bertheau.

44. Charles Bridges, *An Exposition of the Book of Proverbs* (London: Seeley, 1847), 132; Moses Stuart, *A Commentary on the Book of Proverbs* (New York: M. W. Dodd, 1852), 39; Friedrich Bleek, *An Introduction to the Old Testament*, ed. Johannes Friedrich Bleek and Adolf Kamphausen, 2 vols. (London: Bell & Daldy, 1869), 2:256; Carl Friedrich Keil, George C. M. Douglas, and Friedrich Bleek, *Manual of Historico-Critical Introduction to the Canonical Scriptures of the Old Testament*, 2 vols. (Edinburgh: T. & T. Clark, 1869), 1:479–80; Carl Cornill, *Einleitung in das Alte Testament* (Freiburg: J. C. B. Mohr, 1892), 222, 227; Davison, *Wisdom-Literature*, 115; A. Cohen, *Proverbs: Hebrew Text and English Translation with Introduction and Commentary* (London: Soncino Press, 1945), 56; Helmer Ringgren, *Sprüche* (Göttingen: Vandenhoeck & Ruprecht, 1962), 8; Silvia Schroer, *Wisdom Has Built Her House: Studies on the Figure of Sophia in the Bible* (Collegeville, MN: Liturgical Press, 2000), 27; Roland Murphy, *The Tree of Life: An Exploration of Biblical Wisdom Literature* (New York: Doubleday, 2002), 28–9; Samuel L. Adams, *Wisdom in Transition: Act and Consequence in Second Temple Instructions*, JSJSup 125 (Leiden: Brill, 2008), 60.

linguistic agreements in Proverbs 1–9 and 10.1–22.16 to justify assertions about authorship but not to validate or expound the role of Proverbs 1–9.[45] Decades later, Edgar Jones simply states that Prov. 1.1-6 'sets forth the essential aim of the book' and calls Collection I a 'long prologue' that advocates wisdom as the basis of life.[46] For much of the twentieth century, as with centuries prior, interpreters continued to label Proverbs 1–9 an 'introduction', and when they did consider the implications of this label for interpretive issues, they did so primarily with diachronic interests, as in the case of Wildeboer, who aimed to delineate the authorship of Proverbs. But as the twentieth century came to a close, many interpreters became most interested in a synchronic perspective on the book, and in 1986 Magne Sæbø advanced an innovative challenge for Proverbs scholarship with 'the question of how the different units which make up the final shape of the book are related to each other. This question seems to be the most neglected one and has hardly had any substantial impact on the exposition of the book; generally, the units are treated separately, as disintegrated parts'.[47] For Sæbø, the relationship of collections in their 'final shape' and the exegetical significance of their arrangement had been neglected by interpreters of Proverbs up to that point. Since 1986, and, as we shall see, just prior to that year, interpreters have more closely addressed the relationship between the collections and its significance for understanding Proverbs 1–9.

1.4. *Current Interpretations of Proverbs 1–9 as an 'Introduction'*

1.4.1. *Proverbs 1–9 as an Introduction*
Many scholars writing from 1985 to 2017 who affirm the labels of 'introduction' and 'prologue' for Proverbs 1–9 have surpassed previous remarks about how these chapters might function. While very few of them refer to Sæbø's article from 1986, these scholars do attend to the relationship of collections and argue for notable features in how the collections are arranged, especially as Proverbs 1–9 juxtaposes with 10.1–22.16. The bases for connecting these sections of text include metaphor, values and

---

45. G. Wildeboer, *Die Sprüche* (Freiburg: J. C. B. Mohr, 1897), x, xviii.

46. Edgar Jones, *Proverbs and Ecclesiastes: Introduction and Commentary*, Torch Bible Commentaries (London: SCM Press, 1961), 22, 55.

47. Magne Sæbø, 'From Collections to Book – A New Approach to the History of Tradition and Redaction of the Book of Proverbs', in *Proceedings of the Ninth World Congress of Jewish Studies*, ed. Moshe Goshen-Gottstein and David Assaf (Jerusalem: World Union of Jewish Studies, 1986), 99.

aims, literary forms, theology, and character types.[48] Commentators too, who may not systematically demonstrate the introductory function of Proverbs 1–9, treat it as such in their remarks about individual proverbs, while many interpreters say that Proverbs 1–9 'thematically' introduces the book, with some substantiating this comment more than others.[49] Additional perspectives to the question are brought by those who view Proverbs 1–9 in its relation to Proverbs 31 and also those who view 1–9 independent of its relation to other portions of the book, that is, scholars who prefer to interpret Proverbs 1–9 in its own right and who thereby introduce interpretive issues that are potentially unaffected by Proverbs 10–31.

Prior to Sæbø's challenge in 1986, at least one scholar had explored in some depth the neglected question of 'how the different units which make up the final shape of the book, are related to each other' by considering Proverbs 1–9 as an interpretive framework for Proverbs 10–29.[50] It was Claudia Camp, who in 1985 published *Wisdom and the Feminine in the Book of Proverbs* and examined many aspects of Proverbs – its imagery, female figures, and socio-historical context – including the relationship between Proverbs 1–9 and 10–29.[51] She argues that certain metaphors in Proverbs 1–9 substantiate the metaphors of Proverbs 10–29 by supplementing its imagery and providing fresh conceptual relations. The tree

---

48. Regarding the literary form of Proverbs, the works of Christine Yoder (*Proverbs*, AOTC [Nashville, TN: Abingdon Press, 2009]) and Knut Heim (*Poetic Imagination in Proverbs: Variant Repetitions and the Nature of Poetry* [Winona Lake, IN: Eisenbrauns, 2013], e.g. 626–7) are, respectively, suggestive and implicit in the support that they give to the function of Proverbs 1–9. Yoder has proposed that Proverbs 1–9 embeds proverbs within some of its poems in order to show the interpreter how to use the proverbial form of communication (i.e. 1.17; 2.21-22; 3.33-35; 9.7-9), a promising suggestion for how 1–9 might function. Heim has recognized the function of Proverbs 1–9 as a 'hermeneutical introduction' in his work on 'variant repetition', in which he traces the repetition of terms and phrases throughout Proverbs. When set within a diachronic framework, several cases of repetition in 1–9 and 10–29 imply that 1–9 embeds variant passages from 10–29 in a context of fuller explanation. For character types, see Chapter 2.

49. For the latter see, among others, Horst Dietrich Preuss, *Einführung in die alttestamentliche Weisheitsliteratur* (Stuttgart: Kohlhammer, 1987), 32, 60; Markus Saur, 'Die Literarische Funktion und die Theologische Intention der Weisheitsreden des Sprüchebuches', *VT* 61 (2011): 457–8; Waltke, *Proverbs*, 14, 74; Whybray, *Proverbs*, 17; Fox, *Proverbs 1–9*, 323, 325, 346.

50. Sæbø, 'From Collections to Book', 99.

51. Claudia Camp, *Wisdom and the Feminine in the Book of Proverbs* (Decatur, GA: Almond Press, 1985), 191–208.

of life, for example, features in Collections I and II (3.18; 11.30; 13.12; 15.4), and according to her the connotations of its appearance in 3.18 should be informed by the concepts associated with it in 10.1–22.16. Camp also forwards the imagery of Prov. 21.6, which mentions 'treasures' and 'death', to argue that the figures of Wisdom and Folly in Proverbs 7–8 come to mind when reading Prov. 21.6. Despite their intrigue and innovation, these examples attest to the methodological challenges that studies of Proverbs 1–9 have and do face. On the one hand, it seems that Proverbs 1–9 substantiates the imagery of 10.1–22.16 (i.e. 'treasures/ death'), but, on the other hand, Camp seems to show that sayings within 10.1–22.16 also inform the interpretation of material in Proverbs 1–9 (i.e. the tree of life). In other words, the interpretive influence of these sections is bi-directional so that a problem of methodological inconsistency arises. In what follows, it will be worth asking how this problem should be accounted for and if it might be resolved.

Effort has also been spent on the goals and values of Proverbs, with the most thorough investigation of these issues using the book's wealth and poverty language as a starting point.[52] Here, Proverbs 1–9 has been acknowledged as a 'hermeneutical lens' for the book and yet in practice we have little evidence of what that lens might enable interpreters to see in Proverbs 10–31.[53] The aims and goals of Proverbs supply one of the

---

52. Sandoval, *The Discourse of Wealth and Poverty in the Book of Proverbs* (Leiden: Brill, 2006); Raymond Van Leeuwen, 'The Book of Proverbs', *NIB* 5:31; Walther Zimmerli ('Zur Struktur der Alttestamentlichen Weisheit', *ZAW* 51 [1933]: 177–204, esp. 185–92) claimed that Proverbs 1–9 provides motivational grounds for obedience. While he did offer evidence from 1–9 (e.g. Prov. 3.5-9), he mostly appealed to material from 10.1–22.16 to demonstrate his point.

53. See Sandoval, *Discourse*, esp. 56, 118–24, 133, 155, 209. Sandoval's conclusions likely arise in part from his fixation on Prov. 1.3 and its reference to 'righteousness' (צדק). He acknowledges the 'cue to read wisely' in what he calls Proverbs' 'prologue' (1.2-6/7) but gives much more interpretive weight to 1.3, which, according to him, affixes wisdom to 'virtue', especially for establishing 'social justice', and then drives his vision of Proverbial values. My view of Proverbial values differs, due to my own emphasis on the 'cue' for intelligent reading as stated in Prov. 1.2 and 1.6, noted above. R. N. Whybray (*Wealth and Poverty in the Book of Proverbs*, JSOTSup 99 [Sheffield: Sheffield Academic Press, 1990], 64) analyzes the attitudes towards wealth and poverty in Prov. 10.1–22.16 and chs. 25–29, and refers to the 'values' of the speakers. However, he does not synthesize or concentrate on the values with respect to the collection as a whole – except to say that they 'leave a general impression of consistency' – or engage with their rhetorical function. Further, he downplays the significance of Proverbs 1–9 for wealth and poverty language, which Sandoval counters.

most riveting instances of Proverbs 1–9's function, and these are taken up in Chapter 3 of the present work. As for its 'theology', this topic of Proverbs is often grounded on the references to 'God' or 'the Lord' contained therein, which have recently been shown to form a coherent part of the book as a whole.[54] The study that has come closest to the present work arises within this theological discussion, and it is a doctoral dissertation by Hee Suk Kim, who claims that Proverbs 1–9 creates an interpretive framework for 10–29 and conducts a close reading of chapters 1–9 to propose that it establishes a 'faith–consequence nexus' that should overcome the interpretive difficulties within chapters 10–29.[55] While I affirm Kim's core thesis and much of his exegesis as well as his notion of 'interpretive framework', he does not interact closely with texts in Proverbs 10–29 and provides no textual examples to show how 1–9 actually aids interpretation. This omission prompts one of my central efforts: to show how Proverbs 1–9 functions for 10–29 by demonstrating its interpretive role with in-depth examples from both portions of material. The need for this demonstration echoes throughout the current studies of Proverbs that proclaim the introductory function of 1–9, the resolution of which remains to be seen. As with others, theological interpreters provide plausible proposals for how Collection I might function as an introduction but offer limited examples to substantiate it.

What these arguments more positively reveal is the need to supply Proverbs 10–29 with a context of some sort. Theological sayings within those chapters, for instance, might give insight into the bulk of the book's material, especially its 'non-theological' sayings. Perhaps the lectures to a son in 1–9 and then to a man with royal authority in chapter 31, along with its exposé of a mature woman, frame how we ought to view the purpose of 10–29.[56] Or perhaps more discrete challenges arise in 10–29 that receive adequate clarification in Proverbs 1–9.[57] Along with these

---

54. See the discussion in Chapter 4. In addition to the studies mentioned in this section, other interpreters hold unsubstantiated proposals that Proverbs 1–9 functions as a theological framework for the rest of the book.

55. Hee Suk Kim, 'Proverbs 1–9: A Hermeneutical Introduction to the Book of Proverbs' (PhD diss., Trinity International University, 2010).

56. So William P. Brown, *Wisdom's Wonder: Character, Creation, and Crisis in the Bible's Wisdom Literature* (Grand Rapids, MI: Eerdmans, 2014), 29–66.

57. See Tremper Longman, *Proverbs*, BCOT (Grand Rapids. MI: Baker Academic, 2006), 243, 496–7. For his interpretation of Proverbs 1–9 as an 'introduction' that calls for a decision from the young reader to choose between Wisdom and Folly, a feature corroborated by the pathway imagery, see 59–61; so Michael V. Fox, *Proverbs 1–9*,

possibilities, we must also consider if sources external to Proverbs address its hermeneutical challenges in the fullest and most coherent fashion. Most of these endeavours can be explained as attempts to provide some part of Proverbs, especially its sayings material, with a 'context', which in most every case faces methodological challenges. Should Proverbs 1–9 be segregated from the rest of the book, read along with 30–31, read before 10–29 or in light of it? There is perhaps no 'right' answer to these questions, which may be part of the reason why no monograph has been dedicated to the introductory function of Proverbs 1–9. But there is a way of reading the book that I think gives the most advantageous look at how Proverbs 1–9 may function as an introduction.

1.4.2. *Proverbs 1–9 as an Independent Section*
The review of work on Proverbs 1–9 so far may suggest that all studies on these first nine chapters advocate its introductory function, but this would be misleading. A few interpreters examine 1–9 in its own right, either independently of 10–31 or with no interest in its introductory role. Although they do not explicitly object to the notion that Proverbs 1–9 plays a particular role in the book as a whole, these interpreters treat 1–9 with little consideration of its place within the book and thereby offer an important perspective on Proverbs 1–9, exposing the features of this text in a way unclouded by the questions or categories of 10–31. In other words, Proverbs 1–9 develops ideas that may have little to do with the chapters that follow, and such interests must be accounted for if we are to discover its function within Proverbs. For what it underscores in its own right certainly pertains to its function, which may hold little relevance for Proverbs 10–31 and therefore severely question what I am proposing. Hence these proposals require extended attention. Jean-Noël Aletti, Stuart Weeks, and Bernd Schipper all work in this mode, interpreting Proverbs 1–9 as an independent entity and taking long strides towards how it functions on its own terms.[58]

129–30; *Proverbs 10–31: A New Translation with Introduction and Commentary*, AB 18B (New Haven: Yale University Press, 2009), 516, 819, 831–2; Otto Plöger, *Sprüche Salomos (Proverbia)*, BKAT 17 (Neukirchen-Vluyn: Neukirchener Verlag, 1984), 279; Bruce K. Waltke, *The Book of Proverbs: Chapters 15–31*, NICOT (Grand Rapids, MI: Eerdmans, 2005), 286; Plöger, *Sprüche*, 276.

58. Jean-Noël Aletti, 'Seduction et Parole en Proverbs I–IX', *VT* 27 (1977): 129–44; Weeks, *Instruction*; Bernd Schipper, *Hermeneutik der Tora: Studien zur Traditionsgeschichte von Prov 2 und zur Komposition von Prov 1–9*, BZAW 432 (Berlin: de Gruyter, 2012).

1.4.2.1. *J. N. Aletti*

In 1977, Aletti wrote an article entitled 'Seduction et Parole en Proverbs I–IX' in which he looked at the means of seduction in Proverbs 1–9 and their remarkable connection to the words spoken by key characters within this collection. Focusing on the 'youth' (נער) and 'simpleton' (פתי) of Proverbs 1–9, Aletti argues that for the boy 'ce ne son pas les choses ou les êtres qui séduisent.... Le savoir faire est celui de la parole, la séduction s'opère par le dire.'[59] On the one hand, the speech of Prov. 1.22-33 scrambles the values within the son's moral vision by exhibiting lexical confusion, which is compounded by the sage and the female figures throughout Proverbs 1–9 as they forward invitations with similar language but with disparate results. Folly and Wisdom, for instance, use the very same words to call their invitees to dinner (9.4, 16) but end the evening in very different ways, demonstrating a key point for my study: the moral situation is not simple, for what is wrong can sound right, and, consequently, discerning good from bad requires a solution.

Although Aletti focuses on the fact that wrong things sound right, the problem in 1–9 is a broader one of 'moral ambiguity', the solution for which Aletti finds in the divinely given wisdom and the advice of the father. Proverbs 1–9, therefore, functions by establishing a seduction-related human problem and by offering a solution that awaits acceptance.[60] In view of dangerous moral complexity, the pupil must become an apprentice to wisdom that is taught by the father and transmitted by God. Working explicitly with the question of how Proverbs 1–9 functions when interpreted on its own terms, and accounting for much of its material, Aletti adds an unavoidable contribution to my study of 1–9. He elucidates a feature that must be accounted for if its function is to be established responsibly and as robustly as possible. Aletti's work on Proverbs 1–9 does not, I will argue, undermine my larger aim – to establish the function of 1–9 in its relation with other portions of Proverbs – but instead directs attention to unforeseen interpretive issues within Proverbs 10–29, namely, aspects of moral ambiguity. The moral ambiguity laid out in Proverbs 1–9 appears tersely in many proverbs of 10–29, proffering a relationship that is forged in section 3.2. That section further expounds Aletti's contribution in view of my broader argument.

---

59. Aletti, 'Seduction', 129.
60. Aletti ('Seduction', 130) says 'Tel sera donc l'objet de la présente étude: analyser, en Prov. i-ix, comment fonctionne et jusqu'où va séduction de la parole humaine pour en mesurer les effets'.

Alletti's work includes some shortcomings, such as the failure to fully account for distinctions between the foolish characters (i.e. the youth and simpleton) and the audience itself. However, the danger of this conflation does not override the strengths of Aletti's case, the importance of which cannot be overlooked. For it advances a second methodological mode, which first approaches not the interpretive challenges of Prov. 10.1–22.16 but the emphases of Proverbs 1–9, a direction of study fully explained shortly.

1.4.2.2. *S. Weeks*

Like Aletti, Weeks considers Proverbs 1–9 in its own right and is interested in its coherence more than in its inner differences and diachronic features. Weeks dedicates an entire monograph to these chapters to argue two primary theses: Proverbs 1–9 sits within a Jewish context more than an Egyptian or broadly ancient Near Eastern background, and the material of Proverbs 1–9 forms a coherent whole, with the exception of 6.1-19.[61] Both theses are supported by the allusions, terms and imagery within Proverbs 1–9 that connect with OT understandings of law, especially Deuteronomy. Yet the contents of Proverbs 1–9 also connect with each other as the various metaphors, for instance, interrelate and produce a united vision for the audience. The coherence of 1–9 encourages my study and certain details of Weeks' work will lend help to later exegesis, but his insistence on the relation of Proverbs 1–9 with OT law leads to a conclusion that may unsettle the central question of 1–9's role.

According to Weeks, 'If instruction is indeed to be associated with the Law, then wisdom may be the way in which Proverbs 1–9 characterizes not the Law, but the condition achieved by those who have internalized the Law'.[62] Wisdom is not identified with law but is realized by those who receive instruction, that is, '*torah*'. Such a conclusion stems, in part, from the following features: lexical connections between Deuteronomy and Proverbs 1–9, namely, Prov. 3.12 and Deut. 8.5 and their comparison of God with a father; the 'instruction of the Lord' in Prov. 3.11 and Deut. 11.2; the terms תורה and מצות used throughout Proverbs 1–9; and 'tablet' in Prov. 3.3 and 7.3 which appears in Deut. 9.9 and elsewhere, as well as connections throughout the OT between wisdom and instruction.[63] Weeks aligns the receptiveness to parental teaching in Proverbs 1–9 with receptiveness

---

61. Weeks (*Instruction*, 156–8), reasonably, remains unsure about the date of Proverbs 1–9 and suggests no more specific time period than 500–200 BCE.
62. Weeks, *Instruction*, 113.
63. Weeks, *Instruction*, 102–5, also 96–127.

to Deuteronomic law and thereby understands 1–9 as advocating a certain view of law and wisdom. It does not simply champion OT law but casts legal piety in a sapiential mould with special concern for internalization. Proverbs 1–9 functions for the reader in this way, but not, it seems, as an introduction.

As mentioned, Weeks does not entertain Proverbs 1–9 as an introduction to the book of Proverbs, but he does ponder what would happen if we decoupled Deuteronomy from Proverbs 1–9. Once such a background is removed, he says,

> We are still left with a work that repeatedly exhorts obedience to a teaching through which compliance with the divine will may be achieved, and personal security thereby assured. No alternative identification of that teaching is offered, and, for all the attempts to isolate 'wisdom circles' from other strands of Jewish thought, it strains credulity to believe that a contemporary Jewish reader would not have made some link with the Law.... It is relatively straightforward to say that Prov. 31: 1-9, for instance, has no interest in the Law, but much harder to ascertain what assumptions form the basis for, say, the righteous-wicked contrasts that dominate the start of 10: 1–22: 16. It does seem apparent, at least, that no other material in Proverbs seeks actively to draw out and identify the nature of wisdom and instruction in the same way.[64]

By removing Deuteronomy from the picture, Weeks searches for a viable background to Proverbs 1–9 within Proverbs itself and proposes that no material, at least not 10.1–22.16 and 31.1-9, handles wisdom and instruction in a way that explains their relationship in 1–9. Deuteronomy, then, remains the plausible option.

Weeks establishes a function of Proverbs 1–9 that seems unrelated to the rest of the book, and I do not, fundamentally, reject his thesis. However, neither do I find an acceptance of his proposed links between law and Proverbs as detrimental or even alternative to the possibility that Proverbs 1–9 carries a function for 10–29. In the first place, 10.1–22.16 uses the same lexemes that, for Weeks, so firmly relate to Deuteronomy (תורה and מצוה in Prov. 10.8; 13.13-14; 19.16).[65] Now, none of these references 'seeks actively to draw out and identify the nature of wisdom

---

64. Weeks, *Instruction*, 172–3.
65. He does say that 'The place of conventional Jewish piety elsewhere in Proverbs is too big an issue to discuss here, but there are other points in the book (e.g. 28: 4, 7, 9) where we should probably understand there to be an explicit interest in the Law' (Weeks, *Instruction*, 173 n. 44).

and instruction', but such a factor is precisely my starting point for determining how Proverbs 1–9 functions as an introduction: 10.1–22.16 fails to explain certain remarks, remarks that receive a much fuller explanation in 1–9. The sapiential legal piety established in Proverbs 1–9 may very well supply a framework for understanding the terse and undeveloped references to תורה and מצוה in 10.1–22.16.

In the second place, we must be careful not to impose an either/or distinction where it is unnecessary, as if connections in Proverbs 1–9 with OT law consequently disconnect it from Proverbs 10–31. The consequence of Weeks' argument is not that Proverbs 1–9 acquires more independence from the book of Proverbs but that if Proverbs 1–9 does relate to the law then we must determine how its view of the law might relate to 10–31. Proverbs 1–9 may advocate a wisdom version of legal piety, resonating with and depending on other OT texts, and at the same time function as an introduction for Proverbs 10–31. For aside from legal concepts, Proverbs 1–9 retains distinctive connections with the book of Proverbs, not least its character types, certain lexemes, references to the Lord, and visions of education. However, in his later *Introduction* to wisdom literature, Weeks is provoked to doubt connections of 1–9 with other portions of Proverbs:

> It is often suggested, for example, that chapters 1–9 are supposed to serve as a sort of prologue, though that does little justice, perhaps, to the coherence and self-containment of the section. Ultimately, with the book as a whole, as with many of the sections within it, we are left wondering just how much weight we should place on apparent connections, and just how much deliberation has gone into the creation of Proverbs from its constituent parts.[66]

Weeks exposes valid doubts, and these doubts give way to questions about the amount of weight we should place on connections across Proverbs and the deliberateness behind them. Many of the connective features mentioned above will occupy this study, which instead of encountering obstacles and deepening doubts will reveal places that advance the integration of Proverbs and the OT. My study will dispel certain apprehensions about the role of Proverbs 1–9 by suggesting that we can place quite a lot of weight on apparent connections and can detect ample deliberation within and across Proverbs while respecting individual integrity and the possible independence of chapters 1–9.

---

66. Stuart Weeks, *An Introduction to the Study of Wisdom Literature* (London: T&T Clark, 2010), 47.

1.4.2.3. B. Schipper

Schipper has substantiated some of Weeks' views but done so in a largely different mode. Schipper looks at the makeup of Proverbs 2, its place within Proverbs 1–9, and the relationship of Proverbs as a whole to OT law, particularly '*torah*' and Deuteronomy, Psalms 19, 37, and 119, Jeremiah 31 and Isaiah 56–66. For him, Proverbs exhibits a 'Hermeneutik der Tora' by posing different relations of wisdom and law and arranging these alternative views in a deliberate fashion. In that, Schipper comes to conclusions about the message of Proverbs, that, contra Weeks, disclose levels of disunity in its presentation of wisdom and law. For example, the allusions to the *Shema* in Proverbs 3, 6 and 7 all portray the wisdom/*torah* relation differently, while Proverbs 2 and 8 add further differences to these, with Proverbs 28 and 30 adding another – what Schipper considers final – position on wisdom and *torah*.

Again, the details of Schipper's work, especially on Proverbs 2, supply a helpful resource for exegesis, but his overall theses establish a texture for 1–9 that presents an incoherent relationship between wisdom and *torah*. The preceding comments about how Weeks' work does not necessarily hamper my investigation also pertain to Schipper's, as *torah* connections in Proverbs 1–9 do not necessarily disassociate it from 10–31. Schipper likewise passes over pertinent evidence in 10–29,[67] and yet his diachronic vision does result in a proposal for how 10–29 fits within the book. According to him, given that portions of these chapters were composed later than the core sections of 1–9 and that they reduce wisdom's affinity with *torah* and seat wisdom within the context of practical living, Proverbs 10–29 blunts the legal interests of other portions of the book. Yet Schipper nevertheless poses the question of how Proverbs 1–9 relates to the rest of Proverbs as a very live enquiry:

> Wie ist das Verhältnis zwischen 1–9 und 10–31 zu bestimmen, wenn einzelne Kapitel der ersten Sammlung deutlich an Themen und Formulierungen von 10–31 anknüpfen? Bedeutet dies, dass die Lehrreden von Prov. 1–9* von vornherein im Hinblick auf 10–31 komponiert wurden, oder handelt es sich um ein eigenständiges Korpus?[68]

While he concludes that Proverbs 9 transitions from 1–9 to chapters 10 and following, Schipper does not explore the commonalities in these materials other than their conceptions of law, which, according to him, do

---

67. For brief comments, see Schipper, *Hermeneutik*, 84–8, 223 n. 11, 247–50.
68. Schipper, *Hermeneutik*, 187.

not really concern 10.1–22.16. Consequently, he to a large extent leaves the question about the function of 1–9 unanswered.[69] As to the cacophony of wisdom voices in Proverbs, I think certain differences are overstated and that Schipper's attention to diachronic detail would benefit from a study that gives primary attention to macro-diachronic elements of the book. For where he emphasizes the contrast in Proverbs, I will propose how such contrasts contribute to the book's coherence.

Lastly, highlighting the sophisticated features of the text, both Weeks and Schipper argue that someone with adequate intelligence or an educated community fashioned and read the text, which calls for further clarity as to what I do not mean by arguing for a 'didactic' function of Proverb 1–9. 'Didactic' does not, in this study, necessarily correspond to 'clear' or 'simplified for the purposes of teaching', as if to overlook the sophisticated and at times complex texture of the poetry in this biblical material. Didactic, as I indicated earlier in this chapter, refers to the function of Proverbs 1–9, its deliberate aim to teach and, as we will see, to teach interpretive skills. My thesis actually corresponds with the high view of poetry argued for by Weeks, as a didactic function reflects a complex attempt to prepare an able audience to further interpret proverbial material.

Aletti, Weeks and Schipper set aside questions about the introductory function of Proverbs 1–9 and present the salient features of these chapters when considered as a standalone unit. Aletti's attention to moral ambiguity and the need for discernment developed by 1–9 inspire a section dedicated to these ideas in Chapter 3, which bolsters my overall argument by accounting for an alternative methodological starting point. Weeks and Schipper, each in their own way, tie Proverbs 1–9 to visions of *torah* and, rather than silencing the question at hand, show its importance as an independent unit, placing it within a context of ongoing enquiries into how Proverbs relates to the OT and contains possible points of tension within itself. These concerns will arise in several chapters in service to my primary question, and Schipper's work is particularly recalled in my treatment of Prov. 30.1-9 in Chapter 3.

1.5. *Conclusions on Context*

I have told a brief history of how Proverbs 1–9 functions, especially what it might mean for it to be an 'introduction' for Proverbs 10–31. The text of Proverbs itself, especially 1.1-7 and 10.1–22.16, suggests that

---

69. Schipper, *Hermeneutik*, 208–12.

the book contains interpretive challenges and at the same time contains an aid for addressing those challenges. Other 'prologues' in OT texts as well as post-biblical and ancient Near Eastern literature endorse this role and corroborate a methodological starting point for examining various sections of Proverbs. The interpreters of these texts, from as early as the seventeenth century CE, entertained the question of how Proverbs 1–9 or materials therein might function for the rest of the book. The question climaxed in the debate of Heinrich Ewald and Ernst Bertheau, who in 1837 and 1847 respectively proffered contrasting views of Proverbs 1–9. Ewald argued for a coherent introduction, firmly connected to other portions of the book, while Bertheau denied the introductory role of Proverbs 1–9 and attached this role only to 1.1-7.

The debate remained undeveloped until the 1980s when interpreters began to explore the introductory role of Proverbs 1–9. These 'current interpretations' include a notable variety of approaches to how 1–9 functions, as each centres this function on one key area of interpretation, including metaphor, values and aims, literary forms, theology, and character types, as well as the work of commentators and those who view Proverbs 1–9 in its relation to 31. Next to the many stand the few who interpret 1–9 independently of questions about its role for 10–31, and yet, instead of stalling the years of talk about an 'introduction', these few advance the present thesis and the urgency of its question.

This account primarily reveals three points. First, a near consensus expresses the view that Proverbs 1–9 somehow operates as an introduction in the final form of Proverbs. Second, these interpreters reflect a high diversity of perspectives on how 1–9 functions as an introduction. Third, there is a lack of argument that demonstrates the function of 1–9 with an in-depth treatment of examples from 10.1–22.16. In other words, interpreters affirm the introductory function of Proverbs 1–9 but have not defended or systematically explained it. A defence of this function goes hand in hand with an explanation of it, and that is what I propose to do in the chapters that follow, after a consideration of how that defence is best conducted.

1.6. *Methodology: A Macro-Redactional Approach*

It is evident that much of the current scholarship on Proverbs concentrates on the book's final form, especially among scholars from Britain and the United States. Many interpreters, however, not least in Germany, maintain a diachronic methodology, one that predominated in the nineteenth century and continues to appear in works on Proverbs 1–9 and

10.1–22.16.⁷⁰ In view of these traditions, I have made mention of 'synchronic', 'diachronic', and 'final-form' readings of the book, and it is vital to be clear about what exactly I am doing in this study. The question of how Proverbs 1–9 functions is especially difficult in this regard but, in my judgment, it is given its most cogent answer when a few key methodological supports are put in place. On the one hand, diachronic analysis of the detailed textual history of Proverbs will be eschewed. Studies of that quality, for instance, query the unity of Proverbs 1–9, as it has been suggested that 1–9 presents a segment of text largely unified in its purpose, and that 1.1-7⁷¹ and 9.7-12⁷² appeared in the final stage of the book's editorial history, providing advantageous perspectives on the whole of Proverbs and thereby serving particular functions.⁷³ Proverbs 1.1-7 introduces Proverbs and notifies the reader of the material that follows, and 9.7-12 likewise accounts for both Proverbs 1–9 and the text that follows and functions as a transition from the first collection to the second. The suitability of 6.1-19 within 1–9 is much more contentious, and yet convincing arguments for its integrity have been made.⁷⁴ The

70. E.g. Rolf Schäfer, *Die Poesie der Weisen: Dichotomie als Grundstruktur der Lehr- und Weisheitsgedichte in Proverbien 1–9* (Neukirchen-Vluyn: Neukirchener Verlag, 1999); Andreas Scherer, *Das weise Wort und seine Wirkung: Eine Untersuchung zur Komposition und Redaktion von Proverbia 10,1–22,16* (Neukirchen-Vluyn: Neukirchener Verlag, 1999).

71. Magne Sæbø, *Sprüche*, ATD 16 (Göttingen: Vandenhoeck & Ruprecht, 2012), 17–18, 21; C. H. Toy, *A Critical and Exegetical Commentary on the Book of Proverbs*, ICC (Edinburgh: T. & T. Clark, 1904), 4; cf. Fox, *Proverbs 1–9*, 325–6. Those who connect the title (1.1) with 1.8–9.18 consider 1.2-7 as the relevant section.

72. See Toy, *Proverbs*, 192; Hitzig, *Die Sprüche*, 85; Sæbø, *Sprüche*, 140–1. Cf. Fox (*Proverbs 1–9*, 306–7) who sees 9.7-12 as an interpolation with no transitional role. While many argue that it represents a redactional addition, they nevertheless claim that the chapter makes good sense in its final form, most likely functioning as a link between Proverbs 1–9 and 10.1–22.16 (so, e.g., Loader, *Proverbs*, 380–1; Plöger, Van Leeuwen, Waltke). For the integration of this passage with Proverbs 9, see Rick Byargeon, 'The Structure and Significance of Prov 9:7-12', *JETS* 40 (1997): 367–72.

73. On the unity of Proverbs 1–9, see Achim Müller, *Proverbien 1–9: Der Weisheit Neue Kleider*, BZAW 291 (Berlin: de Gruyter, 2000).

74. Hitzig, *Die Sprüche*, 46–7; Fox, *Proverbs 1–9*, 222, 224–5, 227; Weeks, *Instruction*, 224–5. Some see 6.1-19's dissemblance as no problem and propose that, despite its difference from Proverbs 1–9, it serves to warn the son of figures other than the seductive woman who appears in surrounding chapters, elevating laziness (6.6-11) and worthlessness (6.12-15) to the level of wickedness and punishment entailed in Proverbs 5 (e.g. Delitzsch, *Proverbs*, 1:134–5; Loader, *Proverbs 1–9*, 251–2. Cf. Heim, *Poetic Imagination*, 161–6, 174–81). By treating 6.1-19 as a part of chapters

present study treats chapters 1–9 not as a collection of editorial placements but as a unified whole that was then placed at the front of 10–29, which offers promising suggestions for anyone interested in the editorial history of Proverbs.

On the other hand, there is a second question that recurs in diachronic study of Proverbs, which asks how 1–9 functions in relationship to other portions of the book, what might be referred to as the book's 'macro-redactional history'.[75] That level of critical analysis suits my question quite well and, thanks to the work of Milstein, is corroborated by evidence of various textual witnesses in the ancient Near East, and not only perceived inconsistencies within the final form of biblical literature. For Proverbs 1–9 is generally agreed to have post-dated the main sections of 10–29 and is believed to have been composed in view of those chapters.[76] That premise is the foundational assumption for this study. Consequently, Proverbs 1–9 may have been developed with a function that deliberately accounted for the interpretive challenges of 10–29. If Proverbs 10–29 appeared later than 1–9, especially by the hand of a different author, then it would be difficult to demonstrate, on diachronic grounds, that 1–9 functions with interpretive consequences for 10–29. But there are good reasons to think that Proverbs 1–9 was added to 10–29 and done so with a deliberate strategy in view.

1–9 and including portions of that passage in the argument for 1–9's introductory function, 6.1-19 will be shown to have interpretive bearing on chapters 10–29 like the rest of 1–9.

75. On the book's compositional history, see Ewald, *Die poetischen Bücher*, 2–44 (followed by Delitzsch and Zöckler), 28–9; Toy, *Proverbs*, xxx; F. Hitzig, *Die Sprüche Salomo's* (Zurich: Orell, Füssli & Co., 1858), XVII–XVIII; Sæbø, *Sprüche*, 388–9. Such scholars disagreed primarily on how they accounted for the differences within Proverbs, inclining towards either the material's unity or diversity.

76. Schipper, *Hermeneutik*; Wildeboer, *Sprüche*, 1. Cf. Heim, *Poetic Imagination*, 616, 629–30. In contrast to chronological sequence, the actual dates that portions of Proverbs appeared in literary form are largely irrelevant to my question and largely a matter of subjective opinion anyway. The debate centres on an early, including Solomonic-era, time period (Kenneth Kitchen, 'Proverbs and Wisdom Books of the Ancient Near East: The Factual History of a Literary Form', *TynBul* 28 [1977]: 69–114; cf. David Carr, *The Formation of the Hebrew Bible: A New Reconstruction* [New York: Oxford University Press, 2011], 403–29, esp. 403, 410) versus a period beginning in the eighth–seventh centuries BCE and extending into the 'Ptolemaic period' (Fox, *Proverbs 10–31*, 499–505; Leo Perdue, *The Sword and the Stylus: An Introduction to Wisdom in the Age of Empires* [Grand Rapids: Eerdmans, 2008], 86–9, 99). Ultimately, evidence allows quite little certainty for precise dates for either the oral origins or literary beginnings of Proverbs.

In the first place, we have the results of diachronic studies on Proverbs, which, despite their in some cases problematic assumptions, have produced a consensus about the sequential history of the main sections of Proverbs and how they came together. In the second place, Proverbs 1–9 stands at the outset of the book. Whether placed there later, or located there first and then supplemented, those chapters are the first encounter that readers have with the book as it stands, and that location ought to be accounted for.[77] In the third place, as explained in the above discussion about 'revision by introduction', there is precedence for what I am proposing about Proverbs 1–9, namely, that it was attached to pre-existing material with a particular interpretive purpose in mind.

Recalling the evidence for 'revision by introduction' and my macro-scale approach to biblical criticism, Milstein also gives voice to a method of studying textual formation that I would echo.

> I have tried to approach textual transmission not with the aim of nailing down every verse or line, but instead with the aim of identifying the major shifts in perspective that took place in the course of transmission. I have done this with the understanding that these major shifts may well be full of all sorts of other additions and omissions that I could not possibly reconstruct. I have tried to keep my sights, however, on the big picture, in the hopes of getting a glimpse, if but fleeting, of the masters. Toward this end, I chose to focus on revision through introduction because this method so often involved large-scale contributions: contributions that are arguably more detectable, more 'trackable'. This method was apparently employed by Israelite and Mesopotamian scribes alike, as a convenient tool for revamping a work and allowing it to serve new contexts.[78]

So, while various cases might be made for textual changes within Proverbs 1–9 itself, my eyes remain stayed on the larger portions of the book, and with those portions in view, it seems reasonable to begin a study into the function of Proverbs 1–9 by stating that those chapters were placed, at some point, by some person or peoples, at the outset of a pre-existing portion of Proverbs, perhaps 10.1–22.16 and possibly chapters 10–29.

---

77. For Carr (*Formation*, 412), that fronted locale of Proverbs 1–9 is the only justification for acknowledging it as an introduction: 'Whatever introductory function [chapters 1–9] now play vis-à-vis the collection as a whole comes simply as a result of their placement toward the start of Proverbs'. The 'remarkable lack of specific connections to the material they are supposed to have been composed from the outset to introduce' will be shown instead to be substantial, even if not in every case linguistic as Carr may wish, throughout the present study.

78. Milstein, *Tracking the Master Scribe*, 211.

As for chapters 30–31, I am not sure when these came to be. Many have proposed that these chapters form complementary 'bookends' with 1–9, and in Chapter 3 I interpret Proverbs 30 in juxtaposition with Proverbs 1–9, basically in a synchronic relation, to offer several avenues for telling the redactional story of Proverbs 30–31.[79]

In summary, the location of Proverbs 1–9, the results of historical-critical studies on Proverbs, and the socio-historical evidence of other scribe-added introductions form a collective justification for the assumption that Proverbs 1–9 was added to 10–29.[80] Though dictating little about how Proverbs 1–9 came to be and when and how it may have been added to another portion of Proverbs, this evidence grounds the assumption that those chapters were indeed placed at the front of much of Proverbs, and perhaps for some deliberate purpose.

Given this assumption, several caveats come to the fore. First, while my project bumps up against questions about scribal practice and scribal culture, it will remain silent on many of the scholarly debates in this area.[81]

---

79. The LXX arranged sections of Prov. 24.23–31.31 in a different order than the MT (LXX = MT 1.1–24.22; 30.1-14; 24.23-34; 30.15-33; 31.1-9; 25.1–29.27; 31.10-31). While previously thought to mark these sections as independently circulated collections, the sequence of 24–29 and 30–31, which is separated in the LXX yet matches that of the MT, suggests otherwise (Fox, *Proverbs 1–9*, 363). The location of sections in the book of Proverbs tends not to influence views of its redaction, except for its 'bookends', and LXX Proverbs 1–9 shows few substantial differences from the MT (1.7; 3.18; 5.20; 6.6-11; 9.10, 12; the Peshitta and Targum translate even more woodenly). Supported by similar authorial concerns in the Syriac and in medieval commentaries, Waltke's explanation (*Proverbs 1–15*, 4–5) for the LXX order seems possible: to maintain the impression of Solomonic authorship, given the removal of 'Agur' and 'Lemuel' in 30.1 and 31.1, and adding 'Solomon' to 22.17 and 24.23, supported by interlacing chapters 30–31 throughout 'Solomonic' material. Thematic connections may also have motivated the LXX, such as kingship in 30.1-9 and ch. 25 or the wicked man versus the wise woman in ch. 29 and 31.10-31 (for the latter, see Johann Cook, *The Septuagint of Proverbs: Jewish and/or Hellenistic Proverbs? Concerning the Hellenistic Colouring of LXX Proverbs*, VTSup 69 [Leiden: Brill, 1997], 293–315).

80. For a discussion of what I mean by 'historical-critical', see above.

81. The many questions that I am referring to are the existence, roles, and social location of scribes, and the materials and practices associated with them. For an overview of material evidence and writing practices, see Lindsay Askin, *Scribal Culture in Ben Sira*, JSJSup 184 (Leiden: Brill, 2018), 21–31. For an assessment of the mainly textual evidence for 'scribes' in the Second Temple period, see Samuel L. Adams, 'The Social Location of the Scribe in the Second Temple Period', in *Sibyls,*

It, instead, will supply one lengthy case study of a practice that certain scribes exercised: 'revision by introduction'.

Second, the nature of this study's question means that a simple synchronic–diachronic distinction is not feasible. The best answer to how Proverbs 1–9 functions within the book, which must also account for the scholarship that has built up around it, is not given by a baldly synchronic study, whereby Proverbs 10–31 is read in light of Proverbs 1–9 and 1–9 then read in light of 10–31 and assorted readings then tossed together. A strictly synchronic reading would interpret these sections of Proverbs reciprocally, giving priority to neither and consistently interpreting the parts in light of the whole. Although the reciprocity of collections in Proverbs will be attended to in this study, as explained below, it will become evident that this mode of interpretation supports a uni-directional intention for Proverbs 1–9, that it functions as an introduction designed for the interpretation of the rest of the book. That argument, derived from the question of how Proverbs 1–9 functions for the book of Proverbs, operates on the assumption that Proverbs 1–9 was added to Proverbs 10–29, or at least 10.1–22.16. This assumption is the only 'diachronic' principle of thesis; for as independent collections of chapters, Proverbs 1–9 and 10–29 are treated as unified wholes and no attempt is made to investigate the origin or emendation of passages therein, except on a text-critical level for which we have evidence of alternative textual witnesses.[82] Therefore, in this instance, it seems best to avoid the language of 'synchronic' and 'diachronic', to instead observe that we have good reasons to think that Proverbs 1–9 was added to Proverbs 10–29, and to proceed with the question of why it stands at the head of Proverbs.

Third, although I argue that Proverbs 1–9 serves a deliberate and, in some senses, authoritative role for the interpretation of the rest of the book, that is not to say that other sources of interpretive insight are rendered void or that there is a singular intended reading of Proverbs 10–31, only accessible via Proverbs 1–9. My ambitions, in other words, do not operate as if there is one correct reading of a passage over and

---

Scriptures, and Scrolls: John Collins at Seventy, ed. Joel Baden et al., JSJSup 175 (Leiden: Brill, 2016), 22–37. Adams' work shows the lack of specificity with which we can answer questions about who may have added Proverbs 1–9 to the book.

82. This reflects the way in which Sæbø (*Sprüche*, 23) recognizes the priority of the final form: 'Dabei wird man – energischer als früher – nach der hermeneutischen Funktion des Redaktionsprozesses auf die Endgestalt hin fragen müssen, zumal sie letzten Endes die Weisheitslehre und Theologie des Buches mit bestimmt, und die Einheit des Buches erst mit seiner Endgestalt gegeben ist'.

against an accumulation of misguided interpretations. A variety of valid understandings of the biblical material are possible, and, when a particular interpretation is argued for, it simply represents my best attempt to account for the available evidence and the place of Proverbs 1–9 at the outset of the book rather than an attempt to compel a singular meaning. An argument of this sort, though, does become falsifiable, and that very possibility indicates how the introductory function of Proverbs 1–9 becomes not only one possible way of reading the text but one of the most convincing. This line of thought is made evident in view of resources alternative to Proverbs 1–9, that is, other texts or sources of knowledge that might revoke its role as an 'introduction'. As mentioned above, Proverbs 1–9 may help interpreters understand challenging aspects of 10–29, many of which proceed from what I have called 'assumptions', that is, the information or skills that the text requires for interpretation. Put another way, what concepts, background knowledge, or interpretive faculties does this text presuppose? There are many plausible resources for supplying insight into the meaning of individual proverbs, such as other ancient Near Eastern texts, various portions of the OT, and any demonstrably prevalent thoughts or beliefs among the ancient audiences of Proverbs. These other sources of interpretive information provide possible alternatives to 1–9 and therefore might discredit its function as an introduction. For if 1–9 were to function as an introduction, it would be expected to offer a distinct and more coherent contribution than other resources to the meaning of 10–31, though not necessarily an exclusive contribution.

When such alternatives to 1–9, like an Egyptian poem or a biblical psalm, seem to trouble the argument for 1–9's introductory role or to propel it, then that resource is dealt with. For example, if a proverb uses language quite common to the OT, such as 'favour from the Lord' (e.g. Prov. 18.22), then the uses of that phrase throughout the OT should be reckoned with in interpretation before jumping immediately to Proverbs 1–9 to show how it features the Lord's favour and illuminates the interpretation of said proverb. Proverbs 1–9 may provide significant insight on this topic, but it must be considered alongside the additional OT evidence.

This observation is key for anyone interested in querying the introductory role of Proverbs 1–9, which, by nature of the query itself may be difficult to verify in any satisfactory way. Making the case, in some instances, rests on what many literary studies do, namely, demonstrate one possible reading strategy that exposes interesting interpretations of a text. At this, the synchronic method excels, and there is substantial merit to making not an airtight case that 1–9 serves a singular function in Proverbs and serves that function to the exclusion of other resources, but rather to making a case for its introductory function by presenting a collection of viable examples. At the same time, a more definitive case can be made, especially when working from the assumption that Proverbs 1–9 was deliberately placed at the fore of pre-existing material. For in many instances, the query of how 1–9 functions rests upon the possibility of showing that these chapters provide the most advantageous reading strategy among plausible alternatives. It will become evident that Proverbs 1–9 provides exegetical insight into 10–31 in ways that other texts do not, which suggests that it holds, in some cases, a more privileged interpretive position within Proverbs. Only in determining how these other texts contribute to 10–31 can we have a sense for what 1–9 does and does not accomplish in that regard. All things considered, the macro-redactional approach delineated here is the most viable, at least in the first instance of an extensive exploration of 1–9 as an introduction.

1.7. Two Methodological Avenues to Proverbs

Within such an approach, traditional methods of biblical exegesis are employed to interpret the book of Proverbs, including attention to keywords, socio-cultural context, grammatical features, relevant inter-texts, and other sayings within portions of Proverbs. Each of these requires laying out broader methodologies for determining the function of Proverbs 1–9, and in order to account for the material as thoroughly as possible, I approach Proverbs from two directions: primarily starting with 10.1–22.16 and in one instance with 1–9.

For the textual examples found in Chapters 2–4, I primarily approach the material by starting with Prov. 10.1–22.16 and its specific interpretive challenges, and only subsequently move to Proverbs 1–9, where I demonstrate that 1–9 supplies interpretive insights for the challenges of individual proverbs. In short, the primary method moves from Prov. 10.1–22.16 for problems, to 1–9 for solutions, and then back to 10.1–22.16 for resolution, which accords obviously with the assumption that Proverbs 1–9 were added to the book. But, as mentioned previously, the works of Aletti, Weeks and Schipper indicate that Proverbs 1–9 might have its own interests independent of 10–31 and that the interpretive challenges that vex the sentence literature might distort the main concerns of 1–9. This possibility warrants an alternative methodological approach, so, in what follows, two methods are presented: the first starts with 10.1–22.16 and represents the primary approach of my study; the second starts with 1–9 and accounts for works by interpreters like Aletti. Combining these approaches begets the most robust account of how Proverbs 1–9 functions.

Chapters 2, 4, and part of 3, use the primary method, approaching Proverbs first at 10.1–22.16 and then proceeding to Proverbs 1–9. In one portion of Chapter 3, I use the alternative method, entering Proverbs 1–9 before moving to 10.1–22.16. This direction of interpretation may seem to contradict my starting assumption, that Proverbs 1–9 is later than 10.1–22.16. Why would I then start with the later material if I think it may be intended to clarify issues within the older material? Surely, the hermeneutical issues within that older material must be identified first and then Proverbs 1–9 used as an interpretive aid for said issues. While that is, indeed, my primary method – interpreting 10.1–22.16 with 1–9 – the duty to also consider the alternative – interpreting 1–9 with 10.1–22.16 – remains. This alternative point of departure ensures that the primary features of Proverbs 1–9 are accounted for on their own terms. For the main method, which uses 1–9 to address the categories and questions derived from 10.1–22.16, runs the risk of overlooking 1–9's key features. Approaching 1–9 first not only accounts for the material on its own terms, ensuring that aspects are not overlooked, but in doing so qualifies the argument for its introductory function.

On the one hand, it supports the introductory function of Proverbs 1–9 by showing that the autonomous aims of 1–9 disclose correlations with 10–29 that demonstrate its role as an introduction. As shown in section 3.2, when interpreted on its own Proverbs 1–9 depicts the world as morally ambiguous and reiterates this view to the interpreter, also proffering a solution to such ambiguity. Delineating these features from 1–9 first then exposes similar elements of moral ambiguity in 10–29 that in turn glean interpretive insights from 1–9. This alternative method does not represent an alternative argument; it represents an alternative approach to the material in order to make the same argument and so strengthens the overall case in a fresh way.

On the other hand, this method also exposes the limitations of the argument, disclosing certain priorities of Proverbs 1–9 that have little didactic relevance for 10–29. As mentioned earlier, the links of Proverbs 1–9 with law and Deuteronomy may attest not to its introductory function but to its aim of integrating Proverbs with other portions of the OT. The Deuteronomic ties occur in Proverbs 1–9 and 10–31 and in both are largely assumed conceptions, appearing like icebergs, protruding at particular places and harbouring much more underneath. I have called such formations 'assumptions' whereby a little shows atop the text's surface and implies information or a framework that might draw out latent insights. The Deuteronomic allusions often appear in a similar way – as assumptions – not only in 10–31 but also in 1–9. For this reason, Schipper can say that Proverbs 2 portrays an image of wisdom that concludes with the goal of residing in the land (2.21-22), so that, evidently, 'der Verfasser von Prov. 2 eine bestimmte Texttradition und eine Reflexion über Weisheit bereits voraussetzt', and that 'Prov. 2 auf Dtn 28 Bezug nimmt und auch Dtn 4 und 8 voraussetzt'.[83] Themes such as law in Proverbs must first be understood in light of large portions of other OT texts before they can be convincingly applied to the function of Proverbs 1–9 for the book of Proverbs, an intertextual task that lies beyond the scope of my immediate concerns. Therefore, links with law and Deuteronomy, while clearly significant for Proverbs 1–9 and likely significant for its interpretive function in the book, are not the starting point of this study. It begins instead with places where 10–31 clearly makes assumptions that 1–9 does not.

A final question remains about this alternative method: why is it the alternative? Why not use it as the primary approach? First, I start with 10.1–22.16 because this crystallizes the interpretive question for Proverbs 1–9 and facilitates a clearer argument as to how 1–9 functions. Second, the alternative method offers potential objections to the primary argument, and since it may indeed falsify arguments based in the primary method, using the independent concerns of Proverbs 1–9 as a starting point remains essential but secondary.

The preceding remarks concern the initial step of the primary methodological approach to Proverbs: to identify the interpretive challenges of particular passages in Prov. 10.1–22.16. In summary, I consider challenges that are prominent within Proverbs and call upon ancient Near Eastern, biblical, and socio-cultural evidence in as much as it bears direct relevance, most importantly direct objections, to my main concern: the function of Proverbs 1–9 for the book of Proverbs. After uncovering the interpretive challenges of a particular proverb in light of relevant evidence, Proverbs 1–9 is read with these challenges in mind to see if it proffers any insight, asking, what texts in 1–9 address the issues raised by 10–31, and do these texts illuminate any of the questions? I argue that Proverbs 1–9 frequently offers interpretive insight into issues of meaning that arise in 10–31 and in this way functions didactically. It is along this avenue that I argue for the bulk of this study, (1) approaching Prov. 10.1–22.16 to identify interpretive challenges, (2) unpacking evidence relevant to them, (3) then approaching Proverbs 1–9 with questions derived from those challenges and (4) demonstrating the distinctive and coherent interpretive insight that 1–9 supplies for them.

83. Schipper, *Hermeneutik*, 78–9, 153. For a full evaluation of Schipper's interpretation of Proverbs 2, see section 3.1.

The complications faced at the outset of this study that I have taken several pages to detail are, in my judgment, necessary. For in order to answer the question of how Proverbs 1–9 functions, while accounting for its history of interpretation and the claims of the text itself, several decisions must be made, and these decisions are not always straightforward. I have eschewed a strictly synchronic reading and, at the same time, a historical-critical analysis of the more detailed sort, because there is good reason to see Proverbs 1–9 as a unified whole that was later added to some or all of Proverbs 10–29. And although that leads me to wonder if an editor intended a uni-directional purpose for Proverbs 1–9 – that it interprets 10–29 – we cannot entirely do away with reading in both directions. For it is only by considering a bi-directional interpretation of the parts of Proverbs that confident and nuanced claims can be made about if and how Proverbs 1–9 functions in one direction. Thus the possibility that 10–29 informs the interpretation 1–9, and thereby counters or qualifies its function as an introduction, will be considered at various points in what follows, as will the possibility that neither section really lends much help to the other at all. But amidst these possibilities, Proverbs 1–9 will still exhibit its ability to supply distinctive and consistent insights into the interpretive issues of 10–31.

1.8. *Outline of Chapters*

Over the course of this chapter, I have delineated a problem within interpretations of Proverbs and proposed a theory of how to address it, which entailed a look at the text of Proverbs itself, its ancient Near Eastern counterparts, and a review of historical positions on the topic of Proverbs 1–9 as a 'prologue', along with those who do not necessarily view it with that label. A key assumption has been defended about the macro-history of Proverbs, namely that chapters 1–9 were added later, and a pair of interrelated methodologies have also been detailed, which approach the biblical material from two entry points in order to establish a more reliable analysis of the text. My selection of topics from Proverbs, which dictates the shape of the remaining chapters, also aims at reliable and thorough analysis, as each topic accounts for a predominant feature of Proverbs that is present in chapters 1–9 and 10–31. All examples fall under three contexts of interpretation – literary, rhetorical and theological – each of which receives its own chapter.

Over the course of Chapter 2, I explore one of the most palpable features in the book of Proverbs: its characters. The wise, the foolish, the righteous and the wicked show up in most chapters, especially 10.1–22.16, a collection of sayings that has prompted the enquiry into character types. Section 2.1 addresses the question of what these characters are with respect to their identities, which may be exaggerated or real or somewhere in between. Proverbs 10.1-5 poses two particular interpretive challenges, the first being what to make of the 'treasures of wickedness' in 10.2, as it has been debated whether gaining treasures by wickedness is even possible or to be expected. Second, the ambiguous syntax of 10.4a renders two possible interpretations of the line and prompts a larger question of how character relates to behaviour. In view of such questions, Proverbs 1–9 is consulted to determine if it might lend insight into these interpretive issues and into character types more broadly. Proverbs 1.10-19, the scenario in which the Proverbial father warns his son against joining a flagrant gang of greedy sinners, displays an extreme portrait of wickedness, names it as such, labels the culprits 'sinners', and then generalizes from this particular scenario to reveal, for interpreters, that the characters in Proverbs – like these 'sinners' – represent extreme exaggerations of humans rather than the sorts of people that an ancient reader might encounter on a daily basis. With additional support from 6.1-19, Proverbs 1–9 shows that character types are like caricatures of people, though not strictly negative in their portrayal or unreal.

In addition to the identity of these characters, the question of how different character types maintain their identities in relation to each other also arises, quite an important question given the abundance and diversity of character lexemes in Proverbs. Knut Heim has proposed a theory of 'coreferentiality' that interprets Proverbial characters as different portrayals of an ultimately good or bad person. They represent, fundamentally, neither distinct figures nor amalgamations of one person, but rather distinct qualities from different realms of life, unified in their overall characteristic of good or evil. Focusing especially on Proverbs 2 and the conclusion of Proverbs 3 (vv. 31-35), I show that Proverbs 1–9, a section unaccounted for by Heim, affirms and instils this sense of coreferentiality between its characters.

Having discerned interpretive challenges in Prov. 10.1–22.16 and then consulted 1–9, the following step determines how 1–9 might resolve the challenges from 10.1–22.16. As mentioned, Prov. 10.1-5 produced two interpretive challenges, one related to the phrase 'treasures of wickedness' (10.2) and the other to the ambiguous syntax of 10.4, which may render 'a poor man makes a lax palm' or 'a lax palm makes a poor man' and more importantly opens a series of questions about the possibility of character types and their relation to behaviour. As an interpretive framework, Proverbs 1–9 provides insights into these challenges, demonstrating its didactic function. According to Proverbs 1, the wicked can gain treasures, which means that, for prepared interpreters, the possibility for 'treasures of wickedness' comes as no surprise when encountering 10.2. Proverbs 1 also introduces the interpreter to characters like the 'sinners', suggesting that the 'wicked' of 10.2 connotes the wicked character type, an idealized sort of evil person, who accumulates treasure through evil means, deceptive tactics, and possibly tempting partnerships. As for 10.4, the interpreter fluent in Proverbs 1–9 now knows that behaviour and consequences stem from character rather than vice versa, so that, when confronted with syntactical options in the proverb, he or she may conclude that the idle person begets poverty and, more significantly, that the 'sluggard', though not mentioned in 10.4, serves as a likely and suitable character backdrop.

From the question about the characters' identity follows the question of how they are meant to function for the interpreter. Do Proverbial characters compel some sort of response from the reader? Explored in the section 2.2, the question pertains to rhetoric, viewed simply as the aims and means of persuasion. Other interpreters, commenting on Proverbs 10–31, suggest that character types may function as mirrors for emulation and self-evaluation, prompting readers of Proverbs to imitate or steer clear of certain characters and assess themselves in light of them, not least based on affective postures. Holding these suggestions as hypotheses, I consult Prov. 1.20-33 to discover that it presents a set of bad character types: simpletons, scoffers and fools. These people are condemned by Lady Wisdom and distinguished from her primary audience, who, she indicates, should evaluate these characters and use them for self-reflection, ultimately rejecting the simpleton, the scoffer, and the fool in favour of the right sort of person: 'the one who listens' to her.

Returning to Prov. 10.1–22.16, two sayings are examined – Prov. 15.2 and 18.2 – which include character lexemes, namely the wise person and the fool, and state observations about them without giving explicit advice. In other words, when read on their own, without accounting for Proverbs 1–9, the characters of 15.2 and 18.2 compel no response from the interpreter: wise people simply commend knowledge, and fools do not delight in understanding. They give an indicative rather than imperative portrait of people. While these passages, when read independently of Proverbs 1–9, offer valuable insights, when they are interpreted with 1–9 in view, it becomes clear that both 15.2 and 18.2, and later 29.11, harbour rhetorical force because of their character types. As an interpretive framework, Proverbs 1–9 saturates these proverbs with rhetorical implications, prompting interpreters to emulate good, self-evaluate based on character types, and feel particular ways about them. From both literary and rhetorical perspectives, Proverbs 1–9 functions didactically by constructing a framework within which to understand the characters of Proverbs 10–29.

In Chapter 3, I explore the goals and values of Proverbs based on two particular challenges in Prov. 22.1 – 'A name is to be chosen rather than great riches; favour is better than silver and gold'. The first issue appears when 22.1 is interpreted aside Prov. 16.16, which states that 'To acquire wisdom is much better than gold, and to acquire understanding is to be chosen more than silver'. The juxtaposition of these sayings creates a set of potentially competing values – a name and wisdom – which do not receive an ordered relationship when viewed within Proverbs 10–29 alone. The two values might remain in tension, both simply championed by individual proverbs with no other guidance as to how an interpreter might choose between a name and wisdom if given the option. But it is also worth asking if Proverbs harbours some organizing principle or structure for its values, since it does propound comparative, axiological statements so often, lending suspicion to the idea that 22.1 and 16.16 ought to remain in apposition.

Proverbs 22.1 also produces a question about its use of the lexeme שם, which, based on OT evidence and Akkadian *šumum*, refers to 'fame' or 'reputation' without further qualification, such as positive connotations. Other uses of שם in Proverbs attest to this neutral sense, since the lexeme always occurs with a modifier – such as 'the name of the wicked' – except for its absolute appearance in 22.1. These resources, then, do not address the question of what sort of name Prov. 22.1 envisions. It may remain unqualified, as if a name of any sort, even a 'favourable name' in view of 22.1b, should be chosen rather than great wealth. However, when such questions are posed to Proverbs 1–9, Prov. 22.1 receives interpretive insight, and in the remainder of Chapter 3, I show just that.

The two interpretive challenges related to Prov. 22.1 lead to Proverbs 7–8, chapters quite appropriate for these questions due to their highly rhetorical flavour. They persuade, I argue, towards the goals of avoiding folly and embracing wisdom, goals established by the teaching of the Proverbial father, who portrays these correlative aims while drawing attention to his own teaching. Proverbs 7–8 champions wisdom and wise character as the ultimate goals of education and sets prime value on wisdom as a possession and friend, culminating in a scheme of education: through the text's teachings, acquire wisdom in order to grow in wise character.

This provisional conclusion, though convincingly based on Proverbs 7–8, does not account for the remainder of Proverbs 1–9, with Proverbs 2, the 'Lehrprogramm' of 1–9, posing the greatest potential objection to my proposal. With the work of Bernd Schipper, I argue that Proverbs 2 not only affirms the views of Proverbs 7–8 but also supplements them with a theological layer that colours the whole educational model and specifically modifies it to the following: through the text's teachings and the fear of the Lord, acquire wisdom in order to grow in wise character. When this educational framework is applied to the interpretive challenges of Prov. 22.1, it offers interpretive insights into conceptions of value, goals, and lexical developments. The system of goals and values indicates that if faced with a choice, the interpreter should prefer wisdom (16.16) to fame (22.1), and that the 'name' to be chosen over great riches in 22.1 refers to the reputation that arises from wise character. Proverbs 22.1 and related sayings fit snugly into the system of values and educational goals set forth by Proverbs 1–9, revealing its didactic function for the book of Proverbs.

Extending its scope beyond 10.1–22.16, the teleological network established by Proverbs 1–9 operates in a similar way for 30.1-9. In Proverbs 30, Agur expresses a lack of understanding, wisdom, and, it seems, knowledge of God. Although Agur states a problem and a potential solution, he does not provide the context necessary to answer the question of why his problem is a problem: why has a lack of wisdom provoked such a response? Many interpreters cite other OT texts that Prov. 30.1-9 alludes to, especially Job, Psalms and Deuteronomy, and attempt to explain Agur's statements with one or all of the views found in these other passages. The cacophony of allusions in Prov. 30.1-9, though, can leave the intent of these allusions and their interpretive implications unclear. For clarity, I appeal to Proverbs 1–9, which offers a network of goals to suggest that Agur's problem is a problem because he struggles to attain the educational goals of wisdom's schooling. The very lexemes he uses for 'understanding' and 'wisdom', as well as knowledge of God, appear in Proverbs 1 and 2 where they most directly serve to define the educational scheme of Proverbs. Agur may allude to other OT texts, but his comments also bear an unquestionable connection to Proverbs 1–9 and thereby establish a framework that informs one of the central interpretive challenges of Prov. 30.1-9. In addition to the teleological context of Agur's remarks, Proverbs 1–9 provides insight into a detailed difficulty of Prov. 30.3b, which, based solely on grammatical evidence, may affirm Agur's 'knowledge of God' or deny it. Providing more decisive clarity, the educational scheme outlined in Proverbs 1–9 suggests that Agur has not acquired this knowledge, cohering with the hyperbolic register of these statements and the remainder of the passage.

The second section of Chapter 3 executes an alternative methodology that takes its point of departure from Proverbs 1–9 instead of 10.1–22.16 to ensure that the main features of chapters 1–9 are not overlooked, as these features might very well hamper the conclusion that 1–9 functions didactically. Taking 1–9 on its own terms, Jean-Noël Aletti has disclosed some of the section's main features, arguing that it portrays the world as a morally chaotic and ambiguous place where what is wrong sounds right, like the invitations of the temptress who sounds very much like Wisdom. This moral ambiguity creates problems for those unable to distinguish good and bad. The youth of Proverbs 7, for example, falls prey to seduction and, in a word, lacks discernment, which the father of Proverbs 1–9 shows is necessary for navigating the Proverbial landscape.

A similar depiction, albeit terse, appears in Proverbs 10–29, where fools operate with moral confusion, and certain scenarios portray bad things as good things. The latter occurs in Prov. 14.12 and 18.8 in which the way to death 'seems right to a man' and the whisperer's words taste like 'delicious morsels'. The sayings leave few evaluative clues with which to determine how to respond: should I gobble gossip and enjoy it? Do I simply tread through life and hope for the best? Or is there some way to ensure a livelier outcome? Little more can be said in response to these passages except that they require discernment, which, according to Proverbs 1–9, is the faculty for encountering such moral ambiguity victoriously. But Proverbs 1–9 also shows how such discernment is acquired, namely, through the scheme of education outlined earlier in Chapter 3, a scheme that begins with the father's instruction and the fear of the Lord, leading to the acquisition of wisdom and growth in wise character that wisdom facilitates with the Lord's help. In this way 1–9 functions didactically and exposes features overlooked when taking 10.1–22.16 as the sole point of departure. Even when interpreted on its own terms, Proverbs 1–9 still provides an interpretive framework for material in 10–31.

Chapter 4 examines the theology of Proverbs by organising the 57 sayings from 10.1–22.16 that refer to 'the Lord' or 'God' into three categories: human postures toward the Lord; the supremacy of the Lord's wisdom and sovereignty; and the Lord's affection and assessment. Proverbs 15.33–16.9 is found to include material from each of the three categories and to function as a theological 'kernel' for 10.1–22.16, with its use of יהוה or אלהים being the highest concentration of any keyword in Prov. 10.1–22.16. From this kernel, three sayings, each of which represents one theological category, are selected to serve as examples for extracting an interpretive challenge and determining how Proverbs 1–9 might function for the book's theology.

First, Prov. 16.3 represents sayings that refer to the Lord and also portray human postures towards him, such as 'fear' or 'anger' or, in this case, 'trust', as the proverb baldly commands people to 'trust your works to the Lord', who will establish your plans, and thereby assumes that the Lord deserves trust. But why trust the Lord? After exploring Proverbs 10–31 and other potential interpretive resources (e.g. Prov. 12.2; 16.1, 5, 9; 20.22; 21.3), which could motivate trust based on the Lord's supreme wisdom and dispensation of consequences, this question is posed to Proverbs 1–9. The instructions in Prov. 3.1-12 that address why and how the Lord is worthy of human trust proffer reasons that cohere with those found elsewhere, especially from 10.1–22.16, but they also add another reason: trust the Lord because he loves you and delights in you, like a father does his son (3.11-12). Proverbs 3.11-12 instils an interpretive framework that lends interpretive insight into an assumption of Prov. 16.3, substantiating a response to an interpretive challenge fundamental to the saying.

Proverbs 16.9 represents the second category of theological sayings in Collection II, depicting the superiority of the Lord's wisdom and sovereignty, and often juxtaposing these concepts with human wisdom and control. Proverbs 16.9 observes that humans 'plan' their ways in a largely cognitive sense, and that the Lord 'establishes' their steps, a remark about God that entails both his knowledge and power. The interpretive challenge of this proverb turns on the ambiguous relationship of the two lines, which read 'The heart of man plans his way *while* the Lord establishes his steps' and prompt deeper questions of the human–divine relationship in Proverbs 10–29. Interpreters often assert an antithetical relationship between such lines and view humans as primarily depraved operators who plan ways that the Lord then overrides; humans push the envelope of their cognitive and volitional limitations so that proverbs like 16.9 warn against pressing such boundaries. However, by consulting Proverbs 1–9, specifically 3.19-26 and 8.22-31, I argue that wisdom functions as a mediator between God and humans, 'bridging the gap' so to speak between the Lord's prudent governance and human planning, to render them complementary so long as humans heed wisdom. Proverbs 1–9 confirms the interpretive options of 16.9 and in that way displays theological coherence with 10–29, but it more importantly provides a theological backcloth for the passage, detailing how and why the Lord might oppose one's ways, and in what way one can plan in accord with his wisdom and sovereignty. In this way, Proverbs 1–9 functions didactically.

Third and finally, Prov. 16.2 provides an example of those sayings that portray the Lord's affection and assessment, how he feels about and appraises humans and the world. It states that all ways are 'pure' (זך) in the eyes of humans and that the Lord weighs – in the sense of examining and measuring – human hearts, thereby assuming a notion of 'impurity' and posing the question, what is the human problem in the view of this proverb? Lexical and conceptual links derived from Prov. 16.2 lead to the discovery of interpretive contributions from Proverbs 10–31 and the *Instruction of Amenemope* but also direct us to Prov. 3.31-32 and Proverbs 5, as well as 6.12-19, passages that make remarks about human wrong-doing within the context of comments on the affection or assessment of the Lord. These texts indicate that human affections are a key human problem and that these affections ought to align with the Lord's, in light of his omnicompetence and omniscience. In Proverbs 1–9, the Lord sets the standard for morality, particularly hates evil, and wishes people to align with his appraisal of good and evil and with the way he feels toward them. And so, Proverbs 1–9 lays a backdrop for 16.2 with which to see a more substantial vision of the human problem, that is, what it means to be 'impure'.

In this example, the function of Proverbs 1–9 encounters some of its most obvious limitations. While Proverbs 1–9 offers insight into the interpretive problem of Prov. 16.2 and other sayings like it, it at the same time lacks the comprehensive interpretive punch that it delivers for 16.3 and 16.9. The challenges of Prov. 16.2 unveil even more puzzles within Proverbs 1–9 itself, suggesting that 1–9 makes certain assumptions that no part of the book addresses and thereby requires its own resources for interpretation. But these assumptions do not compromise its didactic role; they reveal the ambit of its introductory function, along with starting points for how Proverbs might integrate with other portions of the OT and its ancient context. Again, the focus of each chapter remains on how Proverbs 1–9 functions for the rest of the book, and the scope of features examined in Chapters 2–4 aims to establish that function in its most significant ways, expounding the role of Proverbs 1–9 for the characters of Proverbs, the educational goals of the book, and its theology. For each perspective, Proverbs 1–9 produces a framework that lends interpretive insights for 10–31, like an interpretive tutor, a map or blueprint, a sort of exegetical glossary for the terse Proverbial sayings, and in this way functions as an introduction.

2

CHARACTER TYPES

One of the most prominent features of Proverbs is its characters. This diverse population most frequently includes the righteous, the wicked, the wise and the fool, and less frequently, the diligent, sluggard, and prudent person, among others. The appearance of these characters in Proverbs, many of whom surface in 1–9 and 10.1–22.16, prompts two interrelated questions: who are they and how are they meant to function for interpreters? It is these two enquiries that are explored in this chapter, which addresses the literary identity and relation of Proverbial characters as well as their rhetorical function. In the first section, it will become clear that the presentation of characters in Prov. 10.1–22.16 raises questions about where such characters lie on the spectrum of ideal to real. Should the wise and foolish persons, for example, be understood as idealized, extreme portraits of wisdom and folly, or as examples of realistic human beings? In addition to the identity of these people, 10.1–22.16 raises the question of how different characters relate with respect to their characteristic features. Are the wise, righteous and diligent figures, for instance, all examples of the same person or completely distinct people or forms of both? Such questions are not entirely new among interpreters of Proverbs, and it is, of course, my ultimate aim to suggest that Proverbs 1–9 addresses these questions in some distinctive way, but there is, first, some essential ground-clearing to be done.

A few studies that focused on character types appeared as parts of larger works during the nineteenth and twentieth centuries.[1] From a

---

1. E.g. Karl Gramberg, *Das Buch der Sprüche Salomo's neu übersetzt* (Leipzig: J. A. G. Weigel, 1828), 16–24; W. Frankenberg, 'Ueber Abfassungs-Ort und-Zeit, Sowie Art und Inhalt von Prov. I-IX', *ZAW* 15 (1895): 110–17; Hans-Jürgen Hermisson, *Studien zur israelitischen Spruchweisheit* (Neukirchen-Vluyn: Neukirchener Verlag des Erziehungsvereins, 1968), 73–6; Brian W. Kovacs, 'Is There a Class-Ethic in Proverbs?', in *Essays in Old Testament Ethics*, ed. John Willis and James Crenshaw (New York: KTAV, 1974), 173–89.

brief description of certain wise and foolish types, to the appearance of characters in Proverbs 10–29 and the concentration of righteous/wicked contrasts in chapters 10–11 and wise/fool contrasts in chapters 14–15, interpreters have discovered a firm antithesis between the character types, a polarity referred to as 'binary anthropology'. For some, the characters' attitudes are emphasized more than their deeds or traits, and when such character attitudes are linked with their corresponding outcomes, the relationship becomes known as the 'character–consequence' nexus. While both the similarities and distinctions between the character terms are still contested, the interpretation of Proverbs 10–15 remains preoccupied with antithetical character types and the attitude or character of these types.[2]

Aside from these points of agreement, three lines of enquiry remain inconclusive or unexplored: what exactly these types are, how they relate, and a comparison of their appearance in Proverbs 1–9 versus 10.1–22.16.[3] As to the first, McKane moved beyond studies of character types that focused on their lexemes and offered a theory of how these characters function on a literary level.[4] He comments that 10.1–22.16 gives 'the impression of an unreal black and white schematism' for its characters, and he offers as a 'theory' that 'for the *saddiq* this is the best of all possible

---

2. Interpreters specifically debate whether the terms reflect synonymous types, completely distinct types, or a blend of the two. Most recently, compare Knut M. Heim, 'Coreferentiality, Structure and Context in Proverbs 10.1-5', *Journal of Translation and Textlinguistics* 6 (1993): 183–209; Ruth Scoralick, *Einzelspruch und Sammlung: Komposition im Buch der Sprichwörter Kapitel 10–15* (Berlin: de Gruyter, 1995), 27–43; Sun Myung Lyu, *Righteousness in the Book of Proverbs*, FAT 2/55 (Tübingen: Mohr Siebeck, 2012), 52.

3. Discussion also exists regarding the relation of Proverbial character types to ancient Near Eastern characters. As to the origin and development of the character terms, Nili Shupak (*Where Can Wisdom Be Found?*, 199–212, 231–65, esp. 259–65) has offered the most conclusive study; the debate barely continues. See also Shupak, 'Positive and Negative Human Types in the Egyptian Wisdom Literature', in *Homeland and Exile: Biblical and Ancient Near Eastern Studies in Honour of Bustenay Oded*, ed. Gershon Galil, Mark Geller and Alan Millard, VTSup 130 (Leiden: Brill, 2009), 245–60.

4. Interpreters have widely provided definitions of lexemes that refer to these characters, with descriptions of their contextual and lexical meanings based on different grammatical forms. Among others, see Nili Shupak, *Where Can Wisdom Be Found?*, 199–212, 231–58; Jutta Hausmann, *Studien zum Menschenbild der älteren Weisheit (Spr 10ff.)*, FAT 7 (Tübingen: Mohr Siebeck, 1995), 9–104 (she focuses exclusively on Proverbs 10–31); Michael V. Fox, 'Words for Wisdom', *Zeitschrift für Althebraistik* 6 (1993): 149–65; Fox, 'Words for Folly', *Zeitschrift für Althebraistik* 10 (1997): 4–17; Müller, *Proverbien*, 320; Lyu, *Righteousness*, 46–59.

worlds'.⁵ I understand McKane to mean that the righteous character is portrayed in an ideal existence of flawless actions, attitudes, relationships, and consequences, a proposal that has been expanded by identifying the righteous or wise person in Proverbs as a 'typisches Weisheitsideal'.⁶ Proverbs 10.1–22.16 confirms this possibility, as Prov. 19.24 and 22.13, for example, exaggerate people into 'caricatures' that cannot possibly represent real figures.⁷ The sluggard puts forward a ludicrous notion – 'A lion is outside! In the middle of the market I shall be slain!' (22.13) – and is likewise described in implausibly lazy terms: 'The sluggard buries his hand in the dish, he will not even bring it back to his mouth' (19.24). By labelling such a figure a 'caricature' I do not necessarily mean a negative representation or a misrepresentation, as often appears in modern newspapers, but only an extremely exaggerated form, whether negatively or positively portrayed. Although the sluggard does seem to embody the negative form of a caricature, other characters in Proverbs will embody the positive version of certain extremes. I refer to these portraits as 'ideals', meaning that the characters embody their virtues or vices to the uttermost extent. The sluggard, for example, refuses to work and is lazy to the most thorough and extreme degree. Such thorough embodiment constitutes him as ideal, and his extreme embodiment gives him his caricatured quality. This understanding of characters in Proverbs is still under debate, as Sæbø, for instance, questions whether or not the characters of Proverbs 10–15 represent idealized caricatures: 'Ob die positiven Eigenschaften darüber hinaus ein „Ideal" vom Menschen vorstellen wollen, bleibt trotz gelegentlicher Behauptung fraglich'.⁸ The characters of Proverbs may represent something more 'real' than 'ideal', and their identity remains open to question, and yet within these disagreements about what character types are, Proverbs 1–9 has not been adequately incorporated into the discussion, a discussion that instead tends to concentrate on 10–29 and especially 10–15. It is my contention that Proverbs 1–9 offers guidance in answering current questions about the identity of Proverbial characters.

A second area of interest attends not so much to the real or ideal identity of these characters but more to how they relate to each other. Heim has championed the question and argues that the character terms in Prov.

---

5. William McKane, *Proverbs: A New Approach*, OTL (London: SCM Press, 1970), 16.

6. Hausmann, *Studien*, 346; 'a (stereo)typical wisdom ideal'.

7. McKane, 'Functions', 173. He notes the same observation in Toy, Ringgren, and Gemser.

8. Sæbø, *Sprüche*, 26, see also 27.

10.1–22.16 can be 'co-referential' according to their meanings, syntagms and connotations.⁹ He divides the lexemes from Proverbs 10 into semantic fields of morality, intellect, and diligence, such as the righteous/wicked, the wise/fool, and the diligent/slothful. He then shows how terms from each group occur in similar thematic contexts or in direct parallel, and that each contrasting pair represents both a positive and negative type of character. So, the diligent person and the sluggard, a pair of characters defined by their relation to work, are in one case 'good' (diligent) and in the other 'bad' (sluggard). Likewise, the righteous/wicked refer to moral character, and the wise/fool refer to intellectual, and yet each of them also refers to either a 'good' or 'bad' character type. The specific characters, in other words, are not identical but coreferential. Heim also demonstrates that the character types derive not only from specific lexemes but also from their predicates. For example, the 'prudent son' is 'one who gathers in summer' (Prov. 10.5a), and thus this character is not only referred to by בן מביש ('prudent son') but also by the characteristic attributed to him, as the 'one who gathers in summer'. Accounting for such predicate descriptions furthermore enables one to account for all of a verse's material – its subjects and predicate descriptions – and also reveals the collection's focus on characters. Thus, 10.1–22.16 features character and attitude, portraying types not only through singular lexemes but also through positive or negative predicated descriptions.

I find Heim's argument convincing, commended also by its sensitivity to the linguistic concepts of sense and referent, which allow him to distinguish the terms and phrases themselves from the object referred to and to retain distinction between terms while also identifying their commonalities. His initial article, described above, also accounts for all of the material in Prov. 10.1-5, yielding a focus on character in a passage representative of 10.1–22.16, and thereby providing a starting point from which to approach the sayings material. For, six of the seven characterizations of 'diligence' appear in Prov. 10.1-5 (10.4-5), plus coreferential terms in the intellectual (e.g. wise/foolish) and moral fields (e.g. righteous/wicked).¹⁰ Heim's work does not, however, account for co-referentiality in Proverbs 1–9 or the function of the 'way' metaphor, which is where I aim to take the discussion.¹¹

---

9. Heim, 'Coreferentiality'.
10. Heim, 'Coreferentiality', 199.
11. The function of the way metaphor relates also to the limits of Heim's argument, which could, arguably, be pushed to show that each and every character type does not occur adjacent to another and therefore fails to acquire a coreferential

Third, how do the characters in Proverbs 1–9 and 10.1–22.16 compare? Some suggest that Proverbs 1–9 presents a portrait of characters that is distinct from 10.1–22.16.[12] Others hold that 1–9 plays a significant role for the interpretation of characters in the sayings material, which is a much more convincing proposal, in my judgment. Christopher Ansberry writes that in Proverbs 10–15,

> The 'wise' and the 'righteous' continue to serve as positive archetypes who represent the way of life.... These personages not only bind the collections together through shared vocabulary and imagery, but they also provide a hermeneutical guide for the reader. The prologue describes socio-moral values through a series of characters and root metaphors in order to provide an ethical framework through which to evaluate the sayings in the sentence literature.[13]

Ansberry has articulated a cogent theory about the characters and the function of Proverbs 1–9 and has also attended to the female figures therein. However, the traditional character types that bind 1.1–22.16, such as the wise and righteous, are not addressed, and the focus remains instead on those figures who feature only in 1–9: the two female figures of Wisdom and Folly, the foreign woman, and the simpleton.[14] The scope of characters examined in Proverbs 1–9 needs to be expanded.

Sun Myung Lyu continues with further proposals about how characters function and on the role of Proverbs 1–9:

> Proverbs' character of the righteous is to be studied, mimicked, and internalized in the pupil's life. Proverbs 1–9 gives a structured "theory of learning" and guiding principles for using the raw material in the rest of the book.... The binary anthropology of Proverbs, coupled with its ardent emphasis on wisdom, is the crystallization of Israelite wisdom that enables moral imagination to bloom into moral character.[15]

---

label of good or bad. For example, a fool and the greedy person may be coreferential, but other characters, such as the violent person, may not. They may, instead, stand relatively isolated in Proverbs, even in Proverbs 1–9. As argued below, the use of the way only strengthens the case for coreferentiality.

12. Hausmann, *Studien*, 347; Kenneth Aitken, *Proverbs* (Philadelphia, PA: Westminster Press, 1986), 135.

13. Ansberry, *Be Wise*, 76.

14. See Ansberry, *Be Wise*, 46–69.

15. Lyu, *Righteousness*, 74–5.

Lyu also mentions the more vivid characterization of negative types, such as the gang, in Proverbs 1–9, but does not support or develop his claims about the role of 1–9 in relation to 10.1–22.16. Despite the promising proposals regarding the characters of Proverbs, what remains to be seen is how Proverbs 1–9 functions in this respect, with a detailed examination of characters common to both collections.

There have been several possible explanations for the identities of the characters in Proverbs and how these characters relate, broaching conceptions of idealized portraits and co-referentiality. But there remains no developed demonstration of such identities or a comparison of character appearances that accounts for both Proverbs 1–9 and 10.1–22.16. Consequently, in the first section of this chapter, two overarching questions are posed to 1–9 in order to determine its function for 10.1–22.16: (1) How does Proverbs 1–9 intend to portray its characters, as idealized caricatures or something else? (2) How do the characters relate in view of Heim's coreferentiality theory? A key text from 10.1–22.16 (10.1-5) is outlined in its hermeneutical assumptions and debates, which will supplement this pair of primary questions with two additional subquestions. Having all of these queries in tow, I then consult Proverbs 1–9 and argue that it functions didactically for Prov. 10.1-5, especially 10.2 and 10.4. The second section of this chapter follows up on these conclusions about character identity to argue that Proverbs 1–9 also operates didactically with respect to the overall function of character types.

2.1. *The Identity of Character Types*

2.1.1. *Character Types in Proverbs 10.1-5*

For examining the identity of Proverbial characters in terms of what or who they are, the significance of Prov. 10.1-5 should not be underestimated. The 'righteous' and 'wicked', two of the most prominent character terms in the book of Proverbs, appear with especially high frequency in 10.1–11.13, which contains 30 percent of the total occurrences of these terms in 1.1–22.16.[16] Observing this peculiar concentration, it has been argued that Collection II connects to Collection I via the mention of parents, wisdom, and folly in their initial passages (1.7-8; 10.1) and that

---

16. In Collection I, רשע occurs in substantive (7×) and alternative forms (2×), and in Collection II (54×) with alternative forms (5×): Prov. 10.1–11.13 (18×); chs. 10–15 (40×); 16.1–22.16 (14×). The lexeme צדיק occurs as follows: Collection I (4×); Collection II (49×); 10.1–11.13 (16×); chs. 10–15 (39×); 16.1–22.16 (10×). Thus, Prov. 10.1–11.13 contains 18 of 61 occurrences of רשע in Collections I and II, and for צדיק, 16 of 53. (Statistics are based on Accordance Bible software.)

Prov. 10.1–11.13 operates as a sort of character kernel, a set of neighbouring verses dense with character referents.[17] The character terms of 10.1–22.16 are dominated by the righteous and wicked, along with the wise and foolish, all four of which appear as contrasting pairs in 10.1b-3. In addition to these types, as mentioned above, 10.4-5 contains coreferential terms in the semantic fields of intelligence and diligence, suggesting that 10.1-5 is quite representative of the character population in Proverbs. Based on its connections with Proverbs 1–9 and its cluster of representative character lexemes, Prov. 10.1-5 constitutes a passage well-suited for studying character types in 10.1–22.16.

משלי שלמה פ	10.1	The proverbs of Solomon:[18]
בן חכם ישמח־אב		A wise son makes a father glad
ובן כסיל תוגת אמו		a foolish son is his mother's sorrow[19]
לא־יועילו אוצרות רשע	10.2	Treasures of wickedness[20] do not profit
וצדקה תציל ממות		but righteousness delivers from death
לא־ירעיב יהוה נפש צדיק	10.3	The Lord does not let the appetite[21] of the righteous be hungry
והות רשעים יהדף		but the desire of the wicked ones he thrusts away
ראש עשה כף־רמיה	10.4	A lax palm makes a poor man
ויד חרוצים תעשיר		but the hand of the diligent ones makes rich
אגר בקיץ בן משכיל	10.5	The one who gathers in summer is a prudent son;
נרדם בקציר בן מביש		the one who sleeps in harvest is a shameful son[22]

Heim has summarized the meaning of the passage as a coherent whole: 'Be a wise son and be diligent, because then you will not have to gain

---

17. John Goldingay, 'The Arrangement of Sayings in Proverbs 10–15', *JSOT* 19 (1994): 75–83. Proverbs 10.1-5 operates like the theological kernel of Proverbs (15.33–16.9), a starting point that will prove fruitful in Chapter 4.

18. The LXX and some MSS omit the title, but the LXX's elimination of clearer headings (24.23; 30.1; 31.1) suggests that 10.1a existed in the original.

19. 'Sorrow of/to his mother' could be a mediated genitive. The cola may also render double substantives: e.g. 'A son, a wise one' (though cf. Prov. 25.12; Eccl. 4.13; Job 34.34).

20. The phrase is often rendered, 'Treasures gained by wickedness'. See, e.g., Waltke, *Proverbs 1–15*, 447; ESV.

21. Cf. Prov. 13.25; 16.24; 25.25.

22. The *hiphil* is interpreted to mean that the son causes either his parents or himself shame.

money through unrighteous practices, so your parents can be proud of you and the Lord will bless you!'[23] Aside from any particular quibbles that could be raised against that summary, the passage certainly exhibits characters in theological, practical, and moral realms, particularly the 'son', as he bears some positive or negative relationship to the Lord (v. 3), work (v. 4), and ethically qualified actions (v. 2).[24] Since theological topics are dealt with in Chapter 4 of the present work, I here examine Prov. 10.2 and 10.4 as cases of character types in the pragmatic and moral realms, both of which pose interpretive challenges.

Proverbs 10.2 states that 'Treasures of wickedness do not profit, but righteousness delivers from death'. The proverb provokes questions regarding character types within the realm of ethics, which is clearly evident in a series of comments from interpreters. Tremper Longman claims that the phrase 'treasures of wickedness' surprises the reader, because it indicates that the wicked can gain wealth.[25] Bruce Waltke more neutrally observes that 'The proverb assumes that one can amass a fortune to which wickedness clings', and he, like Longman, appeals to the role of acts–consequence as reason for this surprise: for the proverb 'clearly implies that there is no tidy calculus between virtue and its rewards and vice and its retribution'.[26] Otto Plöger writes that with respect to all three antithetical pairs, Prov. 10.1-5 'jedenfalls weithin irreparabel Züge annimmt'.[27] Each of these interpreters identifies presuppositions within Prov. 10.2, as Longman and Waltke note that the verse assumes that the wicked can become rich, since 10.2 mentions 'treasures of wickedness',

---

23. Heim, 'Coreferentiality', 203. Commentators observe and admire the structural soundness of Prov. 10.1-5, further testifying to its coherence. See Hans Fuhs, *Sprichwörter* (Würzburg: Echter Verlag, 2001), 74–5; Arndt Meinhold, *Die Sprüche*, Zürcher Bibelkommentare: Altes Testament 16 (Zurich: Theologischer Verlag, 1991), 163 (based on characters); Plöger, *Sprüche*, 124 (based on a literary contrast); Scoralick, *Einzelspruch*, 169–74.

24. Independently, interpreters have identified similar thematic categories within Prov. 10.1-5. Meinhold (*Sprüche*, 165) and Goldingay ('The Arrangement', 81, 83) note the sapiential or pragmatic (10.1b, 4-5), the moral (10.2), and the theological (10.3) perspectives. While these divisions only loosely cohere with Heim's three semantic fields of diligence, intelligence, and morality, Goldingay persuades that they appear throughout Proverbs 10–15 (10.23-27; 12.1-4; 14.1-4; 15.2-7). For my purposes, the pragmatic, moral, and theological perspectives provide categories to direct more specific questions about Prov. 10.1-5 and substantiate the two overarching questions posed above.

25. Longman, *Proverbs*, 230.

26. Waltke, *Proverbs 1–15*, 453.

27. Plöger, *Sprüche*, 123.

and Plöger particularly observes that the 'wicked' and 'righteous' presuppose some sort of ethical identity, what he calls 'irreparable traits'. These observations prompt a pair of questions, the answers to which, I would argue, are not entirely clear based on Prov. 10.1-5 alone: should the interpreter be surprised by the wicked gaining wealth, and more broadly, what are we to make of the assumptions behind these characters' ethical identities?

The second example is 10.4, which contains a syntactical abnormality in the second line: ראש עשה כף־רמיה. The Hebrew word order can mean that poverty leads to idleness or that idleness leads to poverty, either, 'a poor man makes a lax palm' or 'a lax palm makes a poor man'. Suggesting that the ambiguity is no self-explanatory issue, Whybray resolves it through the parallel reference in 10.4b, where diligence causes wealth and thereby implies that a lax palm would lead to poverty.[28] 'The hand of the diligent makes rich', and therefore 'a lax palm makes one poor'. Like Longman and Waltke with 10.2, so Whybray here appeals to the role of acts–consequence in his interpretation of the saying. But might it be warranted to give attention to the role of character in this instance and not only to acts-consequence? For the 'diligent' character in colon B implies not only an immediate syntactical solution but also signals that a corresponding character may be at play in colon A. In the first place, the verse contrasts a 'lax palm' with 'the hand of the diligent', showing that the second line, in its mention of 'the diligent', explicitly incorporates character more than the first. Being rich is an outcome for the diligent, and it seems that being poor would, therefore, be an outcome rather than a constitutive element of character. That is, the poverty mentioned in 10.4a most likely refers not to a character type (i.e. the poor person) but rather to an outcome that, according to 10.4b, stems from a certain character type. Second, 'the poor', if it does represent a character type, expectedly appears with 'the rich' person elsewhere in Proverbs, further supporting the view that the 'poor man' is not the primary contrast to the diligent person in 10.4.[29] Lastly, ראש עשה may refer less to a 'poor man' and more to 'poverty' (ESV; NIV) or becoming 'poor' (NASB), indicating that the language used for destitution does not necessarily denote a character type. Collectively, this reasoning warrants the question, to whom, if not the characteristically

---

28. Whybray, *Proverbs*, 158. Proverbs from 10.1–22.16 that contain predicative participles and display similar ambiguity are, unlike 10.4, most often clarified by the nature of the subject and object (11.18; 12.23; 13.3, 18; 14.10; 15.32; 16.17, 27-28; 17.27-28). In two cases, words occur in an abnormal order unexplainable by an appeal to chiasm (17.17; 22.2).

29. Proverbs 13.7; 14.20; 18.23; 22.2, 7; 28.6; cf. 13.8; 28.3.

poor man, does the lax palm of 10.4a belong? The answer seems undisclosed by or perhaps latent within 10.1-5, and the problem leads to a more basic issue about the presentation of character and behaviour in the proverbs. The issue has received contrasting responses: according to Raymond Van Leeuwen, Proverbs 10–15 supposes the concepts of righteousness and wickedness while displaying their behaviour;[30] according to Waltke, in 10.1-5, 'The behaviour of the wise/righteous is often assumed and left undefined'.[31] So, is it the behaviour or the character concepts that are latent within the proverbs? This question is foundational to the dilemma posed by the interpretation of 10.4 – how are its character types and their behaviours meant to be related? And while the acts–consequence nexus has clearly played a lead role in the interpretation of these verses, I would suggest that character types warrant our full attention too. I propose that we consult Proverbs 1–9 for answers to these concerns, enquiring into the relationship it instils between character types and their behaviour in pragmatic realms, such as work and social relations.

My foray into Prov. 10.1-5 lends two additional questions that substantiate the first larger concern:

1. How does Proverbs 1–9 intend to portray the characters? As idealized caricatures, or something else such as realistic personalities?
   a. How does it inform their ethical identities, specifically in relation to wealth?
   b. What relationship does it instil between character types and their behaviour in pragmatic realms?
2. How do the characters relate in view of Heim's theory of coreferentiality?

2.1.2. *Character Types in Proverbs 1–9*

Many, but not all, of the lexemes in Prov. 10.1–22.16 that characterize groups or individuals appear in 1–9. Of the four most prominent antithetical pairs from Collection II, only two occur as pairs within Collection I: the wise (חכם) and the fool (אויל; כסיל), and the righteous (צדיק) and wicked (רשע). The rich (עשיר) and poor (דל; אביון; רש; עני), along with the prudent (ערום), an alternative term for the foolish (נבל), and the diligent (חרוץ) only appear in chapters 10 and following, though the labourer's worse half – the sluggard (עצל) – does show up in 6.6 and 6.9. Proverbs 1–9 also mentions the scoffer (לץ), simpleton (פתי), the one who lacks sense (חסר

---

30. Van Leeuwen, 'Proverbs', 105.
31. Waltke, *Proverbs 1–15*, 101. So Fox, *Proverbs 10–31*, 510.

לב), the upright (ישר), and the understanding (בין). In addition to these, a number of other characters appear only once in Collection I and rarely in Collection II.³² The character types just mentioned signify characters denoted by one or two lexical items, such as רשע for the 'wicked' and חסר לב for 'the one who lacks sense'. Some characterizations in Proverbs 1–9, though, differ from this format and instead provide predicate descriptions of character types, such as 'the men who speak perversity', which seems to substantiate the wicked (2.12b; cf. 2.13-15; 6.19), or the אשרי ('blessed') person who embodies wisdom and equates to the 'righteous' (3.13; 8.32-36; cf. Ps. 1.1, 6). Otherwise, within Proverbs 1–9, characters contribute to a story or an illustration, in either a fictitious (2.19; 6.29; cf. 9.7) or more realistic fashion (6.1; 8.15-16).

As for additional distinctions between Collections I and II, Kenneth Aitken draws attention to 2.20-22 and 4.10-19 to conclude that Collection I portrays the theological dimension of the character types, such as their relationship to God and their righteous mode of acquiring wisdom, whereas Collection II describes their social outworking, perhaps their relationships with others and society as a whole.³³ But in the context of character terms, I do not find Aitken convincing. Proverbs 2.7-9 and 4.16-17 describe the social activities of certain characters, and the first mention of the righteous and wicked persons in Collection II puts them in relation to the Lord (10.3), which amounts to an exact reversal of Aitken's view. A general distinction like Aitken's might hold, but the notable distinction with respect to character terms in Proverbs 1–9 and 10.1–22.16 stems not from a theological dimension but from the literary context. In 10.1–22.16, the terms appear in single proverbs or small clusters that elaborate on the character types. In Proverbs 1–9, the terms appear in much richer literary contexts, embedded in illustrative narratives, lengthy speeches, or extended series of instructions. I contend that these larger

---

32. That is, the sinner (חטא), godly (חסיד), good (טוב), blameless (תמים), treacherous (בגד), man of violence (איש חמס), devious (נלוז), worthless person (איש בליעל), and wicked man (איש און). Collection II also includes rare characters not found in Collection I. However, in each case, the rare type occurs in parallel with a familiar character type, or includes common ethical terms, or reflects a predicate description: godless (חנף, 11.9), man of evil devices (איש מזמות, 12.2; 14.17), one of twisted mind (נעוה לב, 12.8), backslider in heart (סוג לב, 14.14), man of short anger (i.e. quick temper; קצר אפים, 14.17), good of heart (טוב לב, 15.15), man of anger (איש חמה, 15.18; cf. 6.34; 16.32). See also 11.20; 17.20 (cf. 2.15); 12.20 (cf. 3.29; 6.14); 17.4 (cf. 6.17); 19.5, 15; 20.19; 22.14. One of the terms for 'poor' (עני) occurs at Prov. 3.34, but in this context it refers to the 'humble'.

33. Aitken, *Proverbs*, 133.

and richer contexts serve to establish the function of the character terms, portraying them as idealized types or caricatures, each distinct but ultimately coreferential. By developing the caricatured and coreferential quality of the characters, 1–9 functions didactically by preparing the interpreter to understand their function and relationship within 10.1-22.16. The opening lecture from the father (1.10-19) exemplifies the treatment of character types in Proverbs 1–9, so this passage is closely examined, while other key texts that inform the interpretive questions from 10.1–22.16 are then considered.

2.1.2.1. *Proverbs 1.10-19*

The Proverbial father's first lecture (Prov. 1.10-19) contributes most to the first question about the interpretation of character types: how does Proverbs 1–9 intend to portray its characters? Are they idealized caricatures or realistic personalities? The father begins at 1.10 with a call to attention, 'my son', and an introduction to the passage's primary character type: 'if *sinners* (חטאים) entice you, do not consent'. He poses a hypothetical speech of temptation towards the son, where the gang, with flagrant talk, invites the boy to kill the innocent (1.11) and partake of the spoils (1.13-14). Some claim the account resembles realistic scenarios from ancient Palestine, where such violence likely occurred due to regular daytime and night-time foot travel.[34] But while group violence and theft was possible, and perhaps common, the plausibility or frequency of such occurrences should not determine the (non)fictional nature of the passage. The language of 1.10-19 itself suggests that the words of the criminals evoke a fictitious and radical tone, as the gang likens itself to death (1.13) and declares its own act as 'without cause'. Furthermore, the following speech in Prov. 1.20-33 appears fictitious and extreme, where personified wisdom calls out in the city centre and appeals to her audience with dramatic language. Calamity, terror, distress, anguish, whirlwind, and storms threaten those who reject Lady Wisdom, whose personified nature itself suggests that the characters of Proverbs 1 represent something other than strictly realistic figures. The gang, if it is a realistic portrayal, which may in fact be the case, certainly reflects the worst of the worst of such reality. Of Prov. 1.10-19, Johnny Miles has written that 'the father exercises complete control over the speech and description of the criminals as he infuses an element of reality into a hypothetical scenario,

---

34. Van Leeuwen, 'Proverbs', 38; Whybray, *Proverbs*, 42; Philip J. King and Lawrence E. Stager, *Life in Biblical Israel* (Louisville, KY: Westminster John Knox Press, 2001), 186.

which smacks of more than just youthful temptation'.[35] Thus, without denying the reality of such violence, the words in 1.11-14 suggest a fictitious and exaggerated account that the author attributes to 'sinners'.

This example at the outset of Proverbs places a character term (חטאים) in the context of an extreme and exaggerated self-description, portraying the 'sinners' as a wildly violent and fiercely anti-social character type. Proverbs 2 corroborates this method of ethically identifying literary characters by presenting two basic types of people and addressing the question of character identities. On the one hand, in 2.7-8, the author combines the 'upright' (ישרים), those 'who walk in integrity' (הלכי תם), and God's 'saints' (חסיד): 'he stores up sound wisdom for the upright; he is a shield for those who walk in integrity, guarding paths of justice and watching over the way of his saints'.[36] On the other hand, the author presents the 'men who speak perversities' (2.12b), with a series of descriptive actions, such as forsaking right paths, rejoicing in evil, and living deviously (2.13-15), and then presents the forbidden woman, who forsakes her companion and forgets God's covenant (2.16-19).[37] Amidst grouping these people and their behavioural descriptions, the author explicitly labels the characters with ethical terms, in the first place, summarizing upright living as כל מעגל טוב, 'every *good* pathway' (2.9b), and, second, repeating the term רע ('evil') three times in the passage about perverse men (2.12a, 14). The chapter's conclusion (2.20a) echoes an ethical term from 2.9 (טוב), as the son shall walk in the way of good men (טובים), cementing the author's deliberate effort to ethically evaluate the characters of Proverbs 2.

The final verses of Proverbs 2, like the bulk of the chapter, draw attention not to behaviours as such but to the ethical evaluation of behaviours and their association with character types. So 2.21-22 notes the blessed fate of the 'upright' and 'those with integrity' in contrast to the 'wicked' and 'treacherous' who are removed from blessing. For Christine Yoder, the author is naming '*this* wisdom' and '*that* wickedness', and treating 'the wicked' in chapter 2 as 'little more than stock figures', who recall the

---

35. Johnny E. Miles, *Wise King – Royal Fool: Semiotics, Satire and Proverbs 1–9*, JSOTSup 399 (London: T&T Clark, 2004), 49. Also Plöger, *Sprüche*, 15–17, 20; Waltke, *Proverbs 1–15*, 191; Fox, *Proverbs 1–9*, 86, 93.

36. The plural *Qere* (LXX; Syr) is preferable to the MT's singular. For the singular, only the second person suffix is used (Deut. 33.8; Ps. 16.10), and 1 Sam. 2.9 has similar *Qere/Ketiv* alternatives in a clearly plural context.

37. The plural and singular terms (2.15-16) plus the masculine and feminine combination constitute a merism, representing the entirety of the evil population (Yoder, *Proverbs*, 30).

comprehensive corruption of 'sinners' from chapter 1.[38] Therefore, in Proverbs 2, the author intends primarily not to detail ethical or unethical behaviour but to evaluate the ethical identity of character types, generalizing between two polar groups of 'good' and 'evil' people. The function of a similar passage (4.10-19) has been described with a didactic characterization that I argue applies to Proverbs 2: 'The lecture provides no specific guidance on the right and wrong way. Rather, it serves to prepare the son to receive the specific teachings about right and wrong behaviour, extensively given in the collections that follow Collection I.'[39] At least Proverbs 1 and 2, then, aid the interpretation of 10.1–22.16 by familiarizing the interpreter with character types and portraying or describing them in terms of ethical identities.[40]

The opening verses of Proverbs (1.1-7) raise doubts about this conclusion. Surely, goes the objection, the 'wise' and 'foolish' persons mentioned in 1.5 and 1.7 precede the didactic induction of 1.10–2.22 and presuppose from the outset that the interpreter understands how such characters function: 'let *the wise* hear and increase in learning' (1.5a). As I have argued, the 'wise' in 1.5 represents an ideal reader, supported by the fact that 1.2-6 characterizes his basic functions without qualification: he receives instruction (1.2-3a), with practical implications (1.3b), passes it on to others (1.4), and learns (1.5-6).[41] On the back of this characterization, Prov. 1.7 portrays the 'fool' in his fundamental posture – despising wisdom and instruction – implying a total rejection of wisdom and a complete contrast with the wise person. Proverbs 1.2-7, then, does not so much assume the identity of its characters like 10.1–22.16 does but rather didactically develops them, depicting the wise person and the fool in what Proverbs 1–9 shows to be their typical habits. Therefore, instead of countering the pattern of character presentation in 1.10–2.22, Prov. 1.2-7 immediately inducts the interpreter into Proverbs' scheme of character types, who await further formation throughout Proverbs 1–9.

Returning to the interpretive questions of this chapter, I move now to the first subquestion, which asks how Proverbs 1–9 informs the identities of character types, specifically with regard to wealth. The topic of wealth features in 1.10-19, wherein, first, the 'sinners' appear to have access to resources similar to the positive characters in Proverbs, such as money (1.13, 19a), a social circle (1.14), and the intelligence assumed to

---

38. Yoder, *Proverbs*, 35. Also McKane, *Proverbs*, 282, 288.
39. Waltke, *Proverbs 1–15*, 285.
40. I would argue Proverbs 5 functions in a similar way by serving to characterize the 'wicked' (5.22-23).
41. Keefer, 'A Shift', *passim*.

successfully accomplish their plot. They do not seem inherently restricted from gaining wealth. Second, the author not only describes what may appear to be unethical behaviours; he explicitly brands the behaviours themselves as unethical. He calls the group 'sinners', claims their feet run to 'evil' (1.16a), and labels their gains as 'unjust' (1.19a), similar to the predications from Proverbs 2 about the perverse man and forbidden woman. So, with more than a descriptive list of behaviours, the unethical nature of the group is emphasized. For the second subquestion, the nature of behaviour in pragmatic realms, 1.10-19 clearly portrays the gang's behaviour as an extreme case and intends to disapprove of such action.

Proverbs 6 coheres with and supplements the caricatures from 1.10-19. It sets a pragmatic context of economic agreements (6.1-5) and labour (6.6-11), and offers the most detailed description of behaviours in Collection I (6.12-19), characterizing the 'sluggard' (עצל) and 'worthless person' (אדם בליעל). These characters also appear as extreme examples. In Prov. 6.6-11, the appeal to an ant, use of rhetorical questions, and understated jab at the sluggard render the passage comical and exaggerated, much like the satirical lines of Prov. 19.24 and 22.13. But more importantly, the following verses (6.12-19) add a holistic portrait, mentioning the mouth, eyes, feet, and fingers in order to complete the character's evil. Proverbs 6.12-14a describes the 'worthless man' going about 'with a crooked mouth, winking his eyes, shuffling his feet, pointing his fingers, perversity in his heart, devising evil'. Likewise, 6.17-19 mentions a globe of body parts and evil actions, such as 'haughty eyes, a lying tongue and hands which spill innocent blood' (6.17). What appears in 6.12-19, then, reflects much of what appears in chapters 1–2, which deal with generalized personalities rather than with specific persons.[42] As a whole, Prov. 6.1-19 portrays actions in extreme and holistic form and attributes them to character types, cohering with other portions of Proverbs 1–9 and contributing most to this question of behaviour in pragmatic contexts.

The final overarching question for this section addresses the relation of the characters: are they distinct, coreferential, or identical? Proverbs 1.10-19 begins with a particular group lexeme – 'if *sinners* (חטאים) entice you' – yet concludes by universalizing these sinful characters as

---

42. Richard Clifford, *Proverbs: A Commentary* (Louisville, KY: Westminster John Knox Press, 1999), 73. Proverbs 4.14-19 arguably aligns with the views of Proverbs 1–2 in its distinction between the 'wicked' and 'righteous', as the former move along the path of 'evil' (v. 14), do wrong (v. 16a), make others stumble (v. 16b), and drink 'violence' (v. 17). See Clifford, *Proverbs*, 73, 76; Waltke, *Proverbs 1–15*, 336, 341–2; Fox, *Proverbs 1–9*, 219.

a generalized type of person. Starting at 1.10, the father focuses on the 'sinners' as a particular example of temptation and evil, and in 1.18 refers to them when he says: 'But *they*, for their own blood they ambush, *they* lurk for their own lives'. While verse 18 refers to the sinners/gang (i.e. 'they'), verse 19 expands the interpreter's purview by universalizing the gang: 'Such are the ways of *everyone greedy for gain*, it takes the life of its possessors'. Proverbs 1.10-19 substantiates a single type of person for eight verses and then concludes by expanding the particular label to a generalized identity. 'They', the greedy, sinner gang, will tempt and thieve and murder, and this is the way of life for 'everyone greedy for gain'. Such a trend recurs in 2.20-22 and 3.31-35, passages that also inform this final interpretive question.

Again, the final question concerns whether the characters stand in distinct, coreferential, or identical relation. Admittedly, Proverbs 1–9 does retain some distinction between its various types of 'negative' characters. The 'fool', for example, appears as one who rejects the fundamental tenets of wisdom, constituting the unteachable caricature (1.7, 22), while the 'simpleton', though equally condemned (1.32), shows a unique level of gullibility (7.7; cf. 7.8-23). Despite these distinctions, Proverbs 1–9 consistently portrays characters as coreferential, through generalized conclusions that slot the character terms into two basic categories: good or evil. Like 1.19, which explodes the gang into 'everyone greedy for unjust gain', Prov. 1.33 establishes the identity of 'whoever listens' to Lady Wisdom.[43] The pattern of summative conclusion recurs in 2.20-22 and 3.31-35, as, on the tail of a lengthy set of commands and warnings (3.21-30), Prov. 3.31-32 transitions by naming the 'man of violence' (איש חמס) and 'devious one' (נלוז) into a summarized set of contrasts that places many of the characters in parallel throughout 3.31-35: חכמים/כסילים; לצים/ענײם; רשע/צדיקים; נלוז/ישרים.[44] Based on Proverbs 1, it has been argued that characters are distilled into either good or bad persons within a context of clarification, suggesting that the author intends to instil general categories associated with character terms.[45] I would add that characters, sometimes distinct, appear in direct parallel to each other, such as the simpleton, the scoffer, and the fool (1.22; also 4.14; 8.5; 9.7-9), solidifying their common identity.

---

43. Fox, *Proverbs 1–9*, 102; Waltke, *Proverbs 1–15*, 203.
44. There is no apparent reason for the singular of רשע, although נלוז follows on from the singular 'man of violence'.
45. Aletti, 'Seduction', 132, see also 130–3.

2.1.2.2. *Characters and the 'Way' Metaphor*

One final feature of Proverbs consolidates the character types and places them into two distinct groups; that feature is the 'way' metaphor. In Proverbs 1–9, four lexemes refer to 'ways', variously translated as 'pathways' or 'paths' (דרך; מעגל; נתיבה; ארח), and each occur in parallel to each other, evincing no difference in meaning (Prov. 1.15; 2.13, 15; 4.11; 8.20). The way ranges from references to behaviour as a more abstract concept (5.21; 6.6), to more figurative (2.18; 5.5-6) as well as less-figurative uses (7.8, 19; cf. Judg. 5.6). Collectively, these terms occur 54 times in Collection I, 40 times in Collection II, and 14 times elsewhere in Proverbs, with the concentration of terms for 'way' in Proverbs 1–9 signalling its significance therein.[46]

In addition to lexical concentration, an outline of the 'way' language in Proverbs 1–9 demonstrates its prominence and metaphorical contours. Proverbs 1 introduces a criminal scenario (1.10-14) and then admonishes the son: 'do not go in the way with them, withhold your foot from their path' (1.15). This 'way/path' is described by actions of evil and bloodshed, resulting in a loss of life (1.16-19). In Prov. 1.20-33, Wisdom addresses 'ways' explicitly only in her conclusion, where those who reject her will 'eat from the fruit of their way' (1.31) and so die (1.32). Way language explodes in Proverbs 2 and acquires a host of qualities: God protects the 'ways of justice' and the 'way of his godly' (2.8) who then understand 'every good way' (2.9), which contrasts with the way of evil, darkness and crookedness (2.12-15). Concluding statements portray the polarity of these ways and their results: one leads to death, the other leads to life (2.18-20).

In James Loader's comments on Prov. 2.20, he begins to direct interpretation towards 10.1–22.16. He writes,

> [Prov. 2.20] uses the metaphor of the way to categorise all the positive manifestations of understanding wisdom in the most generic manner possible. They all amount to practice "the good" and "the just." This general way of using the metaphor of the way (or of walking) to subsume concrete acts under the headings of being "righteous" or "wicked" is also found in the aphorisms (cf. 10.9).[47]

Such is the pattern that emerges throughout chapters 1–9. As Proverbs 1–2 clarifies, 'ways' functions as a metaphor that represents the collective

---

46. Also notable is the relative absence of female figures for wisdom and folly in Prov. 10.1–22.16 (cf. 14.1; 22.14) but the abundance of its way language (40 occurrences), which suggests that the way is a more integral metaphor for Collections I and II.

47. Loader, *Proverbs 1–9*, 133. See also Waltke, *Proverbs 1–15*, 285

behaviours of persons. And yet despite plural 'ways', Proverbs suggests only two. One is associated with the Lord and wisdom, trodden by good characters and leading to life, the other associates with folly and its character types, ending in death. Further chapters cement this conclusion but also elaborate on the characteristics of both ways. For example, the way of life is a way of peace (3.6, 17, 23; cf. 3.31). In Prov. 4.10-19 one way is smooth and illuminated while the other dark and obstructed (see also 4.26-27; 5.5-6), and the way of wisdom, especially, requires guidance (4.11). Proverbs 1–5 provides a general view of 'ways' that incorporates a few key characteristics, not least that the characters within those chapters trod one of those two paths.[48]

In short, the way constitutes the metaphorical substructure of Proverbs 1–9. And what are its main characteristics? According to Proverbs, all individual ways, which stand for behaviours embodied in characters, fall onto either the way of wisdom or folly and result in either life or death. For in addition to consolidating the two groups of characters in Proverbs, the ways are, in turn, even defined by them – 'the path of the righteous' and 'way of the wicked' (4.18-19) – resolving most doubts about the bipolar classification of these people. These passages exhibit the basic antithesis of Proverbs 1–9 – positive and negative ways of life embodied in character types – and support the claim that 1–9 clarifies and instils characters as general portrayals of coreferential ideals.[49]

2.1.2.3. *Summary*

An investigation has been made, so far, into proposals about what the character types in Proverbs are and how they relate to each other. Proverbs 10.1-5 is a ground thorny with interpretive challenges, producing questions that were fielded by Proverbs 1–9, which, I argued, says quite a bit about character types. Proverbs 1 sets the trajectory for the identity and function of character terms in chapters 1–9, contributing most with its portrayal of the 'sinners' as a literary caricature. As seen also in Proverbs 2, the primary concern of these passages is not to detail ethical or unethical behaviour but to evaluate the ethical identity of character types, generalizing between two polar groups of 'good' and 'evil' people.

---

48. Proverbs 7–9 introduces additional metaphors that are ultimately subsumed by pathway imagery. As Weeks (*Instruction*, 79) notes of Proverbs 1 and 7–9, 'all the settings involve roads, implicitly or explicitly, and in a work that displays a strong interest in the figurative use of ways and roads, it seems unlikely to be a coincidence that the speeches of significant characters are associated with them in this way'.

49. Fox, *Proverbs 1–9*, 168; Van Leeuwen, 'Proverbs', 55; Fuhs (*Sprichwörter*, 34) describes a 'Riß' or 'Kluft' between populations.

These chapters also contribute to the question of behaviour in pragmatic contexts, portraying actions in extreme and holistic form and attributing them to character types, with the final intention to disapprove of them.[50] Proverbs 1–9 reveals some distinction between character terms, but overall it aligns them through antitheses, treating the types as coreferential caricatures for either a good or bad character. The immediate introduction and concentration of character types in Proverbs 1, and their consistent appearance in 2–9 within extended literary contexts, suggests that Proverbs 1–9 may didactically prepare its interpreter for the character terms of 10.1–22.16.

2.1.3. *Character Types Outside of the Book of Proverbs*

We should progress no further with character types in Proverbs without exploring their use in other texts of the OT and ancient Near East. Character types do not appear in all ancient Egyptian instruction texts, but they do appear in *Ptahhotep* and *Ankhsheshonq*, and find fullest expression in *Papyrus Insinger*.[51] *Insinger* presents its wise and foolish persons as correlative to its pious and impious men. For example, 'The evil man is evilly punished because of (his) deceit. Do not trust a fool because he brings you (something) with a blessing' (12.3-4).[52] The evil man and the fool seem united in their character here, a trend not dissimilar from the coreferentiality in Proverbs. *Insinger* also describes the behaviour of these characters, as the evil man in the previous passage is said to practice deceit, and yet the character's moral character itself is ultimately determined not by discrete behaviours but by the totality of their traits. Hence *Insinger* labels these figures with 'pious' or 'fool' or

---

50. Proverbs 6 perhaps contributes most to this point.

51. The *Instruction of Ptahhotep*, from P.Prisse, refers primarily to realistic figures (e.g. a disputant [68] or master [250]) and predicate descriptions (e.g. he who hears [548]; a man who leads [265]). It mentions the 'wise' and 'ignorant' (55), the 'silent man' (167), the 'hot-bellied' (352), and the 'hot-heart' (378), with concluding mentions of the wise person (523-524, 526), followed by a lengthy characterization of that person being a good listener (531-572) and a juxtaposition with the fool (573-574) who is also then described (575-587). Cf. the 'great man' (140-144, 388, 515), and notice that *Ptahhotep* forbids greed without a depiction or mention of the greedy man (298-324). The *Instruction of Ankhsheshonq* also mentions non-caricatured people (e.g. the thief [13.3]; merchant [16.5]) but seems to assume an understanding of its 'wise' and 'foolish' persons (e.g. 5.10; 6.3, 13-14; 13.9; 14.8; 26.9). As *Ankhsheshonq* is a much later text than *Ptahhotep*, understandings of these characters may have developed within Egypt, and the influence of a scribal context would inform how they were interpreted.

52. *AEL* 3:194.

'evil man'.⁵³ Mariam Lichtheim has also noted the exemplary nature of such people in this text: 'morality and piety have been completely fused and they are exemplified in the character of the "wise man"'.⁵⁴ *Insinger* not only supports the coreferentiality of terms in Proverbs, it also reflects the holistic concern for behaviours, their service in emphasizing character, and the exemplar conception of character types. Operating outside of Egyptology while assessing its primary texts, biblical interpreters have produced a consensus that the characters function as ideals.⁵⁵

Characterizing Egyptian characters as ideals, though, is not straightforward. On the one hand, they do seem to portray idealizations, as seen in a number of examples. *Insinger* associates the wise man with perfection: 'When a wise man is tested few discover his perfection' (12.23). *Ptahhotep's* introduction notes exemplar expectations for his son: 'May he become a model for the children of the great' (39). And in *The Instructions Addressed to Merikare*, the wise king receives idealistic accolades: 'As one wise did he come from the womb, From a million men god singled him out' (115-116).⁵⁶ Against this idealization, Lichtheim objects that Egyptians 'had no idea what an "Ideal" was', a statement that I find agreeable if it warns against equating an ideal with moral perfection.⁵⁷ For the wise man in *Insinger* may be harmed because of loving a woman (7.11) or become foolish and inconsiderate in the midst of retaliation (34.12-13), possibilities that make this wise man less than perfect.⁵⁸ The wise person of Proverbs, however, is flawless. He does no wrong and succumbs to no foolishness, supporting the idealized nature of characters in Proverbs and accentuating an important distinction within ancient Near Eastern material. While certain Egyptian texts may not describe ideal characters, they do, nevertheless, portray exemplars.

53. Miriam Lichtheim, 'Observations on Papyrus Insinger', in *Studien Zu altägyptischen Lebenslehren*, ed. Erik Hornung and Othmar Keel (Freiburg: Universitätsverlag, 1979), 291, see also 290–3.

54. *AEL* 3:185.

55. Lyu, *Righteousness*, 99–102, 34–5; Hausmann, *Studien*, 346; Shupak, *Where Can Wisdom Be Found?*, 221, 238–9, 259–61; *AEL* 2:147; Leo G. Perdue, *Proverbs*, Interpretation (Louisville, KY: John Knox Press, 2000), 199.

56. Quotations are taken from *AEL*; see also, *Insinger* 2.10; 3.2-8; 4.9; 12.4, 23; 14.5; 34.11-12; 35.11-12.

57. Miriam Lichtheim, *Moral Values in Ancient Egypt*, OBO 155 (Göttingen: Vandenhoeck & Ruprecht, 1997), 88, see also 83. Cf. *AEL* 2:146 where she distinguishes between the ideal man and a perfect man.

58. Miriam Lichtheim, *Late Egyptian Wisdom Literature in the International Context: A Study of Demotic Instructions*, OBO 52 (Göttingen: Vandenhoeck & Ruprecht, 1983), 119, see also 116–27.

Literary character types and the portrayal of characters in firm antithesis (i.e. 'binary anthropology') also appear in the book of Psalms, Ecclesiastes, and Job. Commenting on Psalm 1, Derek Kidner says that 'The tone and themes of the psalm bring to mind the Wisdom writings, especially Proverbs, with their interest in the company a man keeps, in the two ways set before him (cf. e.g. Prov. 2.12ff., 20ff.), and in *moral types*, notably the scoffers'.[59] So the first verse of the Psalm reads, 'Blessed is the man who walks not in the counsel of the wicked, nor stands in the way of sinners, nor sits in the seat of scoffers'. Psalms 15 and 24 similarly describe the virtuous worshipper in idealistic terms: 'Lord, who shall sojourn in your tent; who shall dwell on your holy hill? He who walks blamelessly and does right and speaks truth in his heart' (Ps. 15.1-2). Furthermore, Psalms 26 and 37 refer to the wicked and righteous in ways reminiscent of Proverbs: 'Do not be angry over the one who prospers in his way, over the man who makes (evil) devices.... For evildoers shall be cut off; but those who wait for the Lord, they shall inherit the land' (Ps. 37.7b-c, 9). The lexeme for 'evildoer' (מרע) here refers to an ethical possibility that is then embodied by those who act accordingly, so that in the Psalms, this person stands for 'every member of the congregation who might deviate from the right path'.[60] The 'wicked' and 'sinner', the one who 'walks blamelessly', and the 'evildoer', understood within the contexts of these psalms, represent character types of extreme and binary people.[61]

In short, certain Egyptian texts seem to portray character terms as exemplars through holistic descriptions of behaviour that champion character,

---

59. Derek Kidner, *Psalms 1–72: An Introduction and Commentary on Books I and II of the Psalms*, TOTC (London: Inter-Varsity Press, 1973), 63 (emphasis my own). See also Erhard Gerstenberger, *Psalms: Part I: With an Introduction to Cultic Poetry* (Grand Rapids, MI: Eerdmans, 1988), 42.

60. Gerstenberger, *Psalms: Part I*, 209. In Ps. 50.16a, Theodore Seidl suggests multiple possible concrete referents for the 'wicked' ('Who Stands Behind the RSH' in Psalm 50.16A? The Ethical Testimony of Psalm 50.16-22', in *Psalmody and Poetry in Old Testament Ethics*, ed. Dirk J. Human [New York: T&T Clark, 2012], 76–92).

61. For a thorough argument on the literary and didactic nature of character types in Psalms 15, 24, 34, and 37, see Daniel C. Owens, *Portraits of the Righteous in the Psalms: An Exploration of the Ethics of Book 1* (Eugene, OR: Pickwick, 2013). Ben Sira (21.12-26; 22.7-15) renders a coherent point of view on the wise and foolish person, and the book of Job contains examples of exemplar types. Kenneth Hoglund, 'The Fool and the Wise in Dialogue: Proverbs 26.4-5', in *Learning from the Sages: Selected Studies on the Book of Proverbs*, ed. Roy Zuck (Grand Rapids: Baker Books, 1995), 339–52, esp. 348–50. Brown (*Wisdom's Wonder*, 15) says, 'much of the literature conveys or models the contours of normative character through literary characterization'. See, e.g., Job 3.17; 9.22; 17.9.

while the book of Psalms and other texts of the OT and Apocrypha at times reflect a binary relationship between character concepts, and employ these terms on a literary level. If such interpretations are plausible, these uses of character types outside of the book of Proverbs may support many of the conclusions derived from Proverbs 1–9. However, on the back of this support comes an objection. For the same evidence may suggest that interpreters of Psalms and *Insinger* understood character terms without an interpretive aid, meaning that ancient interpreters might not have found Proverbs 1–9 particularly helpful or necessary for understanding the characters in 10.1–22.16. But there are a few reasons to think otherwise. First, the Egyptian texts and the Psalms that employ character terms use them in ways most similar to Proverbs 1–9, not 10.1–22.16, placing them within the context of prolonged poetic descriptions. Second, *Insinger* – the Egyptian text that makes most use of character terms, at times in ways similar to Prov. 10.1–22.16 – expounds many of its terms early on. For example, 'Do not let yourself be called 'the bad man' because of merciless evildoing' (3.2; so 3.3-8). This and six parallel statements predicate the nature of certain characters and place them within the context of an explicit command, which would clarify the character terms that recur later in the text on a literary and rhetorical level.[62] Such descriptions suggest that these character types may not have been automatically understood. Finally, Prov. 10.1–22.16, and Proverbs as a whole, stands apart in its predominance of character terms, which, when compared with Egyptian texts, other biblical wisdom texts and Psalms, suggests that Collection II warrants more substantial introductory material. These interpretive resources leave certain issues unresolved within 10.1–22.16 and the nature of character types open to question, creating the possibility that Proverbs 1–9 functions didactically in some distinctive way.

2.1.4. *The Function of Proverbs 1–9 for Proverbs 10.1-5*
I have just posited that in view of pertinent texts other than Proverbs 1–9 information remains latent within 10.1–22.16, interpretive challenges remain unresolved, and the nature of character types open to question. It remains to be seen how 1–9 might address these issues, and in this section I argue that the conclusions developed from Proverbs 1–9 fashion a framework that provides insights into some of the challenges of 10.2 and 10.4. Having culled resources from the OT and elsewhere in the ancient Near East, it should be observed that before interrogating Proverbs 1–9,

---

62. Recall that, unlike for Proverbs, we do not possess the initial portions of the text for *Insinger* or *Ptahhotep*.

the local literary context of the proverbs themselves remains the most viable option among interpretive resources.

With its remark about 'treasures of wickedness', Prov. 10.2 raises at least two interpretive challenges: specifically, should the interpreter be surprised by the wicked gaining wealth, and more broadly, what should we, as interpreters, make of the assumptions about these characters' ethical identities? 'Treasures of wickedness do not profit, but righteousness delivers from death', says the proverb. Longman and Waltke assert that 10.2 surprises the reader, because it indicates that the wicked can gain wealth or presupposes the fact.[63] If this interpretation is to be evaluated, then the nature of this 'wicked' person must first be established based on its local context and then considered in view of 1–9. The first line of 10.2 comments upon 'treasures of wickedness' or 'treasures gained by wickedness' (ESV), and while 10.2 uses רֶשַׁע as 'wickedness', Prov. 10.3 clarifies that this quality implicates full-fledged character types. For the Lord 'thrusts away' the desire of 'the wicked ones' (רְשָׁעִים), a plausible use of character lexemes in view of the wise son (בן חכם) and the foolish son (בן כסיל) mentioned in 10.1. The lexical link of רשע in 10.2 and 10.3 and the overall context of clearer characters in 10.1-5 suggest that Prov. 10.2 involves character types, though such connections do not inform the primary interpretive concerns of this saying.

With a key term for wickedness and a surrounding context of character types, Prov. 10.2 recalls many of the elements in 1.10-19, which, like much of Proverbs 1–9, aims to evaluate the ethical identity of its character types, sorting them into either the good or bad category. Proverbs 1.10-19 explicitly labels its gang as a group of 'sinners' and then generalizes them into anyone greedy for gain, a pattern repeated in Proverbs 2 and 3. Furthermore, Proverbs 1 associates one type, the 'sinners', with money and evil, a group that seems quite capable of obtaining plunder, albeit in an unrighteous manner. When viewed from the perspective of 1–9, Prov. 10.2 does not surprise the interpreter. Rather, the mention of treasures and profit in 10.2, plus the term רשע, calls to mind character types, specifically the scenario from Proverbs 1.

Proverbs 10.2 lacks the extended literary context that could inform the interpreter about what it mentions so briefly, namely, wickedness, treasures, and the identity of those involved. Proverbs 1–9 clarifies the ethical identities that substantiate these associated concepts and generates expectations, as it elaborates on wickedness, as well as the ethical and literary identities of character types. Holding 1–9 in mind as an interpretive

---

63. See respectively, Longman, *Proverbs*, 230; Waltke, *Proverbs 1–15*, 453.

framework, the interpreter, in the first place, encounters 10.1–22.16 not with surprise but with informed expectations. Wickedness can certainly supply treasures, an assumption that 10.2 relies upon to make its point that such treasures 'do not profit'. In the second place, although they have been confirmed as possible, what are 'treasures of wickedness'? According to 10.1–22.16 such treasures may be had by one with a lying tongue (21.6) who possibly does not fear the Lord (15.16). Other relevant passages (e.g. 15.6) rely upon an understanding of character terms, endorsing the interpretive challenge of 10.2 and the strength of Proverbs 1–9 as an interpretive resource. The literary brevity of 10.2 begs for substantiation, and Prov. 1.10-19 provides such substance. The 'sinners' accumulate wealth but they do so through evil means and deceptive tactics, ways possibly attractive to the Proverbial 'son' yet ultimately destined to death. This result suits the second line of 10.2, where 'righteousness delivers from death', as the non-wicked type avoids the fate of greedy, wicked people. With the aid of Proverbs 1–9, the inner design of 10.2 becomes that much clearer: 'Treasures of wickedness do not profit, but righteousness delivers from death'.

In the case of 10.2, parallels between Collection I and II centre upon the ethical terms for wickedness and righteousness. While the character lexemes in 10.2 may at first seem like abstract concepts ('wickedness' and 'righteousness'), the surrounding context (10.1-5) evokes the character types delineated in Proverbs 1–9, and it is 1–9 that provides a coherent interpretive framework for 10.1-5, presenting characters as types of people defined by good or bad ethical identities. Proverbs 10.2 therefore most plausibly surprises the interpreter who is unfamiliar with Proverbs 1–9, since the proverb's character types are more clearly understood in view of the character types outlined therein.

The sayings of Prov. 10.1-5 largely assume the nature of their character concepts, and 10.4, in particular, broaches a debate about whether 10.1–22.16 assumes character concepts, like 'righteous', and then defines their behaviours, or assumes behaviour and then substantiates the concepts. Proverbs 10.4 reads, 'a poor man makes a lax palm' or 'a lax palm makes a poor man', depending on how the apposition is interpreted. Whybray underscores the syntactical abnormality, noting that the Hebrew word order can mean either that poverty leads to idleness or that idleness leads to poverty.[64] Considering questions about the relationship of characters

---

64. Whybray, *Proverbs*, 158; ראש עשה כף־רמיה. These options are also supported by the ancient versions. Cf. the Vuglate's *egestatem operata est manus remissa* and Septuagint's πενία ἄνδρα ταπεινοῖ, χεῖρες δὲ ἀνδρείων πλουτίζουσιν.

and their behaviour, I argued that 1.10-19 does detail the behaviours of its characters but seems more concerned with portraying holistic and extreme wickedness in order to disapprove of the characters who embody it. Proverbs 1.19 generalizes the 'sinners' as 'everyone greedy for gain', a pattern repeated throughout Collection I, while other passages employ detailed behaviours in order to portray a character concept. Consequently, Proverbs 1–9 encourages the interpreter to think in character terms more than in behavioural terms, as if character gives rise to behaviour or perhaps holds ethical authority over human action. As shown in 10.2, the character terms are associated with particular behaviours, such as gaining wealth, but I suggest that it is the character concepts themselves that determine such interpretive conclusions. In short, character concepts outweigh behaviour. If a choice were to be made, then, Proverbs can be said to function more as a portrait of characters – who then direct the interpreter to behavioural traits and preferences – than a guidebook for how to behave. As we shall see in the following section of this chapter, those characters and behaviours remain integrated with the consequences that they produce; that, though, is a question of rhetoric and the reader's motivation rather than the priority that Proverbs assigns to the character and actions of a moral agent.

When using Proverbs 1–9 as a framework, the interpreter knows that behaviour and consequences stem from character rather than vice versa, so that when confronted with syntactical options in 10.4, he or she may conclude that the idle person begets poverty, rather than poverty begetting idleness. This syntactical ambiguity, however, was not the only, and perhaps not even the most significant, issue within the proverb. In view of the diligent hand that makes one rich in colon B, the lax palm of 10.4a may make a man poor (so 'a lax palm makes a poor man'). But the lax palm, in the context of labour, resembles the sluggard of Proverbs – the antithesis of the diligent person – so that the 'slack hand' in 10.4a represents a type of character, plausibly the 'sluggard', who then falls into poverty.[65] The possibility that the 'sluggard' (עצל) stands behind 10.4a becomes a near certainty when read in view of Prov. 6.6-11. The passage bids the 'sluggard' to go and observe an ant, who works without a leader and in the appropriate season, offering a stark contrast to the sluggard himself who fails to work and instead sleeps and comes to poverty. 'A little sleep, a little slumber, a little folding the hands to rest, and your poverty will come like a robber and your need like an armed man' (6.10-11). This advice, of course,

---

65. The character focus is affirmed by the lexical overlap of יד with the human person (Toy, *Proverbs*, 200), though this sense usually occurs with a preposition (e.g. Gen. 16.9; 30.35).

also appears in 24.30-34, wherein the speaker observes a sluggard's vineyard, his negligence and consequent poverty. But unlike this sluggard, the lazy person of 6.6-11 is paired with a positive character, the ant, who works hard and receives equal attention in the passage. A negative character type is placed within a context that develops his behaviours in contrast to a preferable character type, showing particularly that laziness leads to poverty and that diligence should be the norm. The informative import for 10.4 is notable, which also contains a negative and positive portrayal of labour. The proverb hints at what 6.6-11 details, suggesting that Proverbs 1–9 not only coheres with but adds to the meaning of Prov. 10.4. Whybray exposed the interpretive issue by noting the syntactical ambiguity in 10.4a, but I have shown that the issue lies deeper than ambiguous syntax and that when read as a didactic introduction Proverbs 1–9 sheds light on the nature of character and behaviour in the proverb.[66] It instils a framework of character types to associate with 10.1–22.16 and consequently deepens interpretive engagement with it.

The role of 1–9, however, requires more nuance when considering 10.1–22.16 as a whole. Proverbs 10.1-5 sometimes assumes character concepts (e.g. 10.4-5) and sometimes assumes behaviour (10.1-3). As a coherent passage, it in some ways substantiates these assumptions on its own, through the interrelationship of verses as Heim's summary of 10.1-5 showed. However, we do not need to look far into Collection II to find similar assumptions, which appear in contexts much more difficult to resolve. In some cases, behaviour may presuppose wicked character (e.g. 15.25; 22.28), but many behaviours arise in ethically neutral language and consequently benefit from character types in their interpretation: 'work of the righteous' (10.16); 'lips of the righteous' (10.21); 'desire of the righteous' (10.24). What does it mean for a work or desire to be 'of the righteous'? The trend continues throughout 10.1–22.16 and demonstrates how much an understanding of character types and their literary nature would aid in its interpretation. By evaluating holistic character concepts as good or bad, Proverbs 1–9 can be seen to create an interpretive nexus with 10.1–22.16. Proverbs 1–9 does not prompt the interpreter to see an either/or distinction between assumed concepts and assumed behaviours. Instead, it lays a foundation of character types for both, just as 10.1–22.16 sits steadily atop it.

---

66. In line with my comment above about 10.4b, Whybray concludes that 'a slack hand causes poverty' due to the line's parallelism with 10.4b, where 'the hand of the diligent makes rich'. He accounts for the alternative word order as a use of chiasm: object–verb–subject (colon A); subject–verb–[implied object] (colon B).

2.1.5. Conclusion

This chapter has thus far examined the personalities of Proverbs, such as the 'wicked' and 'righteous' persons, by questioning who they are, how they relate, and how to account for the distinctive and common aspects of their appearance in Proverbs 1–9 and 10.1–22.16. Proverbs 1–9 emphasizes the ethical identities of many character types encountered in 10.1–22.16. It evaluates them as good or bad and attributes base-line behaviours, while also portraying character concepts as literary caricatures. Collection II assumes the literary nature of these concepts, and Collection I clarifies that they function on a literary level as idealized types. If we are going to speak of the characters as in some sense 'real', then they should be considered as the best and worst embodiments of their respective traits. For not every depiction seems quite as ridiculous as the sluggard's, who cannot even muster the will to move his handful of food from plate to mouth, but these characters do all attest to the extremes of their character attributes. Finally, Proverbs 1–9 not only matches Heim's notion of coreferentiality in 10.1-5, it deliberately portrays character concepts as coreferential. So while the interpreter may deduce from 10.1–22.16 that such terms corefer, Proverbs 1–9 explicitly and firmly relates the terms as coreferential and groups them as either good or bad. The 'man of violence' causes harm without remorse; the 'scornful' continually holds contempt; and the wicked are never spared of God's curse. With their own qualities, each of these characters shines a distinct light on the Proverbial bad man. In view of Prov. 10.2 and 10.4, Proverbs 1–9 clearly provides faculties that help the interpreter to make sense of the proverbs of 10.1–22.16 on a literary level, serving a didactic function that is supported by the simplicity, clarity, and emphasis with which 1–9 treats character concepts. Though not dictating a singular understanding of the material in 10.1–22.16, Proverbs 1–9 does impose a framework and categories that offer interpretive insights into certain passages.

I have shown how Proverbs 1–9 enables the interpreter to interpret character types on a literary level, answering questions that revolve around what these character types are. But the discovery of their identity and literary function prompts a new question: why have the character concepts been portrayed in the form of idealized literary types? This relates to the rhetorical function of these caricatures, which are explored in the next section.

2.2. *The Rhetoric of Character Types*

In the previous section I examined what is denoted by the character terms and concepts of Proverbs. These 'character types', such as the righteous, wicked, wise, and foolish, incorporate distinct traits but in the end refer to either the good or bad personae of Proverbs. They are idealized or exaggerated embodiments of virtue and vice, what I call 'caricatures', without a necessarily negative connotation. Proverbs 1–9 establishes their identity as idealized, coreferential concepts in both predicate and nominal literary form, enabling the interpreter to see that characters carry a primarily literary identity rather than a 'real' identity that would represent a person or people in historical time and space, such as the 'wicked' enemies that pursue the psalmist (e.g. Ps. 3.8[7]). In Proverbs, the 'sluggard' is far too lazy to be found on Earth, and the wise person far smarter than most. These people seem to embody real qualities to an unreal degree, and at the least symbolize the best and worst of their respective traits. While addressing the question of what these characters are, I did not answer the question of how they function for the interpreter. In other words, why has the author portrayed these types as idealized literary figures? What effect are they intended to have upon the interpreter? What are they meant to do to or for those who encounter them? As we shall see, these questions relate to the persuasive force of the character types and therefore belong to the rhetorical context of Proverbs. Again, interpreters have considered similar questions, especially about Prov. 10.1–22.16, and a look at their answers will aid the direction of these enquiries as they are pursued afresh.

Lyu observes that Prov. 10.1–22.16 praises the righteous person (11.11; 14.34) and affirms the pursuit of righteousness (15.9), concluding that

> the rhetorical function of the discourse of praising the righteous person is to instill in its readers a desire to emulate the idealized character of the righteous person.... we can hope to induce desire *by showing what is desirable*.[67]

I want to consider Lyu's claim – that Proverbs shows what is desirable in order to persuade interpreters to emulate its characters – as a theory of the characters' rhetorical function. The shortcoming of this theory is that it proposes too much based on the evidence. For although the texts that 'praise the righteous person' do speak of the righteous in an approving way, such sayings, even 10.1–22.16 as a whole, do not warrant the confident conclusion: that Proverbs intends its readers to emulate its characters. In view of 11.11; 14.34 and 15.9, why should the interpreter pursue righteousness? 'By the blessing of the upright a city is exalted' (11.11; NRSV); 'righteousness exalts a nation' (14.34; NRSV); the

---

67. Lyu, *Righteousness*, 62 (italics original).

Lord 'loves the one who pursues righteousness' (15.9; NRSV). These texts place righteousness in the context of plausibly positive incentives, but they do not adequately establish the function of characters that Lyu proposes, particularly the assertion that they induce the reader's 'desire to emulate the idealized character of the righteous person'. Other sayings package their characters alongside additional, plausibly motivational rhetorical features, such as value-laden consequences or divine approval, and yet 10.1–22.16 still employs good and bad character terms in addition to these other rhetorical features (also see below). Proverbs 11.11, for example – 'By the blessing of the upright a city is exalted' – depends upon an understanding of 'the upright' person, regardless of whether the outcome of 'exalting' a city attracts the reader or not. Perhaps, as Lyu describes, 'the upright' function in a particular rhetorical fashion, namely by evoking the reader to emulate them, but 11.11 and other evidence from 10.1–22.16 do not provide the resources to argue so. As will become clear, many other sayings do not advocate what Lyu contends about rhetoric in a straightforward manner, though it seems that the characters may serve some motivational role in and of themselves, a query that I will bring to Proverbs 1–9.

Lyu does observe some key assumptions within the sayings regarding the emotions of these characters.[68] He notes that Prov. 21.15 and 21.10 reveal that a flourishing life requires cultivating the right desires. For 'it is a *joy* to the righteous when justice is done but *terror* to evildoers'; and 'the soul of the wicked *desires* evil'. Furthermore, Collection II assumes good and bad desires in its dominant character types: the righteous and the wicked. Thus, 'by their *desire*, the treacherous are captured' (11.6b) and 'the *desire* of the righteous will be given' (10.24b; cf. 10.3; 11.6, 23; 10.24). These observations, which tie emotions to Proverbial characters, support the notion that these characters function in a rhetorical manner by engaging the emotions of the audience. We have a sense that the affections of the treacherous contribute to their capture and that the desires of righteous people will be granted, even gratified. Other than this, Lyu's notions are, at the moment, only suggestions, lacking the textual corroboration and the consideration of Proverbs 1–9 that are required for a solid defence. For now, I hold his conclusions regarding the function of character types as a hypothesis.

While not explicitly claiming a rhetorical approach, Kenneth Aitken has also examined the characters of Prov. 10.1–22.16 and captures, in his words, their rhetorical function:

---

68. Lyu, *Righteousness*, 65-8.

the wise intend their proverbs about the fool and his folly to be a series of snap-shots for people to take a very hard look at to see if they can spot themselves—and be warned!.... [W]e must not forget that these proverbs are connected with the theme of the two ways and have a didactic purpose.... So if these proverbs on the righteous and the wicked are concerned to assert a moral orderliness, it is to strengthen our resolve to 'turn away from evil' (12.26) and to 'pursue righteousness' (15.9).[69]

According to Aitken, the author of Proverbs, in portraying these characters, establishes a moral system that serves a didactic purpose. However, Aitken assumes that the interpreter desires to be the righteous person and avoid the wicked, and furthermore that he or she will self-reflect in light of these caricatured figures based on a few suggestive sayings (12.26; 15.9). Even more problematic for Aitken, 12.26b does not assert 'turn away from evil'; it says 'the way of the wicked leads them astray'.[70] And, as mentioned with Lyu, 15.9 presumes that divine approval will motivate the pursuit of righteousness. In my view the proverbs of 10.1–22.16 reflect on and observe characters more than they explicitly exhort behaviour or emulation. This constitutes an interpretive challenge to their potential didactic, rhetorical function that will be considered shortly.

Aitken and Lyu reveal that Prov. 10.1–22.16 suggests a positive and negative desirability between the interpreter and character types. They also propose that the characters function rhetorically by offering models for the interpreter to emulate or mirrors for self-evaluation, options plausible and well articulated but inadequately defended. More clearly, 10.1–22.16 indicates that its characters harbour emotions that match their moral identities, pushing interpretation toward the realm of rhetoric. In summary, both interpreters largely overlook texts from Proverbs 1–9 and no correlation between the collections is explored. Based on the suggestions and assumptions observed above, the interpretive questions for Proverbs 1–9, which may provide insight into the characters of 10–29, stand as follows:

1. What is the rhetorical function of the character types in Proverbs 1–9?
   a. What is the role of emulation?
   b. What is the role of self-reflection?
   c. What affective posture does Proverbs 1–9 instil in the interpreter towards its characters?

---

69. Aitken, *Proverbs*, 96, 144.
70. The MT reads, וְדֶרֶךְ רְשָׁעִים תַּתְעֵם.

2.2.1. *Character Types in Proverbs 10.1–22.16*

Before exploring Proverbs 1–9, texts need to be selected from 10.1–22.16 so that the most generalizable conclusions can be made. In order to select material most pertinent to the rhetorical function of character types, I have categorized all of the material in 10.1–22.16 based on the two elements that contribute most to a saying's rhetorical function: character types and consequences. The references break down as follows:

Table 2.1

Character only	*Character and Consequence*	*Consequence only*
10.3, 6, 18, 20, 23, 26, 32; 11.12, 20; 12.1, 5, 10, 15-17, 23, 28; 13.1, 16; 14.2, 7-9, 15, 19, 21, 29, 33; 15.2, 3, 5, 8, 9, 12, 14, 19, 21, 26, 28; 16.4, 23, 32; 17.4, 7, 10, 12, 15, 16, 18, 24, 26, 27; 18.2, 5, 9; 19.1, 10, 24, 28; 20.26; 21.4, 8, 18, 24, 26, 27; 22.13	10.1, 4, 5, 7, 8, 10, 11, 13, 21, 24, 25, 27, 29-31; 11.2, 3, 5-11, 16, 18, 21, 23, 28-31; 12.3, 6, 7, 12, 13, 18, 20, 21, 24, 26, 27; 13.2, 4-6, 9, 14, 15, 19-22, 25; 14.3, 6, 11, 14, 16-18, 20, 24, 32; 15.6, 7, 20, 24, 31; 16.14, 17, 21, 22, 27-30; 17.11, 20, 21, 23, 25, 27; 18.6-8, 10, 15; 19.8, 13, 15, 25, 29; 20.3-5, 7, 19; 21.5, 7, 10-12, 15, 20, 22, 25, 29; 22.3, 5, 10, 12	10.2, 9, 12, 17, 19; 11.4, 14, 15, 17, 19, 24-27; 12.2, 8, 9, 11, 14, 19, 25; 13.3, 8, 10, 11, 13, 17, 18, 23; 14.1, 4, 22, 23, 25-27, 30, 34, 35; 15.1, 4, 10, 13, 15, 18, 22, 25, 27, 29, 30, 32, 33; 16.3, 5-7, 15, 18, 20, 24, 31; 17.2, 5, 8, 9, 13, 19, 22; 18.3, 12, 15, 16, 18-22, 24; 19.2, 4-7, 9, 11, 16-20, 23, 26, 27; 20.1, 2, 8, 13, 17, 20-22, 25, 28, 30; 21.6, 13, 14, 16, 17, 21, 23, 28; 22.4, 6, 8, 9, 11, 14-16
		Possibly Consequence: 10.22; 11.13; 12.4; 13.7, 24; 14.12, 13, 28, 31; 15.23; 16.10, 13, 25; 17.6, 14; 18.4, 11, 17; 19.3, 12, 21; 20.11, 18, 24, 29; 21.1, 31

Neither Character nor Consequence	11.1, 22; 12.22; 13.24; 14.5, 10; 15.11, 16, 17; 16.1, 2, 8, 9, 11, 12, 16, 19, 26, 33; 17.1, 3, 17; 19.14, 22; 20.6, 9, 10, 12, 14-16, 23, 27; 21.2, 3, 9, 19, 30; 22.1, 2, 7

It is thought that proverbs in Collection II persuade by means of characters, as the comments of Lyu and Aitken attest, and also by means of consequences. The function of consequences in Proverbs has been stated succinctly: 'Ihre Intention ist, wie bereits dargelegt primär eine pädagogische; es geht darum, Zusammenhänge des Lebens darzulegen, um zu einem entsprechenden Verhalten anzuleiten'.[71] For example, Prov. 20.13 warns, 'Do not love sleep, lest you come to poverty'. A consequence (poverty) is portrayed as stemming from a particular action (sleep), plausibly motivating the poverty-fearing reader to adhere to its command: 'Do not love sleep'. The outcome in 20.13 serves not only an informative but also a persuasive purpose: the threat of poverty motivates people to sleep less. The cursory treatment of this proverb illustrates the way that many sayings within 10.1–22.16 omit character terms and yet nevertheless function rhetorically, often aiming to motivate, or to justify a certain mode of being or activity, by stating the consequences.

With these didactic and rhetorical features in mind, the 375 sayings of Prov. 10.1–22.16 present the following divisions: character only (69); consequence only (101); character and consequence (138); possibly consequence (26); and neither character nor consequence (41). At 82 percent, the overwhelming majority of texts include characters and/or consequences. Setting aside consequences, I here select the passages in 10.1–22.16 that incorporate character types without any clear consequence-related elements in order to facilitate the most effective focus on the topic at hand. Again, this segregation fosters analysis; it is not based on the assumption that motivation in Proverbs is unintegrated, as if characters persuade to some end and consequences to another, each in their own fashion and without overlap. Statistically, these two features cross-pollinate, as the majority of sayings in 10.1–22.16 contain both character types and consequences, indicating that they obviously work together. But those statistics only capture part of the picture. Take, for example, a passage that will be examined below. Proverbs 15.2 mentions that the 'tongue of the wise makes knowledge good', and that 'the mouth of fools pours out folly'. At face value, the statements do not persuade towards one action or the other – they characterize the speech of wise people and fools – but when read in light of 15.1, the interpretive possibilities open up. 'A soft answer turns back wrath, but a harsh word brings up anger'. Deflecting wrath is presumably desirable, and invoking anger, presumably, undesirable, and

---

71. Georg Freuling, *'Wer eine Grube gräbt...': Der Tun-Ergehen-Zusammenhang und sein Wandel in der alttestamentlichen Weisheitsliteratur* (Neukirchen-Vluyn: Neukirchener Verlag, 2004), 104. So Philip Johannes Nel, *The Structure and Ethos of the Wisdom Admonitions in Proverbs* (Berlin: de Gruyter, 1982), 74–6.

such inclinations might motivate someone to speak gently and refrain from lambasting. If one were to associate the actions and motivations of Prov. 15.1 with the 'tongue of the wise' and 'mouth of fools' in 15.2, then we have a clear example of how character types and consequences are integrated across multiple proverbs. Wise people respond tenderly and assuage wrath; fools spill out harsh words and induce anger; do not you, interpreter, want to be like the former? Character and consequences work together, and this is to make no mention of value statements or the book's theology, to which the later chapters of this monograph are dedicated.

Proverbs often function holistically, motivating readers to ways of being and action by means of character types and consequential statements. Any motivations that are proximate to character-based proverbs will be accounted for in this chapter, as seemingly solitary characters must be read in light of any consequence statements within the surrounding proverbs. But my selection of texts remains guided by the distribution of characters and consequences, which will bring into focus those character types that carry the greatest motivational burden. With this criteria, the clearest and most persuasive answers can be given to the question of how the character types function rhetorically.

The character-only passages do not exhibit a clear pattern in terms of content or literary and rhetorical form. Sometimes they present a standard case of the wise or foolish person in nominal form, such as the 'fool' without modification: '*A fool* will not delight in understanding but only in his heart revealing itself' (18.2). Characters often appear in construct form, like the 'tongue of the righteous' and the 'heart of the wicked' (10.20), for instance. Lastly, in addition to mixing character domains, such as the moral/intellectual, theological, and wisdom/pragmatic categories noted earlier (e.g. 14.9), 10.1–22.16 packages its character terms in a variety of rhetorical styles, such as the question, imperative, or quotation.

My selection of texts cannot do justice to all of the variety in content, form, and rhetorical style, so I have chosen texts with an eye towards those that are not used elsewhere in this study and that represent material across 10.1–22.16, which should facilitate the best demonstration of the didactic function of Proverbs 1–9. These include a proverb with the wise and the foolish person in nominal form (18.2) and the same characters in construct state (15.2).[72] The full grouping of texts that use character types without consequence orientation include the following:

---

72. See also different rhetorical styles (14.7; 15.26; 17.7, 26; 18.5; 19.10; 21.27; 22.13; cf. 16.4). For predicate-dominant passages, cf. Prov. 14.2, 21, 29; 15.5b; 16.32; 17.27; 18.9.

Table 2.2

Moral (wise/fool/prudent/ understanding)	Theological (righteous/wicked)	Other (e.g. scoffer)
10.3, 18, 23; 11.12; 12.15-16, 23; 13.16; 14.7-8, 19, 33; 15.2, 14, 21; 16.23; 17.7, 10, 12, 18, 24; 18.2	10.3, 6, 20, 32; 12.5, 10, 28; 15.8-9, 28; 16.4; 17.26; 18.5; 20.26; 21.4, 18, 26-27	14.15; 15.3, 12; 17.4; 21.24 Sluggard: 10.26; 18.9; 19.24; 22.13

Mix of Domains	13.1; 14.9; 15.5, 19; 19.1, 10, 28

Rather than dealing with the particular questions of these passages at this point, I examine Proverbs 1–9 with the three key rhetorical questions noted above, which were derived from scholarship on 10.1–22.16 and offer enough direction themselves for an enquiry into 1–9. The texts from 10.1–22.16 that I have selected are revisited in section 2.2.3, where the particular interpretive issues of 15.2 and 18.2 are expounded and the insights of 1–9 brought to bear upon them.

2.2.2. *Character Types in Proverbs 1–9*

The characters of Proverbs 1–9 make a striking appearance in 1.20-33, as Wisdom denounces simpletons, scoffers and fools in a collective enquiry about their lack of attention to and affection for her. Yet prior to their appearance in Prov. 1.20-33, and with more subtlety, Prov. 1.1-7 introduces character types and encourages emulation of one while portraying the other as unattractive: be like the wise; the fool is not appealing.[73] I have argued elsewhere that the primary audience of Proverbs is not the 'simpleton' or 'youth' of 1.4 but 'the wise' in 1.5 who 'hear and increase in learning'. Proverbs 1.5 'commands and invites the audience to posture themselves not as the fool, simpleton, or youth but as the wise character who heeds instruction'.[74] The wise in this passage operates as an ideal addressee, who always listens and grows in wisdom. He functions as a caricatured, literary type with a rhetorical function intended to inspire

---

73. On the characters of Proverbs 1–9 as an emotional map for interpreters, see Christine Yoder, 'The Objects of Our Affections: Emotions and the Moral Life in Proverbs 1–9', in *Shaking Heaven and Earth: Essays in Honor of Walter Brueggemann and Charles B. Cousar*, ed. Kathleen O'Conner, E. Elizabeth Johnson, Christine Elizabeth Yoder and Stanley Saunders (Louisville, KY: Westminster John Knox Press, 2005), 73–88.

74. Keefer, 'A Shift', 112.

emulation and evaluation. Functioning in the same way but with the obverse effect, the fool who 'despises wisdom and instruction' (1.7) should repulse the interpreter. While clear, the rhetorical intentions of these characters remain undeveloped in 1.1-7, suggesting emulation or avoidance but little more than that. Proverbs 1.10-19 begins to further address the question of emulation, but reading to the end of Proverbs 1 discloses much more about character rhetoric.

Proverbs 1.20-33 advocates self-evaluation in view of its caricatures. The passage portrays a personified female figure of Wisdom who calls out in the city centre, addressing a collection of negative character types in 1.22 – the simpleton, scoffers and fools – and consistently attributing them with particular attitudes. She says they love simplicity, delight in scoffing, and hate knowledge (1.22). They refuse Wisdom's call (1.24), neglect her counsel, and do not consent to her reproof (1.25, 30). They hate knowledge and do not choose the fear of the Lord (1.29), instead turning from Wisdom and remaining complacent (1.32). This passage introduces a representative collection of three character terms and enumerates their attitudes to capture a gamut of negative postures and perhaps to emphasize the holistic corruption of these negative types. The passage clearly sets a context of character types and includes a slew of particular characteristics.

In Prov. 1.22-27, Wisdom addresses the characters as 'you':

> How long, simple ones, will *you* love (תאהבו) simplicity.... If *you* turn (תשובו) to my reproof...*you* will know my words (אודיעה דברי אתכם)...but I call and *you* refuse (ותמאנו)...when *your* dread (פחדכם) comes...when distress and anguish come upon *you* (עליכם).

After addressing the negative characters directly in 1.22-27 with 'you' language, at verse 28 Wisdom shifts grammatical person from 'you' to 'they'.

> Then *they* will call (יקראנני) on me and I will not answer; *they* will seek me diligently (ישחרנני).... *They* did not consent (לא־אבו) to my counsel.... So *they* will eat (יאכלו) from the fruit of *their* way (דרכם) (1.28-31).

What is the rhetorical significance of this shift in perspective? I contend that 1.20-33 shows Lady Wisdom shifting grammatical subjects, because the scene is intended to serve as a lesson for the interpreter. Given the options of the wise and foolish persons, Prov. 1.1-7 has already aligned the audience's identity with the wise and started to detail their traits, but for the fool that passage implies only his dislike for wisdom and the Lord: 'The fear of the Lord is the beginning of knowledge; fools despise wisdom and instruction' (1.7). In 1.20-33 we now see specific features of the foolish population: they neglect, refuse, turn from, hate, and stand complacent towards wisdom. Furthermore, Lady Wisdom draws the interpreter's attention to the fools, whom she addresses as 'you', and then shifts to third-person address to retain a distance from them.[75]

The detail of negative attitudes and the concern of Lady Wisdom to talk *about* rather than *to* character types in 1.20-33 suggests a deliberate rhetorical attempt on the part of the text. Interpreters should evaluate themselves in light of the characters portrayed: looking at these fools, looking at their actions and attitudes, and self-reflecting in light of them. 'The fools' emotions', in 1.22, says Christine Yoder 'variously reveal postures of hubris, wantonness, and animosity. Wisdom holds them responsible. Her rhetorical question stings, her exasperation aims to invoke their guilt, and her words caution anyone within earshot to think twice before adopting such smug ways of being in the world.'[76] I am arguing that the text, without aligning interpreters with its negative character types, encourages the audience to consider these negative characteristics in light of their own. Do I hate knowledge? Do I choose the fear of the Lord? Do I despise reproof? Proverbs 1.20-33 invokes a process of evaluation, whereby the interpreter must consider these negatively caricatured attitudes and assess his or her own affections.[77]

The passage does not maintain an exclusively negative tone but concludes with an attractive alternative to the fools – the one who listens to wisdom: 'But the one who listens to me dwells in security and is at ease from the dread of evil' (1.33). This verse affirms the alignment of the interpreter with the positive characters of Proverbs, even recalling the invitation to hear (שמע) in Prov. 1.5 as Wisdom characterizes her favoured person as 'the one who listens (שמע) to me' (1.33a). Seeing that she wants her audience to listen to her (1.23a, 24b), Wisdom's final comment in 1.33 certainly refers to the sort of people she is looking for – those who pay heed to instruction. As to its rhetorical effect, perhaps her call commends the following: be this sort of person, and assess your attitude towards Wisdom and your capacity to heed her. It certainly contrasts with those who reject wisdom and plausibly prompts interpreters to evaluate their own desire to listen. Towards the fools, however, the interpreter's

---

75. Bernhard Lang, *Wisdom and the Book of Proverbs: A Hebrew Goddess Redefined* (New York: Pilgrim Press, 1986), 42.

76. Yoder, 'Objects', 77; so Fox, *Proverbs 1–9*, 98.

77. Yoder (*Proverbs*, 20–1) rightly warns that this is not a Romantic notion of identifying the 'true' self in isolation. Rather, the process entails community but most importantly prompts the question, who do I want to be like?

posture also receives adjustment due to the extended claims of disaster and mockery that befall them in 1.26-28. The negative outcomes for evil characters instil dread, fostering affections of dislike and apprehension, which has addressed the third and final interpretive question of this chapter: what affective posture does Proverbs 1–9 instil in the interpreter towards the characters? In summary, the caricatures of Proverbs portray idealized selves, meant to attract or repel, while offering mirrors of good and evil with which to evaluate our own character. The speech to fools in 1.20-33 particularly shows that character types function not only as models of emulation but as mirrors for self-evaluation. Cohering with Prov. 1.1-7 and 1.10-19, these conclusions account for the three rhetorical framework questions and, when accounting for the clarity and force of the text, suggest that these passages function didactically.

2.2.3. *The Function of Proverbs 1–9 for 15.2 and 18.2*

To determine if the passages from Proverbs 1–9 indeed function didactically, their insights into Proverbial characters must be brought to bear on 10.1–22.16. The textual examples enlisted from 10.1–22.16 were chosen for their strength as examples and for their grammatical properties. Proverbs 18.2 presents the 'fool' in nominal form, and 15.2 presents a single body part of the wise and foolish persons, respectively, a 'tongue' and 'mouth'. These proverbs pose interpretive challenges particularly related to their use of character types and thereby test the interpretive function of Proverbs 1–9.

לא־יחפץ כסיל בתבונה	18.2	A fool will not delight in understanding
כי אם־בהתגלות לבו		but rather[78] in his heart's exposing itself

Proverbs 18.2 says, 'A fool will not delight in understanding, but rather in his heart's exposing itself'. This proverb mentions the fool in nominal form and simply describes what he does and does not delight in. The fool does not delight in understanding but delights only in making himself known (*hithpael* גלה), that is, in expressing his thoughts and words. Genesis 9.21 employs the only other occurrence of the verb (*hithpael* גלה) to depict Noah's drunken self '*uncovered* in his tent' (cf. Prov. 27.5), so that the fool might in a sense 'uncover' his heart. The כי אם in Prov. 18.2, translated 'but rather', emphasizes the contrast: the fool delights not even in a bit of understanding but only in self-expression. At face value, the proverb does not motivate. It states what a fool does and does not delight

---

78. After a negation, כי אם signals a contrast (JM §172c; Gen. 32.29; Ps. 1.2), often translated, 'but only' (ESV; NRSV).

in, and so seems to convey an observation about the fool and his delights. Waltke, however, comments that the saying 'warns against having a closed mind and an open mouth', implying that the proverb includes not only an indicative but a rhetorical force: it warns.[79] This rhetorical function might be disregarded by insisting that the proverb simply observes, that it tells us what is the case and nothing about what ought to be or what someone should do, placing the burden of proof on those who would argue otherwise. Therefore, I will argue otherwise, not to say that Prov. 18.2 does not make an observation about the world, valuable in its own right, but to say that the proverb carries additional rhetorical force that is acquired via the conception of character types that I have been developing based on Proverbs 1–9.

How, then, does the interpreter discern this rhetorical thrust that is not simply observational? First, we might contrast the fool's lack of delight in understanding, with the commended value of understanding, as advocated by Proverbs 1–9: 'Blessed is the one who finds wisdom' (3.13a), and 'My son, be attentive to my wisdom' (5.1a; so Prov. 2.2-3, 11). In Prov. 18.2, then, the failure to delight in understanding does not cohere with the admonitions elsewhere in Proverbs, so that the interpreter might recognize that when 'a fool will not delight in understanding' this saying portrays a bad attitude. Second, the rhetorical nature of the proverb becomes clearer when the character lexeme ('a fool') is replaced with a generic reference to 'a human': 'a human will not delight in understanding'. From this perspective, with the character lexeme omitted, the proverb carries some, though not as much, rhetorical significance. For even a human failing to delight in understanding receives a negative evaluation elsewhere in Proverbs.

I, nevertheless, contend that a figure as ethically neutral as 'the human' would not harbour the rhetorical force of the 'fool', and that the presence or absence of the character lexeme makes all the interpretive difference for 18.2. Consider the second line: 'a human delights in his heart's exposing itself'. This statement counters much of Proverbs 10–29, which, despite valuing silence (10.8, 19; 18.13; 29.11), advocates human expression, namely of the sort that is based on 'understanding'. For example, 'The lips of the wise spread knowledge; not so the heart of fools' (15.7). This passage and others seem to support the 'heart's exposing itself', as the wise 'spread knowledge', the understanding have wisdom on their lips (10.13), and 'the mouth of the righteous brings forth wisdom' (10.31; so 15.2, 28). Expression in these cases appears to be a recommended activity, suggesting that a human who delights in exposing his heart serves as a positive example for readers. However, each of these sayings incorporates

---

79. Waltke, *Proverbs 15–31*, 69.

character lexemes, so that spreading knowledge seems inseparable from the lips of the wise and abnormal for any fool. The mouth of the 'righteous' brings forth wisdom, and 'the understanding' have wisdom on their lips. Although I have been saying these proverbs 'value' certain forms of speech, such as spreading knowledge, they, like Prov. 18.2, actually state observations about characters, to which forms of speech are bound, and thereby return us to the same issue: what is the rhetorical significance of character types? Proverbs 1–9 provides a remarkable response to this question. When read as an interpretive framework, it imposes a conception of these characters that shapes the rhetorical pulse of 18.2, causing its 'fool' to undergo rhetorical transformation.

Proverbs 1–9 instils an unquestionable repulsion against the fool, so that the interpreter arrives at 18.2 knowing that he or she does not want, or should not want, to be like that character. This response accounts for emulation: do not be like this fool. As for self-evaluation, 18.2 describes attributes that the interpreter must avoid: disenchantment with understanding, and exclusively sharing his or her own knowledge. When and where, asks the self-evaluative interpreter, do I reflect such qualities? The third question for 1–9 assessed the affective implications of characters, combining the aforementioned emulation and self-evaluation. The fool models a contorted affective posture, delighting in the wrong things or in the wrong way, so that the interpreter informed by Proverbs 1–9 is motivated to modify his or her affective posture based on the fool's bad example.

In sum, Prov. 18.2 makes an observation without direct rhetorical force. While it contains qualitative descriptions, such as not delighting in understanding, on the surface the passage does not persuade. But with an understanding of the rhetorical function of character types from Proverbs 1–9, the interpreter can identify and, more importantly, feel the persuasive intent of 18.2 and similar sayings, enfolding within his interpretive scope not only valuable observations about the world but also volitional implications. Therefore, Proverbs 1–9 functions didactically by instilling a rhetorical framework and interpretive categories that account for a latent rhetorical layer within 10.1–22.16.

לשון חכמים תיטיב דעת	15.2	The tongue of the wise makes knowledge good[80]
ופי כסילים יביע אולת		but the mouth of fools pours out folly

---

80. The verb (*hiphil* יטב) is translated 'commend' (ESV) or 'adorn' (Fox; Waltke), communicating a sense of mastery or improvement (Franz Delitzsch, *Biblical Commentary on the Proverbs of Solomon*, trans. M. G. Easton [Edinburgh: T. & T. Clark, 1880], 1:316).

A similar situation occurs in Prov. 15.2, which contrasts the wise and foolish persons, not in a grammatically absolute form but rather in a construct state that associates the characters with particular bodily organs: the tongue of the wise and the mouth of fools. Like 18.2, Prov. 15.2 does not explicitly commend or discourage a course of action. It makes an observation, stating that wise tongues 'make good' or improve upon knowledge and that foolish mouths pour out folly. Also like 18.2, the character terms could have been omitted, so that 'A tongue makes knowledge good, but a mouth pours out folly'. However, that statement would render a contradiction, or at least a puzzling tension. For if the tongue and mouth refer to the same thing, namely a person's speech, then according to 15.2 a human expresses both good and folly.[81] As an observation this proverb would be advantageous, indicating a human practice, even a habit, of speech that plausibly corresponds with life in current and ancient contexts, whereby a person may speak in both good and foolish ways. But the original version of Prov. 15.2, though it still states an observation, includes modifiers, and these modifiers are character terms that, again, make all the difference for its interpretation. 'The tongue *of the wise* makes knowledge good, but the mouth *of fools* pours out folly'.

Now, the character terms do make all the difference for 15.2, but there are proximate sources of motivation that might guide the rhetoric of the proverb. According to 15.1, 'A soft answer turns back wrath, but a harsh word brings up anger'. Assuming the attractiveness of diverting someone's wrath and the unattractiveness of causing anger, an interpreter might favour the 'soft answer' instead of the 'harsh word'. So too, 'A healing tongue is a tree of life, but perversion in it breaks the spirit' (15.4). This proverb works in a way similar to the previous, depicting healing words as a life-giving tree and perverted speech as capable of battering someone's spirit. Both proverbs use consequences to persuade readers towards certain courses of action and away from others: gentle words will turn away wrath and even give life; speaking harshly or with twisted talk will enrage someone and possibly harm him. Consequences inform and motivate, depicting what will happen in most circumstances and thereby disposing one to act in a certain way.

Proverbs 15.1 and 15.4 provide some substance to 15.2. As I alluded to at the outset of this chapter, the preferred ways of speech could be associated with the wise person of 15.2, so long as one knows to prefer wisdom to folly, and that may mean that from 'the tongue of the wise' comes a soft answer and soothing remarks, and that the folly that fools

---

81. The Epistle of James (3.9-10a) states this very point.

'pour out' may sound harsh or perverse.[82] So through a chain of reasoning the characters of 15.2 could be perceived as attractive, and readers who follow that reasoning, scanning around 15.2 and accounting for its statements about speech and its consequences, may then wish to be like the wise person and unlike the fool. In my judgment, that is not unfeasible based on the text we have.[83] The immediate context of the proverb supplies some motivation to align with certain characters and specifies a few forms of communicative conduct. But that still leaves us wondering about how these characters are rhetorically evaluated and whether the associations made from 15.1, 4 would make a reader decidedly pursue one character instead of the other. Furthermore, how ought one to respond to that attraction or dislike, and is the immediate literary context the only guidance we have for deciding how to speak?

Proverbs 1–9 clarified the self-evaluative, rhetorical function of characters, and when viewed within this framework the characters of 15.2 function in the same way. The interpreter sees speech organs associated with character types and respective descriptions, so that with the aid of Proverbs 1–9 the observation becomes a mirror of self-reflection, prompting interpreters to question the wise and foolish qualities of their own speech. Do I improve upon knowledge or pour out folly? Proverbs 1–9 also instils an attraction towards the former and repulsion against the latter so that we feel drawn towards knowledgeable speech and opposed to foolish speech. We not only assess our own verbal habits; we aim to improve them in accord with the characters of 15.2. In short, Prov. 15.2 first relies upon its character terms to ethically qualify different types of talk, and apparently remains indicative rather than imperative until, secondly, Proverbs 1–9 supplies a rhetorical framework for extracting a certain type of applicative force from 15.2. That force is generated also from the consequential statements within 15.1-4, which seem to complement the character instructions of chapters 1–9, and yet Proverbs 1–9 leaves interpreters more decided about the rhetorical question of 15.2.

---

82. So Waltke, *Proverbs 15–31*, 613–14: 'This verse continues the topic of a good "answer" versus a bad "word", mentioning both their instruments, *tongue* and *mouth*, and their sources, which are rooted in the character of the *wise* versus that of *fools*' (italics original; I have omitted parenthetical verse references).

83. The same reasoning applies to those who might listen to these proverbs, hearing 15.1-7, for example, or reciting it from memory and making the connections that I have proposed.

2.2.4. *The Function of Proverbs 1–9 for 29.11*

As shown over the course of this chapter, understanding the characters of Proverbs involves two primary questions: what are they and what are they intended to do for the interpreter? I have argued that Proverbs 1–9 provides a framework that lends interpretive insight into some of the challenges that arise from characters in Prov. 10.1–22.16, wherein they represent caricatured versions of certain qualities that represent distinct facets of the Proverbial good or bad person and deliver a series of rhetorical functions meant to persuade the interpreter into reflection and affective response. Proverbs 1–9, I will argue here, also offers this interpretive framework for Prov. 22.17–29.27, which like 10.1–22.16 often relies upon an understanding of character types.

Proverbs 22.17–29.27 too states observations rather than admonitions about its characters. For example, in 29.11 'The fool brings out all of his spirit, but the wise stills it back'. This saying contributes a valuable observation about fools, wise people, and the relationships they have with their inner lives. The 'spirit' (רוח), which is here 'brought out' by the fool or 'stilled back' by the wise, may refer to anger (cf. 14.29; 16.32; Judg. 8.3; Eccl. 10.4) or to the internal thoughts and feelings of a person (Prov. 1.23; Job 7.11; Ps. 77.7[6]), though in Proverbs it most commonly refers to a person's 'spirit' or 'disposition', which may be crushed (15.13), broken (15.4), trustworthy (11.13), haughty (16.18), lowly (16.19; 29.23) or resilient (18.14a). At this point, there is no reason to translate רוח in Prov. 29.11 as anything other than this sense of 'spirit'. However, interpreters often assume two things about this proverb, first, that it deals with anger and, second, that it delivers an instruction about how to handle such anger. In the first place, the lexical evidence alone does not justify interpreting רוח in 29.11 as 'anger', though it permits the possibility. Proverbs 29.22 states that 'A man of anger (אף) stirs up strife, and the wrathful (חמה) man, much transgression', and while this has been cited as evidence for similar themes in 29.11, verse 22 actually shows that other lexemes were at the author's disposal to denote 'anger' and were not used in 29.11, such as אף and חמה.[84] So רוח in 29.11 may refer to anger but we would expect an alternative term.

---

84. Sæbø (*Sprüche*, 350) connects Prov. 29.8, 11, 20, and 22 with anger and the destabilization of society through speech, but only verses 8 and 22 clearly refer to anger and its socially destabilizing consequences. In 29.22, the phrase בעל חמה, woodenly 'owner of wrath', uses בעל as a noun of relation to denote a wrathful person (see BDB, 127 [I.5]).

For argument's sake, if Prov. 29.11 does refer to anger, then how do interpreters justify the conclusion that the saying delivers an instruction? Plöger, for instance, says that 'Auch der Weise ist nicht frei von Emotionen, aber er versteht es, in der rechten Weise mit ihnen umzugehen'.[85] Notice the evaluative and thereby instructive conclusion regarding the proverb's observation: the wise person deals with emotion 'in the right way'. Plöger and others appeal to the court scene in 29.9 to claim that 29.11 continues the scenario and adds further instructions, not seeming to account for the observational nature of 29.9 and 29.11.[86] For 29.9 only tells us what is the case: 'A wise man argues with a foolish man, and [the fool] rages and laughs, and there is no quiet'. To render imperative force from 29.11, appeal is otherwise made to other proverbs that deal with speech or emotions (e.g. 12.16). While such statements are more directly imperative, they, including 29.9, incorporate character types, which I suggest transform the rhetorical implications of Prov. 29.11, since taken without these terms the proverb does not persuade towards certain action or ways of life.[87] If 'a human' brings out all of his spirit, but 'a human' stills it back, it cannot be known if one or both deals with emotions 'in the right way'. Both expressing one's spirit and withholding it remain morally ambiguous options for how one might speak. As it stands, the proverb may simply describe two types of activities: how the fool acts and how the wise person acts – a plausible and not unhelpful interpretation when read within the context of Proverbs 10–29. However, as with the examples explored earlier (15.2; 18.2), two interpretive manoeuvres carry significant insights on a rhetorical level for Prov. 29.11. First, what happens when the character terms are removed?

If the character terms are replaced with neutral references, then the passage would read, 'One person brings out all of his spirit, but another person stills it back'. The statement recalls Prov. 29.22, where 'A man of anger stirs up strife, and the wrathful man, much transgression'. Like the modified version of 29.11, Prov. 29.22 contains no character lexemes, but unlike 29.11, Prov. 29.22 uses unmistakable terms for anger: אף and חמה, not רוח. Furthermore, 29.22 uses other morally qualified language to portray the consequences of anger as bad, for אף instigates 'strife' and חמה causes 'much transgression'. Such morally charged language and consequences do not appear in 29.11, which, without its character terms simply leaves the interpreter with 'One person brings out all of his spirit, but another person stills it back'.

85. Plöger, *Sprüche*, 345.
86. Waltke, *Proverbs 15–31*, 439.
87. Fox (*Proverbs 10–31*, 838), for instance, appeals to Prov. 12.16.

The saying remains an observation, but if the statements of 29.11 intend not only to describe but to commend and warn, as is often asserted, then it is not clear which colon should be obeyed and which should be avoided. Maybe the first line reflects good behaviour, for even if we interpret רוח as 'anger', Proverbs does not necessarily prohibit the emotion: it praises those slow to anger (14.29; 15.18) and portrays the Lord himself as angry (22.14; 24.18). Hence, letting out all of one's angry spirit could be permissible. Likewise, Proverbs associates the 'cool spirit' and restraint of words with understanding (17.27), also indicating that anger can lead to transgression (29.22), evidence that supports the characterization of 29.11b as positive: 'another person stills [his spirit] back'. Based on passages in Proverbs 10–29, both lines of 29.11 are justifiably appropriate acts when rid of their character lexemes. But again, according to Plöger, the behaviour in verse 11b deals with emotions in the right way, as restraint of anger is commended and its full release, condemned.[88] In other words, line A portrays bad behaviour and line B portrays good. Such a conclusion, though, does not follow from other instructions in Proverbs or from Prov. 29.11 when stripped of its character terms, and therefore it seems that the use of character lexemes offers the only solid ground for making a qualitative judgment about the activities in 29.11.[89] In other words, Prov. 29.11 requires its character terms in order to indicate proper conduct. 'One person brings out all of his spirit, but another person stills it back' leaves the application of the proverb ambiguous, so that the interpreter does not know what behaviour the proverb advocates. Such language would advocate neither behaviour; it would simply observe.

Having levelled our first query into the rhetoric of Prov. 29.11, the second significant question to ask is, what happens when 29.11 is read in light of Proverbs 1–9? Proverbs 1–9 does not simply speak of 'humans' but instead portrays a variety of character types, and it is not content with making observations about these people but instead clarifies who they are, how they relate, and how interpreters might interact with them. Proverbs 1–9 inculcates the interpreter with a hatred and avoidance of the foolish person and a love for and desire to emulate the wise person. With this rhetorical framework, the interpreter of 29.11 knows to avoid actions associated with the fool and to replicate the activity of a wise person. In other words, 'Do not (or, be careful about) bringing out all of your spirit; rather, keep it stilled'. The interpreter also knows that these two figures

---

88. Plöger, *Sprüche*, 345.

89. The main legal material of the OT seldom regulates human emotions, especially anger, which would derive from laws about hatred (Exod. 23.5 [cf. 21.20-27]; Lev. 19.17-18; Deut. 19.11).

represent extreme embodiments of wise and foolish qualities and thus display actions that are, respectively, right and wrong.

At this point, a potential problem arises. With such a positive portrayal of restraining anger in 29.11, how should an interpreter account for other statements in Proverbs 10–29 that, when interpreted within the same Proverbs 1–9 framework, endorse anger rather than condemn it? Proverbs 14.29, for example, attributes 'slow anger' to those with understanding – 'Whoever is slow to anger has great understanding, but he who has a hasty temper exalts folly' (ESV) – possibly contradicting 29.11 when understood to condemn anger.[90] It can be said that Proverbs views both restrained and slow anger as different perspectives of good ways to handle anger, that it neither condemns anger in the absolute nor justifies it at all times but rather suggests that it may be appropriate in certain cases. Proverbs 1–9 does add a key qualification to this seeming generalization: such emotion, bubbling within one's spirit and perhaps akin to anger, is handled rightly only when handled by those with wisdom and understanding. For it is the understanding person who is slow to anger, and it is the wise person who holds back his spirit, activities that, according to Proverbs 1–9, are deemed appropriate because of their association with approved character types. Linguistically, conceptually and ethically, character makes all the difference for matters of speech in 29.11. Without its character terms, and even with them, the indicative statements in Prov. 29.11 do not deliver clear instructions for how to manage anger. While using description only is not necessarily a problem, when the proverb includes character lexemes, and these are interpreted in light of Proverbs 1–9, then the indicative statements take clear rhetorical direction, guiding the affections and behaviours of its readers.

2.2.5. *Conclusion*

The characters within Proverbs are caricatures, not necessarily negative pictures but extreme versions and idealized portraits of the Proverbial population, each of which represents one perspective on a single good or bad person. Rhetorically, they function by prompting interpreters to emulate the positive types, shun the negative, and to self-evaluate in light of the particular features that characters display, stemming from and also guiding affective postures. An examination of Prov. 1.10-19; 15.2; 18.2; and 29.11, as well as 6.1-19, demonstrated that Proverbs 1–9 establishes a framework of rhetorical categories that then produces additional

---

90. The proverb nicely reads more woodenly: 'slow anger is great understanding, but short temper exalts folly' (ארך אפים רב־תבונה וקצר־רוח מרים אולת).

interpretations of Proverbs 10–29. On their own, the proverbs make valuable observations about the world, and when they incorporate character types that are read in conjunction with Proverbs 1–9, their observations also become rhetorically charged statements that persuade the interpreter towards particular ways of being and behaving. In other words, Proverbs 1–9 functions didactically by offering interpretive faculties that uncover, and at times supplement, the persuasive effects of Proverbs 10–29.[91]

Having established the literary and rhetorical nature of Proverbial characters over the course of this chapter, I have not explained how these two perspectives relate. It is likely that they inform each other, as it seems, in the first place, that the embellished nature of the character types facilitates emulation. For given that extreme aspect, portraits of good and evil confront the interpreter in a pronounced way. If the gang in 1.10-19, for example, invited the son to join in petty theft – say, stealing a neighbour's scythe without harming anyone involved – then for the interpreter the father's warning to 'not consent' would likely flag in persuasive effect. It is, plausibly, the radical greed and violence in 1.10-19, the rejection of Wisdom and the incapacity to respond to her in 1.20-33 that so jar the audience into evaluation.

Regarding their identity, it was also concluded that the characters relate to each other in a coreferential manner, where each type – such as the fool, the wicked person, and the sluggard – exhibits a different persona of a singular figure, in this case, the evil person. However, the relationship of this coreferentiality to the author's rhetorical intentions was not made so obvious. How do so many different shades of good and evil contribute to the rhetorical aims of evaluation, self-reflection, and affective posture? The coreferential nature of the characters most plausibly contributes to the author's hope that interpreters will self-reflect in light of the multifarious collection of personal qualities. The 'righteous' prompts self-reflection in the realm of one's relationship to the Lord; the 'wise' in relation to wisdom; the 'diligent' in relation to work; and the 'upright' in relation to justice. I am not saying that these distinctions are fixed or exclusive categories, but they do remain quite consistent throughout Proverbs and most convincingly explain how the characters' coreferential identities relate to their rhetorical function. Therefore, the identity of character types – their caricatured nature and coreferential partnerships – contributes to the function of character types in no trifling way. What these characters are stimulates what they can achieve for those who encounter them.

---

91. Such an argument applies not only for the passages selected here but also, in the vein of 18.2, for Prov. 10.32; 15.2; and 21.18.

The increased variety and occurrences of character lexemes in Prov. 10.1–22.16, relative to Proverbs 1–9, were also noted. This distribution suggests that 1–9 intends to supply the interpreter with an interpretive framework by teaching what characters are and how they function. It presents a simpler set of character types within a literary context of extended poems through which the author can comprehend the nature and function of these types. Proverbs 10.1–22.16 subsequently presents the characters with more variety, and yet less elaboration, so that the interpreter can evaluate and self-reflect on himself or herself in life's many scenarios. In this respect, Waltke has captured the function of Proverbial characters precisely: they stand as 'exemplars by which to judge one's life in many situations'.[92] In these ways, Proverbs 1–9 functions didactically for Proverbs 10–29. The next chapter continues to look at the rhetorical features of Proverbs, though it exchanges character types for the specific aims and goals toward which the material persuades.

---

92. Waltke, *Proverbs 1–15*, 125.

3

EDUCATIONAL GOALS

The aims and values explored in this chapter relate directly to the notions of persuasive rhetoric explained in the previous one. In Chapter 2, I argued that the character types of Proverbs serve a rhetorical function, persuading the audience to emulate or avoid their characteristics. Consequently, when a character term appears within a proverb, which would otherwise make an observation about the world without carrying any persuasive force for the reader, that proverb is now imbued with a new level of persuasive power due to the presence of particular character lexemes. While the focus of that argument was understandably on proverbs that contain characters, the focus of the current chapter must account for the remaining material, which will expose additional rhetorical features.

One of those rhetorical features includes consequences, as shown in proverbs that motivate by means of correlating a consequence with a particular command or observation.[1] 'Wealth will not profit on the day of wrath, but righteousness will deliver from death' (Prov. 11.4). By declaring the futility of riches during the 'day of wrath' and the advantage of righteousness in the face of death, this proverb uses consequences to motivate one towards righteousness and away from putting too much stock in prosperity. As in Chapter 2, this material must be set aside in order to concentrate on another rhetorical element: the value statements of Proverbs. What the book values often correlates to the goals that it sets for its pupils. It holds up wisdom, for instance, as both a high value and prime educational achievement, and the same could be said of accepting instruction, which is valued and aimed for by the Proverbial teacher. By examining such values and interrelated aims, and not focusing on character types and consequences, this chapter explores the larger rhetorical mission

---

1. See the statistics and references in section 2.2.1.

of Proverbs to further determine the function of chapters 1–9. In the first section, the didactic role of Proverbs 1–9 is demonstrated with respect to these goals through Prov. 22.1 and 30.1-9. The second section then recalls Aletti's understanding of Proverbs 1–9 and its conception of moral discernment as an educational goal, thus also contributing to the enquiry into the aims and values of Proverbs.

3.1. *The Aims and Values of Proverbs*

I have mentioned the many means that Proverbs employs to persuade its audience, including character types, consequences, and direct commands, among others. A closer look at these features prompts the topic of this section – what Proverbs aims for and what it values – offering a window through which to analyse the relationship of Proverbs 1–9 and 10–31. The aims and values of Proverbs are bound together, and by attempting to structure them within Proverbs 10–31, especially within 10.1–22.16, their interpretive challenges become clear.

3.1.1. *Educational Goals in Proverbs 10.1–22.16*

When the sayings of 10.1–22.16 that contain consequences are combined with those that use character terms, they total 82 percent of the whole.[2] Of the remaining material, a number of sayings make comparative statements, often with language of 'better than', in order to directly commend one object over another, as in Prov. 22.1 – 'A name is to be chosen rather than great riches, favour is better than silver and gold'. A proverb like this, and others that use the language of 'better than' (טוב...מן...) – e.g. 'To acquire wisdom is much better than gold, and to acquire understanding is to be chosen more than silver' (16.16) – imply some system of values. At the very least, they make value judgments: for 22.1, 'a name' is more valuable than 'great riches', and 'favour' carries more value than 'silver and gold', creating a microcosm of axiological order where values fit into a type of hierarchy. The value statements in 22.1 prompt the question of whether 10.1–22.16 harbours a larger, endorsed system of values. That is, do the 'better thans' and comparative values of this entire collection fit within a hierarchy of goods and ends? The question becomes more acute when several value judgments in 10.1–22.16 are considered.

---

2. See Table 2.1 in section 2.2.1.

3.1.1.1. *Competing Goals in Proverbs 10.1–22.16*
We might take a closer look at Prov. 16.16 and 22.1:

קנה־חכמה מה־טוב מחרוץ	16.16	To acquire wisdom is much better than gold,
וקנות בינה נבחר מכסף		and to acquire understanding is to be chosen more than silver.
נבחר שם מעשר רב	22.1	A name is to be chosen rather than great riches,
מכסף ומזהב חן טוב		favour is better than silver and gold.

Both proverbs indicate that something is 'better than' precious metals, making statements of value that imply, respectively, that wisdom holds more value than gold (16.16) and that favour holds more value than gold (22.1). These axiological premises form part of a network of values that, within Proverbs, may or may not be coherent. A coherent network of values would be ordered in a hierarchical fashion that attributes certain things with more value and other things with less.[3] For example, making money could be the prime goal, while working hard holds second place and acquiring enough rest stands in the third, creating a structure of values that might direct one's daily life. An incoherent network would contain competing values, without deliberate order, that are simply left in tension. So rather than financial acquisition being better than hard work, the two are both commended, along with adequate rest, and yet no deliberate order of their importance is indicated. It is worth asking whether a coherent structure appears in Proverbs, that is, whether it organizes its values in a particular fashion. In addition to Prov. 16.16 and 22.1, three references to the Lord expose the importance of this question:

> No wisdom, no understanding, no counsel can avail against the Lord. (21.30, ESV)

> The rich and poor meet; the Lord makes all of them. (22.2)

> The consequence of humility and the fear of the Lord is riches, honour and life.[4] (22.4)

---

3. In contrast to constructing an absolute hierarchy, some things might have equivalent value or variable value depending on the person or situation. For example, good physical fitness would be more valuable for a soldier than for the scribe, who conversely values penmanship above physical fitness.

4. On this translation, see Waltke, *Proverbs 15–31*, 193 n. 6; cf. Delitzsch, *Proverbs*, 2:85–6.

If 16.16 values wisdom more than gold, then 21.30 and 22.2 suggest that the Lord is more valuable than either of these: for no wisdom can avail against him, and he is the creator of people who possess all ranges of wealth. Proverbs 16.16; 21.30 and 22.2 establish a coherent structure of values, from gold to wisdom to the Lord, but this structure is put into question by 22.4, which states, 'The consequence of humility and the fear of the Lord is riches, honour and life'. If the fear of the Lord results in riches and honour and life, then might these products carry more value than the Lord himself?[5] Proverbs 22.4 certainly seems to present them as outcomes of fearing the Lord, perhaps placing a superior level of value upon them and indicating that they may hold an ultimate level of value or desirability. In other words, the Lord seems to operate as a means to an end here, perhaps several ends, and therefore takes an ancillary place to the more valuable aims of riches, honour and life. Elsewhere in 10.1–22.16, life, wealth, favour, honour, and even the family's prosperity and security appear as desirable and attainable goals with little hint as to how they should be organized (e.g. 10.2, 4; 13.15; 14.26; 20.13, 20-21).

The cacophony of goals in 10.1–22.16 and the tension that they create in view of a possibly coherent network of values in Proverbs raise the interpretive challenge of whether we should establish such a coherent system or leave the tension in place. Pragmatically, if both wisdom and favour are better than gold, what happens when someone must choose between wisdom and favour? Does Proverbs view one as more valuable than the other, and does it intend for interpreters to know? Likewise, the Lord, on the one hand, appears supremely valuable – for he stands above wisdom (21.30) and riches and poverty (22.2) – but, on the other hand, it is through the Lord that one acquires riches and honour and life (22.4), which at the least leaves interpreters unclear as to what holds or should hold most value.[6]

---

5. Accepting the alternative translation, that 'the reward of humility is the fear of the Lord, riches, honour and life', simply compounds the problem at hand, namely, the disorder or unclear organization of ends in Proverbs 10–29.

6. Bálint Károly Zabán (*The Pillar Function of the Speeches of Wisdom: Proverbs 1.20-33, 8.1-36, and 9.1-6 in the Structural Framework of Proverbs 1–9*, BZAW 429 [Berlin: de Gruyter, 2012], 282–4) assesses the treasure imagery in Proverbs 1–9 and 16.16, and discounts a connection between Proverbs and the reference to silver and gold in Job 28.15-19 based on the maritime context of the latter, a disassociation further supported by the commonality of references to these and similar precious materials in ancient Near Eastern literature, to which Zabán calls attention (e.g. Ps. 68.14[13]; Zech. 9.3).

We might express these questions about value in a simpler way: what are the goals of Proverbs? Proverbs 10.1–22.16 suggests that someone might live in order to acquire wealth, honour, wisdom, 'life', or a certain relationship with the Lord, all of which are presented as goals of its educational paradigm. Unless the text suggests otherwise, I assume that the priority of a goal is inseparable from its value, so that each end to which Proverbs persuades corresponds to its respective worth. Does Proverbs harbour a coherent system of goals that structures its values in a consistent way? Or, lacking such a framework, does it arbitrarily make statements of value that should simply be left to stand in tension? Proverbs 22.1, when compared to 16.16, offers a clear example that provokes such questions: if wisdom is better than gold (16.16) and if favour is better than gold (22.1), then how do we relate wisdom and favour? Perhaps they carry equal value, and yet if forced to choose between them, perhaps Proverbs would commend one over the other. As suggested, an answer to this question does not arise from 10.1–22.16 alone, and I will contend that the question is addressed by Proverbs 1–9 as it offers a framework of goals with which to structure 10.1–22.16.

3.1.1.2. *The 'Name' in Proverbs 22.1*

Before consulting Proverbs 1–9, consider one other interpretive challenge posed by Prov. 22.1, derived from its language of 'name': 'A name is to be chosen rather than great riches; favour is better than silver and gold'. The 'name' (שׁם) in this case occurs in conjunction with 'favour', values that interpreters often equate to a good and full life, as if the goal is '*überzeugend und gut zu verhalten*' or, as McKane puts it, to be a person of 'engaging personal qualities', or, as the LXX succinctly augments, to choose, not ὄνομα, *but* ὄνομα καλόν.[7] To the broad positive qualities associated with a 'name' in Prov. 22.1, Waltke adds that it aligns with good character that depends on wisdom, supporting such associations with passages from Proverbs 1–9 and 10.1–22.16.[8] I will examine the material in Proverbs 1–9 closely and suggest that other passages within those chapters also address the challenges of 22.1. For the moment, however, this 'name' is considered in view of 10.1–22.16 and other pertinent evidence.

---

7. Meinhold, *Sprüche*, 363; McKane, *Proverbs*, 566; so Toy, *Proverbs*, 413.
8. Waltke, *Proverbs 15–31*, 199. According to Plöger (*Sprüche*, 253), Prov. 22.1 is not about wisdom or the goods it conveys but is rather a declaration that the popular man and what emanates from him are more impressive than silver and gold.

Waltke aligns a 'name' with wisdom-dependent good character primarily based on the semantic quality of שׁם as well as its use in Prov. 10.7; 18.10 and 21.24, since each of these sayings mentions שׁם. In his words, 'A good name represents a person's good character and his memory (see 10.7; 18.10; 21.24) and depends on his wisdom (3.1-4)…wisdom, a co-referential term for a "good name"'.[9] However, even though these sayings share a lexeme with Prov. 22.1, their use of this lexeme, as well as the broader linguistic evidence, differs in ways critical to Waltke's conclusion. For each of the passages from Collection II – as well as the other relevant uses of שׁם in 22.17–31.31 (30.9) – qualifies the lexeme rather than stating it absolutely as 22.1 does. It is the name 'of the wicked' (10.7), 'of the Lord' (18.10; cf. 30.9), or 'his name is scoffer' (21.24) that these passages present instead of 'a name' in the abstract, which, I will contend, harbours no inherent qualitative value. In short, the passages from Proverbs 10–31 that use שׁם qualify the type of name in question, unlike 22.1 which more simply states that 'a name is to be chosen rather than great riches'.

The meaning of 'name' may receive substantiation when considered within the OT as a whole, wherein שׁם takes a connotation of 'fame' or 'reputation'. So the warrior Abishai in 2 Sam. 23.18 wielded a spear against 300 men and a received 'a name', which, as the following verse makes clear, entailed the honour that he received from others. For he was the most 'renowned' (נכבד) of the thirty men (23.19), acquiring honour, perhaps fame, in the eyes of the community. The 'men of name' in Num. 16.2 and 1 Chron. 5.24 seem to be in some respect famous, and in other passages 'a name' is associated with 'a praise', similar to the honour bestowed on Abishai in 2 Samuel 23 (Deut. 26.19; Zech. 3.19-20; cf. Jer. 13.11). It might seem that the connotations of שׁם with fame and reputation in these passages entails an inherently positive quality, as if Abishai had a good name and the 'men of name' represented men of good repute. But such positive connotations are not a given. The 'men of name' in Num. 16.2 refer to those well-known Israelites who followed Korah and challenged the authority of Moses and Aaron, an act and context that suggest their 'name' was not a good one in the eyes of the author. According to Numbers 16, rebels might be famous men but not necessarily good men; they were burned alive (16.35).

Speaking of Solomon, 1 Kgs 4.31 records that 'his name was in all the surrounding nations', which indicates a name with positive connotations, due not to the use of this lexeme but due to the comments earlier in the verse: 'He [Solomon] was wiser than all other men, wiser than Ethan

---

9. Waltke, *Proverbs 15–31*, 199.

the Ezrahite, and Heman, Calcol, and Darda, the sons of Mahol, and his name was in all the surrounding nations'. 1 Kings 4.31 establishes its own context that then qualifies the sort of 'name' in question, in this case, a reputation of astounding wisdom. The inherently unqualified nature of שם is further exhibited in passages that explicitly modify the term: Nehemiah recounts that his enemies 'might give me a bad name [שם רע] in order to taunt me' (Neh. 6.13); and Qohelet says, 'a good name [שם טוב] is better than good oil' (Eccl. 7.1). Interpreters most often cite Eccl. 7.1 as support for seeing a 'good' name in Prov. 22.1, but Eccl. 7.1 obviously does not find שם sufficient to make its point and instead clarifies that 'a *good* name is better than good oil'.[10] The same trend appears in Sirach 41.11-13 (טובת שם; שם חסד) and *Pirkei Avot* 4.13 (שם טוב). In Akkadian, the lexeme *šumum* is used, which, like שם, may refer to 'fame' or 'reputation': 'the diviner will become renowned' (*bārû šum damiqtim ileqqe*); 'the house of Mari is famous' (*bīt Mari šumam išû*).[11] However, to convey a qualitative sense of 'name', *šumum* is modified with *ṭābum* or *damqum*, clarifying that such repute is 'good'. For instance, 'your reputation is good' (*šumka damiq*); 'that house will acquire a good reputation' (*bītu* MU *damiqti* TUK-*ši*); '[I know] that your reputation with the king is bad' (*kīma lamin* MU-*ka ana panī šarri*).[12]

The Akkadian lexical evidence, along with the material in Proverbs and the OT, supports the unqualified nature of שם in Prov. 22.1 and only enhances the interpretive challenge of the saying, namely, what sort of 'name' does it have in mind? Interpreters attach a variety of positive characteristics to this lexeme that receive little support from the evidence examined here. With no other indication of the sort of 'name' intended by Prov. 22.1, the second line of this saying provides one modifier – 'favour' (חן), which is better than silver and gold – and thereby suggests that a 'favourable name' is to be chosen rather than great riches. However, similar to fame, favour might arise from the Lord (Prov. 12.2; רצון) or from a generous man (Prov. 19.6), and, although pleasant, it does not disclose a necessary justification or advisable limitations. A favourable name can simply mean a name favoured by anyone for any reason – like the honour associated with שם – and not necessarily a good reason or, in the sight of the author, productive of the right kind of favour. Hence, Prov. 22.1's interpretive challenge remains unresolved, so that the 'name' might

---

10. See, among others, Ewald, *Die poetischen Bücher*, 199; Fox, *Proverbs 10–31*, 694.
11. See *CAD* 17/3, 292–4 and references there.
12. The logogram MU signifies, among other terms, *šumum*.

simply indicate that a reputation, of any sort and based on any grounds, is to be chosen in preference to great riches, or that the name is somehow favourable, though why and to what extent it is not clear.

On the other hand, there are interpreters who have suggested positive connotations in 22.1 by incorporating Proverbs 1–9, but these claims appear largely unsubstantiated. Waltke gets closest in his reference to 3.1-4 and 3.14, a direction that I will continue in conjunction with my broader concerns for the goals of Proverbs and the questions about what sort of value system might lie behind the axiological remarks of 10.1–22.16. The interpretive challenge, then, distils into one question: what are the educational goals of Proverbs that organize its various values? If an answer to this question can be discovered, it will offer insight into the place of Prov. 22.1 within what appear to be competing assertions of value in Proverbs 10–31 as well as insight into the challenge of what 22.1 means by 'name'. I pose the question of goals to Proverbs 1–9, asking, toward what goal or goals do these chapters persuade?

3.1.2. *Educational Goals in Proverbs 1–9*

Proverbs 22.1, within the context of Proverbs 10–31, has presented two interpretive challenges: the structure of values in Proverbs and the nature of the 'name' mentioned in 22.1. Both issues relate to the educational goals of Proverbs – what it advocates and persuades towards – and while it is reasonable to ask if Proverbs harbours an organized set of values, it may very well be the case that no such order can be found. That is, the goals and values of Proverbs might simply remain in tension and, for all we know, may have been intended to remain so. However, interpreters have suggested Proverbs 1–9 as a fruitful place to look for such a value system, and while not capitalizing on these chapters for the interpretive challenges of 10–31, they have posed a question similar to my own.

Interpreters interested in the goals of Proverbs 1–9 often couch their studies in terms of Collection I's pedagogical aims or how it shapes the desires of its audience, using different language to answer the current question: what are the overall rhetorical aims of Proverbs 1–9? Responses, detailed below, typically mention four characteristics, sometimes hierarchically related and at other times simply listed. These include wisdom, the father's instruction, God or the fear of the Lord, and character formation. While interpreters also use a variety of methods to determine the persuasive *telos* of Proverbs 1–9 and offer a swathe of conclusions, their differences do not so much reveal disagreements as they do alternative points of emphasis. Consider a sampling: Daniel Estes claims that while character formation constitutes one of many pedagogical goals, the greatest goal is to know God, which then allows the audience to assimilate wisdom, the prime virtue of Collection I.[13] Glenn Pemberton employs Aristotle's categories of logos, pathos, and ethos across Proverbs 1–9 to conclude that it persuades the audience to accept the father's instruction (i.e. wisdom) and avoid the seduction of folly.[14] Michael Fox argues that the author, with his rhetorical tools, intends his audience to strive for wisdom, which equals moral character and prepares them for 10.1–22.16.[15] According to Sun Myung Lyu, Proverbs 1–9 persuades towards wisdom which leads to character formation, and for Bálint Zabán internalized instruction establishes a relationship with wisdom and induces ideal character.[16] In these studies, wisdom, the father's instruction, God or the fear of the Lord, and character formation arise in different forms and fashions, but they arise consistently to create a constellation of concepts seemingly significant for determining the persuasive aims of Proverbs 1–9. R. N. Whybray's comments reveal the preponderance of these concepts when, referring to Collection I, he writes that the interpreter

> will see all its teaching as directed towards *the formation of the complete person*, both wise and pious.... In their present form these chapters serve both to elevate the character of *the wisdom teacher* who, it will be assumed by the reader, is responsible for everything which follows, and, at the same time, in impressive and mysterious, quasi-mythical language, to stress *the intimate relationship of wisdom with God*, its attractiveness to the learner, and the indispensability of its acquisition.[17]

---

13. Daniel J. Estes, *Hear, My Son: Teaching and Learning in Proverbs 1–9*, New Studies in Biblical Theology (Leicester: Apollos, 1997), 45, 63–86, 148.

14. Glenn D. Pemberton, 'The Rhetoric of the Father in Proverbs 1–9', *JSOT* 30 (2005): 63–82.

15. Fox, *Proverbs 1–9*, 348–51.

16. Lyu, *Righteousness*, 5; Zabán, *Pillar Function*, 286–342. See, among others, James Fleming, 'Some Aspects of the Religion of Proverbs', *JBL* 51 (1932): 31–9; Dave Bland, 'Formation of Character in the Book of Proverbs', *ResQ* 40 (1998): 221–38; Christine Yoder, 'Forming "Fearers of Yahweh": Repetition and Contradiction as Pedagogy in Proverbs', in *Seeking out the Wisdom of the Ancients: Essays Offered to Honor Michael V. Fox on the Occasion of His Sixty-Fifth Birthday*, ed. Ronald L. Troxel, Kelvin G. Friebel and Dennis R. Magary (Winona Lake, IN: Eisenbrauns, 2005), 167–84; Alice M. Sinnott, *The Personification of Wisdom* (Aldershot, UK: Ashgate, 2005), 19–21, 53–87; Maurice Gilbert, *L'Antique sagesse d'Israël: Études sur Proverbes, Job, Qohélet et leurs prolongements*, EBib (Pendé, France: Gabalda, 2015), 38–47, 206.

17. Whybray, *Proverbs*, 17 (italics added).

When noting the persuasive aims of Proverbs 1–9, Whybray incorporates wisdom, God, the instructor, along with the teacher's instruction specifically, and character formation, those ingredients that seem closely related to wisdom and integral to the persuasive goals of Collection I.[18] In addition to these four emphases, many studies on the rhetoric of Proverbs 1–9 focus on the collection's feminine imagery, given its persuasive pungency.[19]

I affirm the palpability of this conceptual set and the persuasive force of the females in Proverbs 1–9. In pursuing an answer about the collection's goals, these elements do seem to be accounted for in a coherent manner, and yet it remains to be seen whether or not Proverbs 1–9 validates such coherence. Aside from 1.20-33, I have given little attention so far to the female figures of Proverbs 1–9, so in this section Proverbs 7–8 is examined and the four elements of persuasive vision accounted for: wisdom, the father's teaching, God, and character. By incorporating another portion of the text, the choice of Proverbs 7–8 further strengthens the case for the didactic function of Proverbs 1–9.[20] But a discussion of this text must also account for Proverbs 2, which makes, perhaps, the most logical case for an educational framework in Proverbs, and so in what follows I navigate a relatively lengthy discussion of Proverbs 2, 7–8 in order to return to Prov. 22.1 and address an issue prevalent in Proverbs 10–29, of which 22.1 is a representative.

3.1.2.1. *Proverbs 7–8*

Proverbs 7–8 portrays Wisdom and Folly at length and with literary artistry, suggesting a heightened effort to persuade the audience. In brief, Folly appears unattractive and dangerous, while Wisdom presents herself

---

18. Whybray (*Proverbs*, 4) does remark that, as a whole, the purpose of Proverbs 'is to persuade the reader to acquire wisdom'.

19. Margaret Odell Gilchrist, 'Proverbs 1–9: Instruction or Riddle', *Proceedings, Eastern Great Lakes & Midwest Bible Society* (1984), esp. 141, 143; Lang, *Wisdom*, 50, 72, 104, 107; Hennie Viviers, 'The "Body" and Lady Wisdom (Proverbs 1–9)', *OTE* 18 (2005): 879–90; Weeks, *Instruction*, 67–155; Pete F. Wilbanks, 'Non-Proverb Proverbial Bookends: A Possible Lens for Viewing the Book of Proverbs' (paper presented at the Southwest Regional Meeting of the ETS, New Orleans, LA, 26 March 2000), 1–45; Gale Yee, 'I Have Perfumed My Bed with Myrrh: The Foreign Woman (*'iššâ zārâ*) in Proverbs 1–9', *JSOT* 43 (1989): 53–68; Scott C. Jones, 'Wisdom's Pedagogy: A Comparison of Proverbs VII and 4Q184', *VT* 53 (2003): 65–80; Mark Sneed, 'White Trash Wisdom: Proverbs 9 Deconstructed', *JHS* 7 (2007): 1–10.

20. Proverbs 9 continues the rhetorical point developed by Proverbs 7–8 but adds little for the concerns of this section. I account for Proverbs 9 in section 3.2.1.

as attractive and beneficial, composing two portraits that, I contend, aim to persuade the audience towards a single but two-sided goal: embrace wisdom and avoid folly. For wisdom is a friend, a lover, a protector and provider. Folly appears friendly, lovely and beneficial but ultimately leads to destruction. Although these twin portraits feature in Proverbs 7–8, both chapters include the four aspects apparently integral to Collection I – wisdom, teaching, the Lord, and character – and it is these aspects that must be considered under the rubric of 1–9's educational goals. In my examination of Proverbs 7–8, I attempt to capture the overall thrust of the material rather than exegetically mining particular passages. Such an overarching approach reliably determines the rhetorical effort of the text, while a more detailed attack will be reserved for Proverbs 2, which raises a potential objection to my views of Proverbs 7–8.

Proverbs 7 contains two primary levels of discourse. First, it portrays a youth who wanders the street and falls prey to the seductions of a temptress who looks good, smells good and promises a delightful experience (7.6-23). This scenario of seduction and attraction constitutes the story of chapter 7 that is told by the Proverbial father. Around this story, the father structures the second level of discourse, as he forwards commands to his son and adds commentary about the tale, prefacing it with commands to 'keep my words' (7.1-3) and concluding with a similar injunction: 'listen to me and be attentive to the words of my mouth' (7.24).[21] By drawing attention to his words, the father not only persuades the son to peruse the story but also persuades the son to hear those very words that immediately follow the father's calls to attention. This noteworthy material appears in 7.4-5 and 7.25-27, which offer complementary positive and negative instructions about wisdom and folly. The first passage, 7.4-5, tells the son to embrace wisdom: 'Say to wisdom, "You are my sister", and call insight a relative' (7.4). The following verse then gives one reason why the son should befriend wisdom and insight: 'to keep you from the alien woman and from the foreigner, her smooth words' (7.5). In Prov. 7.4-5, after calling attention to his teaching, the father presents two goals – embrace wisdom and avoid folly – and indicates that wisdom, in some form, is the means to achieving these goals, for it 'keeps you from the alien woman'.

In Prov. 7.24, the father reinforces attention toward his teaching and in verse 25 follows with a warning: 'do not stray into [Folly's] paths'. Why? 'For she has caused many wounded to fall, and all her slain are mighty. Her house is the way to Sheol, going down to chambers of

---

21. For another perspective on the significance of these scenes and the father's commentary, see section 3.2.

death' (7.26-27). The father wants to persuade his son to avoid folly primarily because she is dangerous, as she captures boys like stags, slaughters them like oxen, and takes advantage of their oblivious flight into her snare.[22] Avoid such temptations, says the father, and achieve this goal, he implies, by heeding my instruction which leads to wisdom. As folly's dangers and the father's teaching remain at the forefront of this passage, embracing wisdom stays in the background, and 7.4 allows for little distinction between the father's teaching and wisdom as we will come to know her in Proverbs 8. Nevertheless, the persuasive aim of Proverbs 7 places an avoidance of folly as primary and an awareness of the father's teaching as the means of accomplishing this.

In Proverbs 8, and on the tails of the father's stern warnings about the lady of temptation, we meet wisdom (חכמה) and understanding (בינה), remarkably similar to the wisdom (חכמה) and understanding (תבונה) of 7.4, but now raising their voices and calling to those who will listen: 'Does not wisdom call, and understanding give her voice?' (8.1). The initial alert and scene setting (8.1-3) move into a direct address by Lady Wisdom, who now contrasts with the woman of Proverbs 7. The persuasive force of chapter 8 and perhaps chapter 7 now increases since they have been read sequentially, and their rhetorical features become more prominent in light of the thematic and lexical links. Folly appears quietly in the darkness of the city (7.12-13), while Wisdom stands boldly at its heights (8.2-3). Both women call (7.13-20; 8.3-4) and advertise their possessions to their audiences (7.16-18; 8.10-11), and both texts include terms for 'mouth' (7.5, 21; 8.1, 6, 7a) and conclude with a reference to 'death' (7.27b; 8.36b). These parallels between Proverbs 7 and 8 suggest not only a conceptual contrast but a rhetorical effort that bolsters the persuasive aims of the author. Avoid folly and embrace wisdom.[23]

In Proverbs 8, the father's voice fades and the voice of Wisdom swells, as she makes four points. First, she aligns herself with all things right and knowledgeable, especially her words: 'Hear, for I will speak noble things, and from my lips is uprightness' (8.6). She also underscores her role: 'by

---

22. Christl Maier (*Die 'fremde Frau' in Proverbien 1-9: Eine exegetische und sozialgeschichtliche Studie* [Freiburg: Vandenhoeck & Ruprecht, 1995], 209) says 'Ziel der ganzen Rede Prov 7 ist nach Ausweis von v. 25 die eindringliche Warnung, den Weg der "Fremden" einzuschlagen'.

23. For Maier (*Die 'fremde Frau'*, 214), the comparison of wisdom and folly in Proverbs 7 prepares the way for their contrast in Proverbs 9. However, wisdom, particularly as a personified figure, remains unobtrusive in Proverbs 7 until she is foregrounded in chapter 8.

me kings rule and rulers decree rightness' (8.15; so 8.6-9, 12, 14-16, 20). Second, wisdom puts herself in relation to high value goods, on the one hand, saying that she possesses riches, honour and prosperity (8.18), but, on the other hand, labelling herself as more valuable than these things:

קחו־מוסרי ואל־כסף	8.10	Take my instruction and not silver,
ודעת מחרוץ נבחר		and knowledge rather than choice gold.
כי־טובה חכמה מפנינים	8.11	For wisdom is better than jewels,
וכל־חפצים לא ישוו־בה		and all desires do not compare with her.
טוב פריי מחרוץ	8.19	My fruit is better than gold, even fine gold,
ומפז ותבואתי מכסף נבחר		and my produce than choice silver.
בארח־צדקה אהלך	8.20	I walk in the way of righteousness
בתוך נתיבות משפט		and in the midst of the paths of justice,
להנחיל אהבי יש	8.21	To give an inheritance to those who love me,
ואצרתיהם אמלא		and fill their treasuries.

Wisdom is 'better than' jewels, and her productions outshine the most glamourous gold, offering more than silver can buy. Wisdom constructs a system of value and presents herself within it, placing herself and her teaching at the top. Yet rather than condemning less valuable things, such as wealth and honour, she asserts that these things are supplied by her: 'to give an inheritance to those who love me, and I will fill their treasuries' (8.21).[24] In Prov. 8.1-21, then, she is more valuable than wealth and honour, and to love her marks the ultimate goal.

After her clarion call in 8.1-21, Wisdom, thirdly, recounts her role in the Lord's ancient acts of creation, accentuating her age and her proximity to him. She was set up 'ages ago' (v. 23) and worked 'beside' God as his delight (v. 30).[25] From a rhetorical perspective, Prov. 8.22-31 accentuates

---

24. Sandoval (*Discourse*, 89–101) focuses on the 'symbolic' significance of wealth imagery in Prov. 8.10-11 and 8.18-21 and argues that this imagery does not refer to the actual goods produced by wisdom but instead to all that is desirable. Although he concludes this with appropriate qualification (100–101), I do not find it convincing that the metaphorical presentation of Wisdom leads to metaphorical conceptions of wealth and possessions in this passage. While the silver mentioned in 8.10 may not be necessary for the wise person, based on Sandoval's wooden interpretation of 'take my instruction and [do] not [take] silver', this does not undercut the comparative statements made by Wisdom in the following verses.

25. On the phonetic and semantic options for אמון in Prov. 8.30, see Fox, *Proverbs 1–9*, 285–7, and Arthur Keefer, 'Sound Patterns as Motivation for Rare Words in Proverbs 1–9', *JNSL* 43 (2017): 46. None of the lexeme's possible meanings ('master worker/constantly/ward') take away from my point or the thrust of the passage, that

the attractiveness and status of Wisdom, who commends herself based on her antiquity and intimacy with God.[26] From the perspective of theology, and material and immaterial goods, Wisdom rises as the goal that her audience ought to desire and acquire. In the final portion of Proverbs 8, she situates herself next to teaching and another educational goal, distilling her point to a single line: 'hear instruction and be wise' (8.33).

Wisdom here clarifies the goals of Proverbs 1–9 and the structure of its values, forwarding instruction as a means to grow in wisdom, that is, to become wise, which seems to be the ultimate outcome of fellowship with her. Becoming wise in 8.33 mirrors the concepts that follow in 8.34-35, namely, the 'happiness' of those who listen to wisdom, the life that they find when they find her, and the favour that the Lord bestows: 'hear instruction and be wise [v. 33]…happy is the one who listens to me [v. 34]…. For whoever finds me finds life and obtains favour from the Lord [v. 35].' Based on the structure of these concepts, Magne Sæbø has concluded that 'Den Weisen galt sonst immer das Leben als das vor allem zu sichernde *summum bonum*'.[27] Wisdom upholds 'life' as the greatest good. Yet the Lord ascends to the same status by granting favour and so seems to accompany becoming wise as a final end for Proverbs 1–9. On this view, wisdom and growth in wise character would enable the interpreter to secure the ultimate end of Proverbial education: 'life'.[28] However, perhaps 'being wise' results not only in 'life' but in life and favour and happiness, as seems evident from the macarisms that surround the injunction to 'hear instruction and be wise' (8.33); for those who keep Wisdom's ways and listen to her are 'blessed' (8.32b, 34a). Perhaps 'be wise' represents the educational goal of the passage, while the results of obedience, or the effects of wisdom, are presented as motivating ends with a value equal to growing in wise character. Most clearly, the prime value and aim of Prov. 8.32-36 is attending to wisdom and becoming wise; the other ends presented boost the attractiveness of this prospect. This interpretation is most convincing given the grammar of verse 33, which contains the imperatives of the passage and repeats the call to 'hear'

Wisdom bears a close proximity to God and a privileged presence during the time of creation. Although the different meanings adjust how her function is understood, they do not necessarily affect her attractiveness.

26. On the rhetorical significance of Wisdom's partnership with the Lord, see the discussion on Proverbs 2 below and section 4.2.2.

27. Sæbø, *Sprüche*, 125. Sæbø (124) affirms that 'be wise' in 8.33 indicates the purpose of listening to wisdom (שמעו מוסר וחכמו).

28. On the meaning of this concept in Proverbs, see Waltke (*Proverbs 1–15*, 104–5) who identifies it with 'wisdom's reward' and binds it to 'fellowship with God'.

from verse 32, and is endorsed by the clarity that it brings: 'be wise'.[29] Rhetorically, then, wise character seems to be the aim of the passage, though other ends and values, serving a motivational function in the poem, may stand adjacent to this aim in an absolute sense.

At the conclusion of her speech, Wisdom spreads a constellation of values that centre on a single educational goal: becoming wise. For growth in wisdom is what she commands in verse 33 and from there other benefits accrue, such as happiness, life and divine favour. Therefore, growth in wise character stands as the ultimate educational goal, achieved by listening to instruction and consequently embracing Wisdom, who facilitates such growth.[30] A structure of goals begins to emerge: through the text's teachings, love and pursue wisdom in order to grow in wise character.

3.1.2.2. *Proverbs 2*

This order of educational goals has been developed based upon Proverbs 7–8, but in order to establish it as representative of Proverbs 1–9, the remaining material ought to be considered. Proverbs 2 presents the greatest potential obstacle for the posited educational system as derived from Proverbs 7–8. Well known among interpreters as the 'Lehrprogramm' of 1–9, Proverbs 2 constitutes a 22-verse poem from the Proverbial father with a coherent and tightly knit structure.[31] As the program of education goes, if the son attends to the father's words and seeks wisdom (2.1-4), then he will understand the fear of the Lord (v. 5), who gives wisdom and protection (vv. 6-8), and will also understand every good path (v. 9), with wisdom entering his heart (vv. 10-11) to deliver the boy from evil (vv. 12-19) in order to walk in the way of good people, who inhabit the land (vv. 20-22). This long chain of reasoning offers multiple possible goals, and if Proverbs 2 functions as an educational blueprint for 1–9, then its educational aims must be compared with those from Proverbs 7–8.

Bernd Schipper has examined Proverbs 2, and its place within Proverbs 1–9 as a whole. Regardless of his preoccupation with diachronic details, Schipper contributes exegetical insights that bear significance for the question of what goal or goals Proverbs 1–9 promotes. According to him, the reasoning in Proverbs 2 culminates in verses 20-22, which state the final aims of its educational program:

---

29. See Schäfer, *Poesie*, 224–5.

30. For more on the study of character formation in Proverbs, see Anne Stewart, *Poetic Ethics in Proverbs: Wisdom Literature and the Shaping of the Moral Self* (New York: Cambridge University Press, 2016); Brown, *Wisdom's Wonder*, 29–66.

31. Meinhold, *Sprüche*, 43, 62–4.

> In order that [לְמַעַן] you might walk in the way of good people,
>   and keep the paths of the righteous.
> For [כִּי] the upright will dwell in the land,
>   and the blameless will remain in it.
> But the wicked will be cut from the land,
>   and the treacherous will tear away from it. (2.20-22)

Schipper contends that 'Dieses Ziel – das Bleiben im Land – ist aber nicht im Sinne eines zukünftig zu erwartenden Handelns zu verstehen, sondern erscheint als logische Folge des gegenwärtigen Agierens'.[32] For Schipper, Proverbs 2 works towards the ultimate goal of remaining in the land, which he sees as something not necessarily achievable in the immediate term but a 'logical consequence of the present action', action spelled out especially in verses 12-19. Focus on the land, of course, and other key terms in 2.21-22, broaches debate about the place of Proverbs in the canon and its relation to themes of the covenant.[33] These issues are intriguing but tangential to the present question, so my focus remains on the educational aims of Proverbs 2, what it ultimately persuades the interpreter towards, and how these goals match or disrupt those outlined by Proverbs 7–8.

While Schipper's treatment of Proverbs 2 has much worth commending, commendations that are capitalized on shortly, his interpretation of 2.20-22 is in discordance with my argument, possibly due to our different interpretive interests. The problem stems from confusing certain consequences in 2.20-22 with the rhetorical purpose of the passage, as if the final outcomes noted in a text must constitute its aims of persuasion. This issue relates to an oversight of the grammatical features in these verses as well as the central concepts of the chapter. In the first place, 2.20 begins with לְמַעַן, which most likely depends on the entire exordium of 2.1-11 and particularly the resultant protection of wisdom promised in 2.11 (so 2.12, 16), rendering the following: 'discretion will watch over you, and understanding will guard you [2.11]…in order that you might walk in the way of good people and keep the paths of the righteous [2.20]'.[34] Proverbs 2.20, therefore, not 2.21-22, expresses the purpose of the educational

---

32. Schipper, *Hermeneutik*, 75. See also Sæbø (*Sprüche*, 59–60), who asserts that the dichotomous people types in v. 20 draw attention to the 'land' and the dichotomy in vv. 21-22.

33. Cf. Fox, *Proverbs 1–9*, 122–5. Schipper considers intertextual relations in his third chapter, after his treatment of Proverbs 2.

34. See, among others, Waltke, *Proverbs 1–15*, 216–18; Sæbø, *Sprüche*, 58–9; Schipper, *Hermeneutik*, 67–71. God may simultaneously function as protector throughout Prov. 2.12-19.

model outlined in Proverbs 2. It is not securing residence in the land that the program aims for but rather placing one on the right path of life. That the chapter's goals appear in 2.20 is further supported by the כי that starts verse 21: 'For the upright will inhabit the land and those with integrity will remain in it'. The כי here grounds the purpose statement of verse 20, and for two verses (21-22) it governs an explanation and, most of all, a motivation for the hope that the pupil will 'walk in the way of good people'. Based on these grammatical features, Schäfer rightly calls 2.20 a 'Hauptfinalsatz' and verses 21-22 the 'Schlußmotivation'.[35]

The grammar of Proverbs 2 affirms part of Schipper's conclusion about verses 20-22, namely, that verses 21-22 are a 'logical consequence' of the present action, but the grammar does not support these consequences as the 'Ziel' of the chapter. The purpose arises in verse 20, joined by its motivating consequences in verses 21-22. As consequences, the statements in verses 21-22 can be considered 'ends', but they should not be confused with the goal or educational aim of the preceding instructions. This interpretation is supported by the primacy given to character types and moral categories like good and evil in Proverbs 1–9, including Proverbs 2, as Schipper himself observes and my argument from Chapter 2 fortifies.[36] Proverbs 2 is concerned less with particular behaviours and more with becoming a particular type of person and bearing a particular relationship towards good and evil. In this vein, Schipper makes an astute observation about 2.1-11 when he says that 'Der in Prov 2,1 entfaltete Gedankengang findet in V. 11 ein vorläufiges Ende, indem das, was der Weisheitsschüler als Subjekt tun soll, ihm nun als Objekt widerfährt – er ist gleichsam am Ziel angelangt, nur dass dieses bislang nicht näher konkretisiert wurde'.[37] The son pursues wisdom (vv. 1-5) but also stands as the object pursued by wisdom (vv. 9-11), a symbiotic educational syllabus that Schipper calls the 'erstes Ziel' of Proverbs 2. The description of this first goal sounds much like 'character formation', which is facilitated by the son's search for and discovery of wisdom. Wisdom's protection helps to transform the pupil into the sort of person who 'walks in the way of good people'. Aside from specific instructions about pursuing wisdom in 2.1-4, Proverbs 2 largely describes the benefits that the Lord and his wisdom hold in store, noting that the one who acquires such benefits will live a life of and

---

35. Schäfer, *Die Poesie*, 64–6. Meinhold (*Sprüche*, 63, 70) calls 2.20 an 'abschließenden Zielangabe' with 2.21-22 continuing the conclusion.

36. Schipper, *Hermeneutik*, esp. 67–71, 77–9. He draws attention to the 'Vorbilder' (role models) of the chapter.

37. Schipper, *Hermeneutik*, 53.

among the good. Yes, he may consequently inhabit the land, but the whole of Proverbs 2 aims to instil a desire for wisdom in order to accomplish its primary goal: character formation.

In my judgment, the educational program laid out by Proverbs 2 looks much more like the one developed by Proverbs 7–8 than a vision of land residency mentioned in 2.21-22.[38] The other elements that Proverbs 2 addresses at length, especially the evil people and forbidden woman from whom Wisdom delivers (vv. 12-15, 16-19), do not counter the educational goals established so far but rather support these goals by elaborating on the guardian role of Wisdom, unpacking, in other words, how Wisdom facilitates growth in wise character. She protects those who know her, so that they might become the sort of people who 'walk in the way' of good folk. In all, the chapter depicts the father's teaching as a means to loving and pursuing wisdom, which is intended to produce growth in wise character.

The remaining element noted by Schipper, but not yet discussed, stems from the theology of Proverbs 2. The father says, that 'if you seek [wisdom] like silver and search for it like hidden treasure, then you will understand the fear of the Lord and find the knowledge of God' (vv. 4-5). He continues by saying that the Lord 'gives wisdom' and 'guards' the way of his saints (vv. 6, 8), indicating that wisdom comes from the Lord, who gives it to those who seek it. This mutual human–divine relationship in the school of wisdom, though not yet made lucid in Proverbs 2, permits the following conclusion:

> Es dominieren im ersten Teil der Lehre weisheitliche Begriffe, allerdings werden diese durch den Bezug auf JHWH religiös eingefärbt. JHWH ist der Geber von Weisheit, so dass die Lehre, die hier durch den Weisheitslehrer vermittelt wird (V. 1), eine theologische Dimension erhält. Dabei sind sowohl die Unterweisung des Weisheitslehrers, als auch das Lernen des Weisheitsschülers und die Bestimmung der Weisheit von JHWH her aufeinander bezogen.[39]

However, it is clear that the fear of the Lord, which at the least indicates a relationship with God, marks the starting point of wisdom (1.7) and is encountered by the boy on his search for wisdom (2.4-5). Therefore, to the human instruction that serves as a means to wisdom we might add a relationship with the Lord. The Lord also functions like wisdom in

---

38. Dwelling in the land resembles the promise of material and immaterial goods bestowed by Wisdom in Proverbs 8. See section 4.2.

39. Schipper, *Hermeneutik*, 54.

Proverbs 2, by protecting those he knows and thereby enabling them to achieve the same goal as wisdom: growth in wise character.[40] The Lord saturates the educational process envisioned by Proverbs 2, supplementing the current system of educational goals to produce a revised version. The original scheme of ends stated that through the text's teachings, one would love and pursue wisdom in order to grow in wise character. Given the Lord's role in Proverbs 2, the plan becomes slightly adjusted: through the text's teaching *and the fear of the Lord*, love and pursue wisdom in order to grow in wise character.[41]

Rather than being undermined by alternative educational goals or value structures, the educational paradigm derived from Proverbs 7–8 is fortified, even supplemented, by Proverbs 2, the 'Lehrprogramm' of Proverbs 1–9. The set and sequence of educational goals argued for here answer the question that arose from Prov. 22.1, and other material in Proverbs 10–31, concerning the book's vision of values and aims, and their relationship. The sayings material indicates that such values may stand in tension without a clear structure to order them. However, it also suggests that an organization of values might be latent within its sayings, as if they assume and partially indicate a network of ordered values. Proverbs 1–9 organizes values by making comparative statements and by presenting the goals of Proverbial education in a consistent and ordered fashion, persuading the interpreter toward these goals and introducing the necessary means to achieve them. Upon returning to 22.1, the question remains as to how the educational vision of Proverbs 1–9 might function didactically for 10–31.

3.1.3. *The Function of Proverbs 1–9 for Proverbs 22.1*

Proverbs 22.1 prompted two questions, one dealing with an overall perspective on the material in Proverbs 10–29, which presents a plurality of values that either lie in tension with each other or presume a system of values that would organize them. The other question deals with a particular, though related, issue in 22.1 – what sort of 'name' does it have in mind, given the unqualified nature of שׁם? As argued above, the lexeme שׁם connotes neither a good nor a bad name, a neutrality not resolved by appealing to the second line of the proverb to make the name a 'favourable' one. The first interpretive challenge was approached from two interrelated perspectives, that of value and that of ends (i.e. goals),

---

40. On the similar functions of Wisdom and the Lord, see section 4.2.
41. Wisdom, in this formula, subsumes the teaching of the father, which is at times referred to as 'wisdom' (Fox, *Proverbs 1–9*, 359; Sæbø, *Sprüche*, 122, 125).

and at this point two interpreters will help develop these perspectives and demonstrate the extent of the interpretive dilemma when Proverbs 10–29 is examined apart from 1–9.

Zoltan Schwab considers proverbs that compare values, such as 16.16, and attempts to establish a hierarchy of ends based on material in Proverbs 10–29. He appeals to humility's association with honour and other comparative statements in the collection, as well as sayings in 16.16's nearby literary context.[42] Backed by a detailed outline of the 'results' and 'effects' of wisdom throughout Proverbs, that is, the ends of wisdom based on occurrences of חכמה, Schwab concludes the following:

> Therefore, at least part of the answer to the question regarding why good human character is more valuable than riches is that which I have stated above: because it leads to protection, honour, and riches… [T]his is not often stated explicitly in these sentences, rather, it is conjectured by the reader from the context of some of them. Would not we expect more explicit praise of protection and honour in these sentences if their provision is the only reason for a good character's superiority to riches? There is an intrinsic openness of formulation in these verses that invites more than one interpretation.[43]

Such a point is quite plausible based on the generous connections that Schwab sees in the text, though this does not resolve the issue at hand about how Prov. 16.16 and 22.1 might relate. For when it comes to wisdom, reputation, and the quality of this reputation, Proverbs 10–29 leaves interpretation in the realm of, in Schwab's words, 'conjecture' and implicit evidence. Widening the angle on Proverbs, Schwab accounts for every effect of wisdom to find that 'Proverbs does not offer an explicit, systematic hierarchy of ends. However, it does provide a plurality of ends. Furthermore, even if these ends are not ordered clearly and explicitly into a strict hierarchy, there are certain hints in the text that point in the direction of such a hierarchy'.[44] The book of Proverbs exhibits a 'plurality of ends' with no 'explicit, systematic hierarchy' to order them. The 'hints' in Proverbs of such a hierarchy entail Schwab's previous remarks based on a perusal of interrelations in Proverbs 10–29, which still obscure a

---

42. Zoltan Schwab, *Toward an Interpretation of the Book of Proverbs: Selfishness and Secularity Reconsidered*, JTISup 3 (Winona Lake, IN: Eisenbrauns, 2013), 125. Stewart (*Poetic Ethics*, 126) does not explore the collections separately, but in view of Proverbs' motivating values – wealth, honour, protection and life – she assumes that wisdom is 'the *highest* reward'.

43. Schwab, *Toward an Interpretation*, 125.

44. Schwab, *Toward an Interpretation*, 158.

clear system of ends and only accentuate my initial interpretive question: do goals remain in tension or are they organized? Close attention to Proverbs 1–9, and not only a look at its use of חכמה, reveals a consistent and rhetorically hammered set of goals that, I contend, will offer insight into the plurality of ends that populate Proverbs 10–29. Before attending to this proposal, we need to consider the second perspective on our interpretive challenge, which approaches the material not with language of 'ends' but with language of 'value'.

Claus Westermann has also examined proverbs of value judgment ('die Sprüche der Wertung') within Proverbs 10–29, and when interpreting 22.1 and 16.16 he distinguishes such sayings based on the status of the value presented and how the interpreter ought to respond.[45] According to Westermann, proverbs like 22.1 do not express fixed advice; they provoke the interpreter to contemplate his or her situation and determine what is good and less good based on the saying's value judgment. So 'A name is to be chosen rather than great riches, favour is better than silver and gold' calls one to ponder over these values and discern how one of them or another might be preferable in a certain situation. Proverbs like 16.16 (i.e. 20.15) present wisdom as an 'abstraction' that holds 'objective value'. In his words, 'In den Sprüchen der Wertung ist die jeweils empfohlene Entscheidung die weise, die klügere Entscheidung; in den nachgeahmten Sprüchen ist die Weisheit ein abstrakter Begriff und zum objektivierten Selbstwert geworden'.[46] So 'To acquire wisdom is much better than gold, and to acquire understanding is to be chosen more than silver' attributes not circumstantial worth to wisdom and gold but an absolute amount of value. I agree that value statements, like so many proverbs, prompt the interpreter to contemplate action or attitude in his or her particular situation, but I see no reason to view the value statements in Proverbs as of two sorts, as if 16.16 means 'better than' in a way that differs from the 'better than' of 22.1. Both make statements of comparative value, and these two particular sayings leave interpreters with the indeterminate values of 'a name' and 'wisdom'.

Westermann denies that Proverbs offers a system of values to order such a dilemma: the 'vergleichendes Fragen unterscheidet sich grundlegen von einer statischen Wertelehre, in der, was gut und was schlecht ist, ein für allemal festgelegt wird'.[47] Proverbs 10–29 does not, it seems, offer a completely ordered system of values, and the values that it presents may

---

45. Claus Westermann, *Wurzeln der Weisheit: die ältesten Sprüche Israels und anderer Völker* (Göttingen: Vandenhoeck & Ruprecht, 1990), 83–8.
46. Westermann, *Wurzeln*, 86.
47. Westermann, *Wurzeln*, 86.

very well, as Westermann says, prompt a 'constant weighing against each other, about what was good and less good', rather than a fixed hierarchy.[48] However, once Proverbs 1–9 enters the picture, it transforms the interpretation of 10–29 and its assortment of value judgments. Westermann, like Schwab, makes valid conclusions based on an interpretation of Proverbs that focuses on chapters 10–29, with little consideration of 1–9, fortifying the interpretive challenge that has driven this chapter and pressuring certain conclusions on the part of the interpreter. I would argue not that Westermann and Schwab are wrong in their interpretations but rather that these interpretations stem from a view that removes Proverbs 1–9 from the picture. Once this missing element is relayed, it imposes a framework on Proverbs 10–29 that offers interpretive insight into the challenges that trouble both interpreters.

To summarize the point, Proverbs 1–9 lays out a consistent and clear network of values by persuading the interpreter towards certain goals and establishing the means by which those goals are accomplished. It presents the father's teaching and the fear of the Lord as means, to direct the interpreter towards and successfully acquire Wisdom, who then facilitates growth in wise character. These elements undoubtedly interrelate, and Proverbs 1–9 presents them in a poetic and highly rhetorical register rather than in a formulaic account of values and ends. Nevertheless, an order appears consistently and constructs a framework that coherently organizes the apparently competing values of Proverbs 10–29.

According to Proverbs 1–9, wisdom is the greatest value and it helps one to achieve the highest end of these opening chapters: to grow in wise character.[49] Thus, 16.16 firmly aligns with 1–9 when it states, 'To acquire wisdom is much better than gold, and to acquire understanding is to be chosen more than silver'. Proverbs 1–9 affirms this (3.15; 8.10-11) but it also gives a reason for such an admonition. For instead of acquiring wisdom for its own sake or due to the many wicked reasons that interpreters might devise, which is quite possible based on 16.16 alone, wisdom is acquired in order to grow in wise character, since wisdom and character, both more valuable than precious metals, stand as the ultimate goals of the Proverbial educational program. In the case of 16.16, the program established in Proverbs 1–9 provides a hierarchy of ends and an axiological organization.

---

48. Westermann, *Wurzeln*, 86. The community assessed values 'dass man ständig gegeneinander abwog, was gut und was weniger gut war'.

49. Character formation might be the highest value also, but it seems that wisdom and character form an indissoluble union in Proverbs. See more below.

3. *Educational Goals* 115

Proverbs 1–9 also addresses the question of interpreting 22.1 in light of 16.16. Instead of the wisdom extolled by 16.16, Prov. 22.1 presents 'a name' as more choice-worthy than metals: 'A name is to be chosen rather than great riches, favour is better than silver and gold'. When 22.1 and 16.16 are collocated, this 'name' (שם), referring at least to fame or reputation, stands next to wisdom in its value. What is 'to be chosen', though, if the choice lies between reputation and wisdom? An interpreter familiar with Proverbs most likely points to wisdom instinctively, asserting that 'Proverbs would of course value wisdom above personal fame or reputation'. But, I wonder, where does such an instinct come from? It does not most plausibly come from Proverbs 10–29, which, as seen throughout this chapter, generates more questions than answers about its values. It is by viewing Proverbs 1–9 as an interpretive framework, which presents goals and an organization of values with rhetorical force and sufficient clarity, that the interpreter of 16.16 and 22.1 would, or should, choose wisdom.

The choice of values seems unquestionable in light of Proverbs 1–9, and yet the nature of the reputation mentioned in 22.1 remains at best morally neutral, and its precise relation to wisdom, uncertain. Proverbs 1–9, however, does not simply frame the interpreter's understanding of values in 10–29, it also informs the understanding of the 'name' itself. As argued at the outset of this chapter, 22.1 uses the lexeme שם, and this lexeme does not inherently indicate a moral or value-related quality, such as a 'good name', and at most connotes a name or reputation recognized as honourable. However, such renown may arise from good or bad reasons, like the 250 rebellious men who join Korah and yet have a 'name' among the people (Num. 16.2). Bad acts, not just good, can make someone famous. Otherwise, שם is explicitly modified in biblical Hebrew, in contrast to its absolute form in Prov. 22.1 (so Eccl. 7.1), and the semantic question of 22.1 receives no further clarity from Proverbs 10–31. In contrast to the resources in 10–31, Proverbs 1–9 offers a clear understanding of both the content and sources of 'a name' in 22.1.

Placed within the teleological structure of Proverbs 1–9, a name in the book of Proverbs connotes a person's character, and this name would not include someone with a notoriously foolish character or wicked character, even if such qualities proved that person famous or reputable. The name endorsed by Proverbs 1–9 includes personal character developed by the wisdom that stems from the authoritative teachers of Proverbs and a relationship with the Lord, which indeed stands above the values of silver and gold. In other words, when interpreted within the frame of Proverbs 1–9, Prov. 22.1 places value on a person's wise character, acquired through a religious and human-mediated education. This insight also explains why a name and wisdom stand at similar places within the network of value judgments created by 22.1 and 16.16. For they seem to be competitors, if not equals, in terms of their worth. In the system of values and ends established by Proverbs 1–9, a name and wisdom also stand on similar ground, but their relationship is contextualized: wisdom begets wise character (i.e. a 'name'), which itself embodies that Wisdom who makes it possible. Without wisdom, we can presume that one's 'name' might be malformed and if renowned then perhaps renowned for the wrong reasons. A fool, for instance, could have a 'name', but Proverbs 1–9 indicates that one's name is not to be pursued by such unwise means. With wisdom comes a good reputation, and this good reputation stems from one's wisdom-infused character. Again, Prov. 22.1 may intend to promote any sort and source of fame over precious metals, but when placed in view of Proverbs 1–9 – the proposed introduction to the book – an alternative interpretation arises. Proverbs 1–9 functions didactically for 10–29 by formulating a structured set of values and persuading towards a particular sequence of goals, which have offered insight into certain interpretive challenges of Prov. 22.1 and related sayings. The final example of this section moves beyond the bounds of Prov. 10.1–22.16 into Proverbs 30 to see if Proverbs 1–9 functions didactically for the words of Agur.[50]

3.1.4. *Proverbs 30*

The final example of Proverbial goals turns attention away from competing values and visions and towards the very question of a goal itself. Proverbs 30.1-9 is examined due to its particular interpretive challenge, as it expresses an epistemological dilemma: Agur says he has no knowledge. However, the passage seems to lack a context within which to explain why Agur's problem is a problem. Why does his lack of knowledge vex him so greatly? Before pressing further into 30.1-9, a word should be said about the nature of Proverbs 30–31 as a whole and its relation to the approach taken so far. These final chapters do not contain as many assumptions as Prov. 10.1–22.16 or, in my judgement, as 22.17–29.27 and are comprised of longer, more coherent poems. In this way 30–31 resembles Proverbs 1–9 and provides, rather than assumes, much of its own interpretive context. For example, 31.1-9 depicts a mother speaking to her royal son, maintaining a case for how he should rule his people. The familial and royal contexts are established, as are the audience and solution that the king must address. In this way, 31.1-9 provides much

---

50. For a discussion of Prov. 22.17–29.27 see section 4.2.5.

more of a framework for interpreting its particular statements than do the sayings contained within Proverbs 10–29.⁵¹ But even though the poetic form of Proverbs 30–31 eliminates many hermeneutical challenges, it does not clarify every interpretive issue that arises within these chapters.

3.1.4.1. *The Epistemological Problem in Proverbs 30.1-9*

One such challenge appears in Prov. 30.1-9, a passage that contains 'the words of Agur son of Yakeh'. These words form part of a chapter that includes an opening confession and dictum (30.1-9), an assortment of instructions (30.10-17, 20) and numerical sayings (30.18-19, 21-33), all cohered by the concepts of pride and humility.⁵² The chapter starts with the confession of Agur (vv. 1–9), which poses special challenges for translation and interpretation. One such challenge especially demonstrates the role of Proverbs 1–9, namely, the question of why does Agur have a problem?

He says the following:

דברי אגור בן־יקה המשא	30.1	The words of Agur, son of Yakeh; the oracle.⁵³
נאם הגבר לאיתיאל		The utterance of the man: I am weary, O God;⁵⁴
לאיתיאל ואכל		I am weary, O God, and wasted away.
כי בער אנכי מאיש	30.2	For I am too brutish for a man;
ולא־בינת אדם לי		and I do not have the understanding of a man;
ולא־למדתי חכמה	30.3	And I have not learned wisdom,
ודעת קדשים אדע		and knowledge of the Holy One I do not know.⁵⁵

---

51. Similarly, given the uncertain diachronic relationship between 1–9 and 30–31, they will be treated as simultaneous additions to Proverbs 10–29 and read, more or less, in a synchronic relationship. On this, see Chapter 1.

52. For the many views on how to structure Proverbs 30, see Fox, *Proverbs 10–31*, 851; Ansberry, *Be Wise*, 163–4.

53. המשא may refer to 'the Massahite' but would be its only occurrence. For 'Lemuel, king of Massah [למואל מלך משא]' in Prov. 31.1, the term modifies 'king' and lacks the article. To render 'the Massahite' in 30.1, we expect המשאי or ממשא, and 'oracle', widely attested elsewhere, suits the reference to the 'words' of Agur and the נאם of 30.2.

54. For the 'utterance', see Num. 24.3, 15; 2 Sam. 23.1. The oddity of a repeated 'to Ithiel', and the clause starting with כי in v. 2 (Delitzsch, *Proverbs*, 2:269), which supposes a prior statement, favours the majority interpretation presented above. The meaning of אֻכָל is unknown, and revocalizing it as a form of כלה renders a sensible translation, hence the LXX's καὶ παύομαι (see Fox, *Proverbs 10–31*, 850, 853–4).

55. See the explanation below.

מי עלה־שמים וירד	30.4	Who has gone up to heaven and come down?
מי אסף־רוח בחפניו		Who has gathered the wind in his fists?
מי צרר־מים בשמלה		Who has wrapped the waters in a garment?
מי הקים כל־אפסי־ארץ		Who has established all the ends of the earth?
מה־שמו ומה־שם־בנו		What is his name, and what is the name of his son?
כי תדע	30.5	Surely, you know!
כל־אמרת אלוה צרופה		Every word of God is refined;
מגן הוא לחסים בו		he is a shield to those who seek refuge in him.
אל־תוסף על־דבריו	30.6	Do not add to his words,
פן־יוכיח בך ונכזבת		lest he reprove you and you be proven a liar.

After Agur bemoans his lack of knowledge and energy (vv. 1-3), he attests to the otherness of God and the strength of God's words: 'Who has gone up to heaven and come down?.... Every word of God is refined; he is a shield to those who seek refuge in him' (vv. 4a, 5). While the puzzlement and theology of 30.4-9 may accentuate the epistemological problem stated in 30.1b-3 or formulate its solution, Agur is nevertheless weary, brutish, and ignorant, and one question remains unanswered. As one commentator put it: 'Why this complaint?'[56] The negative statements of Agur, his weariness, lack of understanding, and failure to learn wisdom offer no assertion about why Agur's problem is a problem. He clearly has one, if not many, but does not situate it within a context that explicates his justification for having such a deep-seated lament. According to André Barucq,

> Il n'est pas aisé de rattacher logiquement ce passage au début des 'paroles des sages'.... Ces diverses péricopes font l'effet d'extraits ayant appartenu à un ensemble plus vaste. On les aurait juxtaposés comme en une anthologie sans prendre soin d'en recréer le contexte.[57]

Barucq questions not only the context of Agur's words, he questions how other portions of Proverbs might recreate the context and doubts that they have done so. The significance and difficulty of my question is revealed by the efforts of many interpreters to situate the passage within a background other than Proverbs.

Interpreters offer, deliberately or accidentally, an answer to the question of Agur's problem in one of three ways. First, many explain the significance of this passage by appealing to links with other OT texts, such as Raymond Van Leeuwen who says, 'Reference to other passages of Scripture is an essential feature of this passage, and these allusions

---

56. Delitzsch, *Proverbs*, 2:272.
57. André Barucq, *Le Livre des Proverbes* (Paris: J. Gabalda, 1964), 221.

and quotations have a deliberate theological and canonical function'.⁵⁸ Such intertextual links do provide insights into the interpretation of Prov. 30.1-9 but not, I will argue, for one of the primary questions raised by the passage, namely, why does Agur have a problem? Job 38–39 contains many connections with the questions posed in Prov. 30.4, but Job does not simply want knowledge, as it seems Agur does; he wants vindication before God.⁵⁹ For instance, in addition to the context of the whole book of Job, the remarks in Job 40.2, 7b-8 show that Job desires to be in the right rather than, primarily, to find knowledge and wisdom. According to the Lord,

> Shall a fault-finder dispute with the Almighty?
>   He who reproves God, he shall answer it...
> I will question you and you make it known to me.
>   Will you even frustrate my judgment?
>   Will you condemn me that you might be in the right?

The problem that vexes Job stems in part from a lack of knowledge but primarily from the way that he has been treated in light of his prior character and actions. Job pleads for a hearing with God to vindicate his integrity, which leads to humility, whereas Agur admits failure, finds confidence in God's supremacy, and maintains a humble attitude.

The questions in Prov. 30.4 appear elsewhere in the OT and other ancient Near Eastern literature, attesting to what Van Leeuwen sees as three 'topoi' of such texts.⁶⁰ One pertains to the extension of stature and

---

58. Van Leeuwen, 'Proverbs', 251. See also Rick D. Moore, 'A Home for the Alien: Worldly Wisdom and Covenantal Confession in Proverbs 30,1-9', *ZAW* 106 (1994): 96–107. His comments on page 104 begin to account for Proverbs 1–9. Outside of the biblical evidence, *Insinger* concludes with declarations of piety (35.2-12; *AEL* 3:213).

59. Cf. Barucq, *Proverbes*, 219. In support of the claims in this paragraph: Job defends his innocence (6.8-10, 24-25, 30; 9.21-24; 16.17; 23.11-12; 27.5-6), rebukes his friends (13.4-12; 16.2-4; 17.10; 21.7, 34), rages at God (7.17-21; 9.16) and demands a trial with the Lord (13.1-3; 19.25-27; 31.35-37). I am not saying that a 'courtroom narrative' controls the entire book of Job, but Job does perceive his problem within a largely legal framework (cf. Tremper Longman III, *Job* [Grand Rapids: Baker Academic, 2012], 34–7; Michael Dick, 'The Legal Metaphor in Job 31', *CBQ* 41 [1979]: 37–50).

60. Raymond C. Van Leeuwen, 'The Background to Proverbs 30.4aα', in *Wisdom, You Are My Sister: Studies in Honor of Roland E. Murphy, O.Carm., on the Occasion of His Eightieth Birthday*, ed. Michael L. Barré, CBQMS 29 (Washington, DC: Catholic Biblical Association of America, 1997), 102–21.

grasp, especially a god's; another depicts a hero ascending to heaven and descending to earth or the underworld; and the final, the most relevant to my question, regards 'the cosmic scope of the god's *investigative knowledge*, in contrast to other gods or humans who lack such knowledge'.[61] This third topos includes exclusively biblical and apocryphal evidence, notably Job 11 and 28, while no Mesopotamian or Egyptian texts are put forward. The pertinent evidence would suggest that Agur's problem is a problem because he strove for the 'investigative knowledge' of God and has failed to attain it. Job 11.7, for example, asks 'Will you find the searches of God? Will you find unto the end of *Shaddai*?' While questioning the extent of human epistemological capacities, the passage specifies the 'deep things' (ESV) or 'searches' (חקר) of God himself, and verse 6 mentions the 'secrets of wisdom', making it likely that the puzzlement in Job 11 regards not the 'wisdom' and 'understanding' that Agur lacks but something of a different quality.[62]

Job 28 also contributes, according to Van Leeuwen, to the background to Prov. 30.4, and, as a well-known chapter in the book of Job, recounts the poetically exalted search for wisdom: 'where can it be found?' But Job 28 does not so much express the extent of God's wisdom and the lack of man's as it does the thirst for God's wisdom and a human definition of it. The author wonders about wisdom's source: 'but where shall wisdom be found? And where, then, is the place of understanding?.... God understands its way, and he knows its place' (28.12, 23). The author does not bemoan the inaccessibility of wisdom or the challenge of acquiring it. After all, he concludes with a definition of wisdom, with no suggestion about its remoteness: 'Behold, the fear of *Adonai*, that is wisdom, and to turn from evil is understanding' (28.28b-c). It is possible that Agur's problem arose due to his failure to find the source of wisdom, as if a successful quest would have manifested in a confession similar to Job 28, but I hope to show that another explanation is more plausible. While Agur and the book of Job state profound questions about wisdom, both human and divine, the connections between these texts do not furnish Prov. 30.1-9 with a background that explains one of its key assumptions.

61. Van Leeuwen, 'Background', 107–8 (italics original).
62. See, among others, Friedrich Horst, *Hiob*, BKAT 16/1 (Neukirchen-Vluyn: Neukirchener Verlag, 1968), 169–70. Job 11.7-11 more closely aligns with Psalm 139, which expresses not the absence of human wisdom but the supremacy and inaccessibility of God's complete wisdom (for this intertextual relationship, see Will Kynes, *My Psalm Has Turned into Weeping: Job's Dialogue with the Psalms*, BZAW 437 [Berlin: de Gruyter, 2012], 112–15).

The pleas for knowledge and the recognition of God's word and refuge in Psalms 73, 92, and 139 are also forwarded to explain Agur's cry. Yet the psalmist's remarks too arise from problems that do not cohere with Agur's situation: vindication before accusers (Ps. 139.19-24), salvation from enemies (Ps. 92), and the psalmist's envy of the wicked (Ps. 73).[63] To Job and Psalms, Van Leeuwen adds Deuteronomy: 'the specific focus of Agur's ignorance appears to be his failure to learn the wisdom that Moses taught to Israel (Deut. 4.1, 6) and for which one does not need to ascend to heaven (Deut. 30.11-14)'.[64] With Deuteronomy as a third and final OT background for Prov. 30.1-9, Van Leeuwen suggests that the link of law and wisdom in Deut. 4.1, 6, and the geographical references in 30.11-14 and Prov. 30.4, cloak Prov. 30.1-9 with a framework of law-keeping that then explains Agur's problem as his failure to obey the Mosaic law. In short, Van Leeuwen sees a coherent relationship between Deuteronomy and Prov. 30.1-9. This Deuteronomic framework is also championed by Bernd Schipper, but instead of placing Prov. 30.1-9 in a coherent relation to Deuteronomy, he sees Agur's lament as denying what Deuteronomy so confidently proclaims.[65] In its allusion, Prov. 30.1-9 recognizes the existence of an 'authoritative tradition' in Mosaic *torah* yet claims that such a tradition cannot be grasped by human wisdom and, moreover, 'geht nicht davon aus, dass die göttliche Weisheit vermittelt werden kann'.[66] The 'canon-formula' in Prov. 30.6, according to Schipper, places Agur at odds with the Deuteronomic view of human wisdom, opposing any *torah* interpretation and mediation from one generation to the next. Consequently, the common intertextual connections that Van Leeuwen and Schipper appeal to render alternative interpretations of Prov. 30.1-9, to which other conflicting versions of biblical echoes could be added.[67] To reconcile the Joban and Deuteronomic interpretations of Prov. 30.1-9, it would need to be shown that Job's answer about the source and nature of wisdom also incorporated *torah* and that Deuteronomy reciprocated by connecting wisdom and *torah* in this way. While these interpretations are not out of the question, there is one overlooked, and perhaps simpler, direction of argumentation, namely, bringing Proverbs 1–9 into consideration.

---

63. See, e.g., Fox, *Proverbs 10–31*, 854, 862; Van Leeuwen, 'Proverbs', 252.
64. Van Leeuwen, 'Proverbs', 252. Sæbø (*Sprüche*, 366) mentions Deut. 8.12-14.
65. Schipper, *Hermeneutik*, 250–5.
66. Schipper, *Hermeneutik*, 256.
67. See Ansberry, *Be Wise*, 163–9, among others.

Interpretations of Prov. 30.1-9 are as manifold as the inner-biblical and extra-biblical allusions that appear in the text, which make it difficult to determine the design of the textual allusions and how they relate. Certainly, law, covenantal themes, and other perspectives on wisdom congregate in Prov. 30.1-9, and my aim is neither to refute these nor to offer a comprehensive account of how they might inform Agur's message. Many current treatments of these intertexts, however, seem to champion one element over another, run counter to each other, and offer little grounds for how allusions ought to be established and interpreted within Proverbs. The legal, Deuteronomic interpretation seems the most plausible candidate for offering a framework to answer the interpretive challenge of Prov. 30.1-9 – why is Agur's problem a problem? – but it has not done justice to the connections of this passage with other portions of Proverbs.

It should be said, though, that Schipper does not completely side-line inner-Proverbial allusions in preference for inner-biblical allusions, for he identifies linguistic connections in Prov. 30.2-3, 5b and 2.1-7. Proverbs 2.1-5 calls for 'understanding' (בינה) and turns an ear to 'wisdom' (חכמה) to find the fear of the Lord and knowledge of God. The search for wisdom leads to a relationship with the Lord, and such aims are promised in Prov. 2.1-5. In 30.2b-3a, Agur denies these very concepts: 'I do not have the understanding (בינה) of a man; And I have not learned wisdom (חכמה)'. Schipper says this language 'wirkt fast wie eine Anspielung auf Prov. 2,1-5' and concludes that 30.2-3 denies what 2.1-5 promises.[68] Likewise, the likening of God to a 'shield' in 2.7 is transformed in 30.5b, as such protection comes, in the former (2.7), to those who adhere as upright human beings to the wisdom doctrine and, in the latter (30.5b), to those who subordinate themselves to God's word 'unter Negierung der eigenen Erkenntnis'.[69] Agur's words counter the optimism of Proverbs 2, negating and denying the very things that it promises, and ultimately, according to Schipper, displaying the 'bankruptcy of wisdom' in favour of the eminence of *torah*.

Schipper's interpretation accounts for Proverbs 2, which creates a framework for understanding Agur's comments and dovetails with Agur's concerns about wisdom and law. In summary, Agur negates the optimistic assertions of 2.1-7 and favours divine law over human wisdom. The question of why his problem is a problem, though, receives only an implicit answer: perhaps he found wisdom insufficient for life and found a solution in God's law. Furthermore, the connections with Proverbs 1–9 warrant an

---

68. Schipper, *Hermeneutik*, 251.
69. Schipper, *Hermeneutik*, 283.

additional look. The cluster of lexemes in Prov. 30.2b-3 – דעת, חכמה, בינה – occurs elsewhere in the OT only in Prov. 2.6 and 3.19-20 (both תבונה), and Isa. 11.2 (cf. Dan. 1.4; 2.21), yet the lexical items or their roots also appear in Prov. 1.2-7, especially in 1.2, which inaugurates the stated goals of Proverbs: לדעת חכמה ומוסר להבין אמרי בינה. These lexemes, therefore, relate 30.2b-3 not only with Proverbs 2 but also with 1.1-7, a passage that, I contend, offers a key interpretive context for Agur's dilemma. According to Prov. 1.2, acquiring knowledge, wisdom and understanding constitutes the aim of Proverbs, an aim that I spelled out in more detail earlier in this chapter and established as consistent with Proverbs 2, namely, through the text's teachings and with the fear of the Lord, love and pursue wisdom in order to grow in wise character. Functioning didactically, Proverbs 1–9 as a whole offers this larger framework within which to view Agur's claims and gives a firm sense for why his problem is a problem. It is not that human wisdom has gone bankrupt but that Agur himself has struggled with the aims set out in Proverbs 1–9. He does not deny these aims; he confesses his inability to fully realize them. 'I am weary, O God, and wasted away. For I am too brutish for a man; and I do not have the understanding of a man; And I have not learned wisdom.' Agur's lament makes sense within the framework of goals in Proverbs 1–9, as he does not bemoan a failure to understand as such but bemoans a failure to achieve the book's aims. Agur confronts his stupidity, a problem that is a problem because it leaves the educational vision of Proverbs unaccomplished.

3.1.4.2. *The Grammatical Problem in Proverbs 30.1-9*

The function of Proverbs 1–9 is further demonstrated when we consider a related interpretive challenge of 30.1-9, this time a grammatical detail in verse 3:

ולא־למדתי חכמה ודעת קדשים אדע

The interpretive question here is how to translate the second colon (ודעת קדשים אדע). This colon (v. 3b) forms part of an explanation, started by כי in verse 2 and continued in verse 3a with a *waw*. Consequently, Agur says, '[v. 2] For I am too brutish for a man, and I do not have the understanding of a man; [v. 3a] and I have not learned wisdom'. These statements are followed by the line in question: ודעת קדשים אדע, which as it stands seems to read, 'and I know knowledge of the Holy One'. The sequence of 'do nots' that precede this statement – 'I do not have the understanding of a man, and I have not learned wisdom' – makes a negative in the final line plausible: '[v. 3b] and I [do not] know knowledge of the Holy One'. Negating the verb suits the grammatical context and flow of thought in 30.1-4, also corresponding to the acknowledgment that concludes 30.4 in response to the verse's series of questions: 'Surely you know'. This choice finds further support in clear examples where a negative particle in the initial line governs an unmarked second line (Isa. 38.18; Pss 9.19[18]; 35.19).[70]

The viable alternative to negating 30.3b by grammatical subordination is to subordinate it semantically, interpreting the line as expressing the intention of verse 3a: 'I have not learned wisdom *that I may know* knowledge of the Holy One'.[71] Lamentations 1.19 uses a similar construction to express such a meaning, and nothing in Prov. 30.1-9 opposes it. At the same time, nothing in 30.1-9 facilitates a confident conclusion about the interpretation of 30.3b, which when left on its own or when left to grammatical analogues in biblical Hebrew offers three plausible interpretations:

I have not learned wisdom *but I know* knowledge of the Holy One.
I have not learned wisdom *so that I might know* knowledge of the Holy One.
I have not learned wisdom *and I do not know* knowledge of the Holy One.

The cluster of lexemes just noted and the inclusion of 'knowledge of the Holy One' provide firm grounds for consulting Proverbs 1–9 in order to answer this grammatical question. Proverbs 9.10b itself, which uses this phrase – 'knowledge of the Holy One' – offers a little clarity on the issue, asserting that 'knowledge of the Holy One is insight' (ודעת קדשים בינה). This statement equates knowledge of God with insight to suggest that Prov. 30.2-3 would treat them as equals. As I argued earlier, Collection I as a whole indicates that no true wisdom or instruction is had without the fear of the Lord, a relationship with the Lord, even if not further specified, that starts and maintains growth in wisdom. Therefore, unless 'knowledge of the Holy One' refers to a special sort of knowledge, in distinction to the fear of the Lord, the second interpretation proposed – 'I have not learned wisdom that I may have knowledge of the Holy One' – becomes problematic.[72] For it implies that wisdom begets knowledge of God, rather than, in harmony with Proverbs 1–9, the knowledge of God being the starting point of wisdom, and thereby in some way begetting it. Agur may negate his wisdom and affirm his knowledge of God; yet Proverbs 1–9 gives no reason to think that such a situation is possible.

70. So Fox, *Proverbs 10–31*, 854–5.
71. Delitzsch, *Proverbs*, 2:273; Plöger, *Sprüche*, 351.
72. Fox (*Proverbs 10–31*, 855–6) sees the wisdom of Prov. 30.3 as different from the wisdom of Proverbs 2, but based on the grammar itself rather than the other way around.

If Agur does affirm knowledge of God, he does not, in the view of Proverbs 2, proclaim the bankruptcy of wisdom or the power of *torah*. Instead, such a theological affirmation within the context of 30.1-9 would imply a failure on God's part; for in Proverbs 2 those who search for wisdom receive it from God, who, as its source, gives wisdom to those who desire it. Agur's denial of wisdom coupled with a knowledge of God would mean that God himself has failed to proffer what Proverbs 1–9, not to mention 10–29, promises he will. However, this scenario, that is, a denial of wisdom and an affirmation of God who then fails to deliver wisdom, is inconsistent with the rest of Agur's remarks. For Agur, in his very confession of ignorance, reflects the posture of wisdom depicted in Proverbs 1–9, where the depths of ignorance are admitted only by those not 'wise in their own eyes' (3.5-7).[73] Such people trust not in their own 'wisdom' or insight but in the Lord, who himself provides wisdom to the humble and straightens their paths. As to the place of God in wisdom education, 30.5 seems to make his protective role contingent upon subordination to his words: 'Every word of God is refined; he is a shield to those who seek refuge in him'. To cohere with Proverbs 1–9, these words of God need an analogue therein, and what are the words of the Proverbial father and Wisdom herself in 1–9 if not the words of God? Schipper himself says 'die Lehre des Weisheitslehrers in Prov 2 eng mit der Lehre JHWHs verknüpft ist. Die Weisheit, die er mitteilt, ist letztlich die Gabe JHWHs'.[74] Neither the nature of Agur's confession nor his theological point of view obstructs a connection between his poem and Proverbs 1–9. Based on the rest of Agur's words and theological statements in Proverbs 1–9, it seems that Agur struggles with attaining wisdom but does not declare it bankrupt. All of this is driving towards the grammatical question in 30.3.

The first option for translating 30.3 – affirming a knowledge of God without wisdom – produces theological incoherence between Proverbs 1–9 and 30.1-9. The second option relates wisdom as a necessary condition for knowledge of God – 'I do not have the understanding of a man *so that I might know* knowledge of the Holy One' – which offers a possible interpretation but again finds discord with the rest of 30.1-9, its reflection of knowledge of God, and the rest of Proverbs. When Proverbs 1–9 interjects as an interpretive framework, it places option three as the most likely interpretation: I do not have the understanding of a man *and I do not know* knowledge of the Holy One. Agur's wholesale denial of wisdom

---

73. Longman, *Proverbs*, 520–1.
74. Schipper, *Hermeneutik*, 71.

and knowledge of God reflects a failure of the educational goals outlined by Proverbs 1–9, remains consistent in how it relates those goals, and also receives grammatical support from other biblical passages. Negating the verb in 30.3b, then, seems the most plausible interpretation: 'I do not know knowledge of the Holy One'.[75]

Can this statement, though, really be understood as an absolute denial of wisdom and the knowledge of God? Such denial does not accord with 30.5-9 and all of its theological affirmations, but neither does it accord with 30.1-4 itself. For 30.1b-c addresses God with an expression of weariness: 'I am weary, O God; I am weary, O God, and wasted away'. Consequently, many view the subsequent denials in verses 2-3 as hyperbolic statements borne of Agur's desperate state.[76] I would add that such desperate calls find a place in the framework of Proverbs 1–9, which indicates the goals of wisdom, the way of wisdom, and the challenges entailed in heading its direction, which reasonably warrant an outburst like Agur's. Expecting wisdom and striving for understanding, he cries out in exhaustion of what appears to be a failed education. He is weary; he is brutish; and, in his view, he has no understanding. Agur's lament and his confidence in 30.1-9 accord with the framework of goals set out in Proverbs 1–9, which functions didactically by providing a plausible context to explain why Agur's problem is a problem and shed a bit of light on a grammatical issue in 30.3b. With this interpretation, I do not mean to silence the intertextual appeals made by many scholars or to assert the grammatical solution to 30.3b as irrevocable. However, Proverbs 1–9 does offer a cogent account of 30.1-9 and establishes a coherent relationship between both passages, perhaps lending some credibility to the idea that Proverbs 1–9 and 30–31 frame the book in a way significant for its meaning.

3.1.5. *Conclusion*

Having arrived at the end of this chapter's first section, we ought to take stock of where the argument has come so far. The chapter started by observing the plurality of ends in Proverbs 10–29 and offering two explanations about their relationship. The ends, or values, seem to remain in tension when viewed within Proverbs 10–29 alone, but they also prompt

---

75. Whichever option is selected must reason with the apparent discord between 30.1-4 and 30.5-9, which laments a lack of knowledge and, in my view, knowledge of God (vv. 1-4), and joins this with quite certain points of understanding and relationship with the Lord (vv. 5-9).

76. Hans-Friedemann Richter, 'Hielt Agur sich für den Dümmsten aller Menschen? (Zu Prov 30,1-4)', *ZAW* 113 (2001): 419–21; Van Leeuwen, 'Proverbs', 252.

the question as to whether an organization of values is latent within Proverbs. Posing the question of what end or ends Proverbs 1–9 persuades toward, I argued that 1–9 guides the interpreter towards particular goals that correlate to its vision of values. It establishes such guidance in Proverbs 7–8, which contrasts Folly and Wisdom to advocate friendship with the latter and avoidance of the former. These chapters likewise establish a preliminary educational program: the father's teaching operates as the educational starting point that directs the interpreter to wisdom who then facilitates growth in wise character. Proverbs 2 presents the most probable objection to this system, especially given its reputation as a 'Lehrprogramm' for Proverbs 1–9.

Developed most recently by Bernd Schipper, work on the educational plan of Proverbs 1–9 draws attention to the goals of Proverbs 2 and the means that accomplish these goals, on the one hand affirming the conclusion derived from Proverbs 7–8, such as the role of the father's teaching and the aims of wisdom and wise character, yet on the other hand presenting a potential alternative to the system established so far. Schipper sees Prov. 2.21-22 as the ultimate goal of Proverbs 2 – that is, to dwell in the land – a proposal that I argue against on grammatical, conceptual, and literary grounds, maintaining my original educational program. However, Proverbs 2 supplements this educational paradigm by interpolating the Lord into the values and goals of Proverbial education. The Lord now joins the father's instruction as the starting point of wisdom and the companion who aids in the realization of the ultimate goal of wise character.

This framework of ends and values offered interpretive insight for Proverbs 10–29, providing an ordered set of ends that structures the apparently unordered values of 16.16 and 22.1 – wisdom and fame/reputation (שׁם) – and offering a teleological scheme with which to interpret 'a name' in 22.1. In view of 1–9, this name refers to the reputation built by wise character, which is comprised of wisdom and its foundation of Proverbial teaching and a relationship with the Lord. Proverbs 1–9 does not deny other methods of interpreting sayings like 22.1, but when accounted for, it does impose a framework of ends and values that, I suggest, provides insight into the interpretive challenges of Proverbs 10–29. Proverbs 30.1-9 also provoked an interpretive challenge derived from the lament of Agur who bemoans his lack of wisdom and then affirms the centrality of a relationship with God, leaving the question of why Agur's problem is a problem unaddressed. Intertextual appeals to Job, Psalms and Deuteronomy do not furnish an answer to this question with as much consistency as the book of Proverbs itself, especially Proverbs 1–9. This 'introduction' again functions didactically by providing a framework that explains why Agur's problem is a problem, setting it within a network of educational goals, and offering insight into a grammatical issue in Prov. 30.3. Despite its interpretive fruit and broad scope, this section on the rhetorical aims of Proverbs does not account for every educational goal in Proverbs 1–9. To discover this, Proverbs must be approached from an entryway other than 10.1–22.16, and to this the following section is dedicated.

3.2. *Discerning Moral Ambiguity*

The first half of this chapter explored the, at times disparate, aims and values of Proverbs 10.1–22.16 to discover that Proverbs 1–9 outlines persuasive educational goals, creating a structure of values and a hierarchy of ends that organize the features in 10–29. The scheme produced by Proverbs 1–9 can be summarized as follows: through the father's teaching and fear of the Lord embrace wisdom in order to grow in wise character. This educational framework derives from Proverbs 2 and 7–8, chapters that contain the collection's 'Lehrprogramm' and contrasting female figures, which offered interpretive insight for 16.16 and 22.1. It developed out of this study's primary starting point, namely, the interpretive challenges of 10.1–22.16 which then determined the interpretive questions to be brought to Proverbs 1–9. As indicated in Chapter 1, this method does not distort the text, but it does run the risk of overlooking the most salient features of Proverbs 1–9. For instance, while Proverbs 7–8 clearly presents a contrasting pair of persuasive female figures to organize the values and ends of Proverbs, these figures, when read apart from 16.16 and 22.1, might also serve other purposes. Taken on their own account, the females might have a more significant or at least equally important role.

The present section of this chapter considers just such an alternative function by starting not with Prov. 10.1–22.16 but instead with Proverbs 1–9. When interpreted independently of the rest of Proverbs, what do the book's first nine chapters emphasize? How do the women, in particular, function within 1–9 when examined on their own terms and without the interpretive priorities of 10.1–22.16? I will argue that they still inform the educational goals of Proverbs but that they do so in a way overlooked by the previous section. That is, the women maintain their rhetorical potency but employ it for reasons yet unaccounted for. Accounting for this alternative entry point – Proverbs 1–9 – by extracting its additional rhetorical features fortifies my argument, setting it more firmly on exegetical ground and within scholarly discussion on Proverbs.

This section, however, does not remain within Proverbs 1–9. Those chapters serve as a starting point that leads to 10.1–22.16. In short, the emphases of Proverbs 1–9 will prompt questions about material in 10.1–22.16 that have so far been overlooked. Proverbs 1–9 itself determines how it might function as an introduction by prompting interpretive priorities that disclose interpretive challenges in 10.1–22.16. The interpretive priorities of 1–9 come to the fore in an article by J. N. Aletti, who in 1977 argued that the presentation of speech in Proverbs 1–9, especially the words of the women, functions to persuade the interpreter towards a certain outlook on morality.[77] Aletti's article on 1–9 will be unpacked to expose two proverbs from 10.1–22.16 that are then examined to demonstrate the function of Proverbs 1–9 (14.12; 18.8).

3.2.1. *Moral Ambiguity in Proverbs 1–9*

Treating a generous scope of material in Proverbs 1–9, Aletti's primary contention is that the seduction portrayed in these chapters poses a threat to the simpleton, and that this seduction comes not by means of certain objects, like financial reward, or by the seductive beings themselves, such as the temptress, but rather through the actual words of seduction. That is, it is the words themselves that seduce. Aletti focuses on three features, the first being the linguistic chaos that ensues, especially in 1.22-33. The chaos is evident due to the selection of lexemes in the passage, its tone of urgency, and the multiple substantives that connote panic (e.g. פחד; איד). Second, he concentrates on the means of seducing the simpleton or youth in 1–9 and, third, on the solution to this seduction, that is, the means by which one might avoid the fate of the simpleton. Seduction targets the simpleton or youth of Proverbs 1–9, and as mentioned Aletti argues that it is not the objects or the beings themselves that seduce, it is rather the words spoken. For example, evil characters and good characters use similar words to persuade their audiences.[78] The gang of Proverbs 1 tempts the boy with promises that 'we shall fill (נמלא) our houses with plunder' (1.13), while Wisdom promises to fill (מלא) the treasuries of those who love her (8.21). The proverbial father says that a man should 'always be intoxicated in her love (באהבתה)' (5.19), that is, the love of one's wife, while the temptress declares to the youth: 'let us delight ourselves with love (באהבים)' (7.18). Lastly, the invitations of Wisdom and Folly in Proverbs 9 include identical phrasing, as both 9.4 and 9.16 state,

---

77. Aletti, 'Seduction'. On the significance of this article for the present study, see the discussion in Chapter 1.

78. Aletti, 'Seduction', 133.

'Whoever is simple, let him turn here. To the one who lacks sense, she says....' In each case, a good and an evil tempter use the same language to persuade their audiences. Gangs and Wisdom promise to fill treasuries; a wife and an illicit temptress say they can delight a man with love; and the figures of Wisdom and Folly announce an identical invitation to dine with them. Aletti rightly concludes that in many respects the speakers of Proverbs 1–9 use the same means of temptation: words.

The fact that they use not only words but the same words in different and similar situations leads to Aletti's second insight: the solution to seduction. In the last section, two layers of discourse were distinguished in Proverbs 7: on the one hand the reader encounters a story about a youth and his temptation, and on the other hand encounters the father's commentary on this story. The previous section focused on the latter, the father's commentary, but Aletti accounts for both, especially the narrated scenario itself. The boy in Proverbs 7 is seduced by the temptress (7.21-23), listening to her words and spiralling to death, apparently unaware of her moral quality and the consequences that she expedites. Such lack of awareness might be called 'stupidity', and Aletti observes that within such stories and elsewhere, the author notes two things: the haste of such acts (1.16; 7.22-23; cf. 6.18) and the stupidity of the agents (5.22-23; cf. 1.7). Haste and stupidity, accentuated more than the evil or rebellious attitude of the youth, disclose the solution to seduction.

For Aletti, this solution resides in listening to the teacher: 'Seule l'observation minutieuse des mots et des choses, ainsi que l'écoute patiente des maîtres (iv 13), permet de déjouer la séduction'.[79] In light of the chaotic presentation of language and competing sets of appealing words, Wisdom and the teacher endorse the truth of their words (Prov. 4.1-9; 8.6-7) and draw attention to them throughout Proverbs 1–9 (e.g. 1.8, 22-24). As a part of this strategy, the father exhorts his son to hear and says, 'For I give you good teaching; do not forsake my *torah*' (4.2).[80] Then, appealing to the grandfatherly source of his instruction (4.3-4), he draws attention to seduction's solution:

> Acquire wisdom; acquire insight.
> Do not forget and do not turn from the words of my mouth.
> Do not forsake her, and she will keep you;
> love her and she will protect you. (Prov. 4.5-6)

---

79. Aletti, 'Seduction', 140.
80. Aletti, 'Seduction', 141.

The authority and reliability of the father's teaching dovetail with the power of wisdom, all of which corroborates the educational paradigm outlined in the previous section: through the father's teaching and fear of the Lord embrace wisdom in order to grow in wise character. As Aletti recognizes, the solution to seduction also requires a divine helper – the Lord who gives wisdom to humans – leaving my original educational paradigm undisturbed.[81] However, Aletti's work on Proverbs 1–9 does add a component to the ultimate goal of 'growth in wise character', namely, the faculty of discernment. As mentioned, 'Only the meticulous observation of words and matters…makes it possible to elude seduction'.[82] Gaining such discernment requires, Aletti suggests, a long process of training:

> de même que la valeur symbolique des êtres et des choses ne peut être découverte qu'à la fin d'un long apprentissage (lorsque le regard s'est exercé au discernement), de même, ce n'est qu'à la fin du livre lui-même, lorsqu'il a pu aiguiser son jugement à la lecture des proverbes, que l'élève sait reconnaître en cette femme de valeur le symbole de la sagesse et qu'il chante sa louange.[83]

Discernment comes by sharpening one's judgment through the reading of proverbs with the aid of God-given wisdom. It is the means proposed in this formula that is key for determining how Proverbs 1–9 functions: judgment is sharpened by means of reading proverbs ('à la lecture des proverbes'), that is, the proverbs contained in Proverbs 10–29. These proverbs may hone the moral faculties of a reader now prepared by 1–9 for moral ambiguity. Such moral ambiguity appears to be a hermeneutical bridge between Proverbs 1–9 and 10–29, a connection that Aletti addresses with only a brief comment. My question, therefore, is whether 10–29 contains or displays similar moral confusion, and how this material relates to 1–9.

Aletti has disclosed a key aim of Proverbs 1–9: it depicts the world as morally ambiguous, a place where, like the words of competing voices, bad things look good and good things may, therefore, look like the bad. Illustrated most clearly by the use of words in 1–9, where what is wrong sounds right, the moral landscape is convoluted and those who traverse it need skill to discern good from bad and bad from good. Without the

---

81. Aletti, 'Seduction', 142–3.
82. Aletti, 'Seduction', 140.
83. Aletti, 'Seduction', 144.

queries of Proverbs 10–29 in mind, Proverbs 1–9 renders the world morally ambiguous and proposes a solution in divine wisdom. If 1–9 functions didactically for the book in this regard, then it ought to relate to some such moral ambiguity in 10–29.

3.2.2. *Moral Ambiguity in Proverbs 10–29*
In view of the main points of Aletti's argument, which concentrate solely on Proverbs 1–9, it is remarkable to find that 10–29 displays moral ambiguity of a similar shape. Quite a few proverbs portray fools as morally confused: 'The wisdom of the prudent is to discern his way, but the folly of fools is deceit' (14.8); 'Folly is a joy to the one who lacks sense, but a man of understanding walks straight'[84] (15.21); 'Thus is the way of the adulteress: she eats and wipes her mouth and says, "I have not done wrong"' (30.20). Some passages also suggest that bad things look good, or that bad things taste good as 20.17 would have it: 'Bread of falsehood is sweet to a man, but afterward his mouth will be full of gravel'. Proverbs 10–29 portrays evil characters as morally distorted, with fools taking joy in folly rather than acting like the prudent person who discerns his way. Certain passages imply that the world is a morally ambiguous place, a place where falsehood tastes sweet, and telling right from wrong is not necessarily easy.

Matters of moral ambiguity in Proverbs are matters of the moral self. Though not focussing on Proverbs, Carol Newsom has formulated three essential features of the moral self in the OT: 'desire, knowledge, and the discipline of submission to external authority'.[85] That trio does a decent job at reflecting the moral self of Proverbs and is helpful for anatomizing moral agents that encounter moral ambiguity. But with such anatomization comes the risk of artificial segregation. So, as with the classification of character and consequence in Proverbs, a caveat applies to the elements of the moral self: they are not permanently or functionally segregated, as if moral problems are only problems of knowledge or desire or external authority. As Newsom herself says, 'Moral failure generally involves a combination of these three elements, though one or another may be stressed'.[86] It is that stress which interests me and, I would argue, is evident in the passages about moral ambiguity in Proverbs.

---

84. Delitzsch (*Proverbs*, 1:327) rightly sees לכת as an accusative, as in Prov. 30.29 and Mic. 6.8.

85. Carol A. Newsom, 'Models of the Moral Self: Hebrew Bible and Second Temple Judaism', *JBL* 131 (2012): 12.

86. Newsom, 'Models of the Moral Self', 13. It should be remembered that moral ambiguity is only one aspect of moral failure in Proverbs, which encompasses a far

The stressed element of moral disfunction that I am homing in on, and I think Aletti points to, is knowledge. Good and bad are ambiguous because people cannot perceive them correctly. Good sounds like evil; it is unfamiliar, misperceived, or misunderstood. But that knowledge problem, like the wider scope of moral failure in Proverbs, depends upon desire and external authority. For moral agents are portrayed as confused about right and wrong not only because they are ignorant, but because they desire the wrong things and resist sanctioned sources of moral authority. And yet cognitive confusion still seems to hold a first-place position. So where desire is clearly involved – 'folly is a joy to the one who lacks sense' (15.21a) – even that enjoyment, which is a delight in folly, is felt by the one who 'lacks sense'; he has an intellectual problem.[87] Similarly, Prov. 14.15 suggests that heeding too many voices can lead one along the wrong path: 'The simpleton believes every word, but the prudent understands his steps'. Here, the simpleton is blamed for accepting all sources of moral direction, making his flaw one of external authority. However, the prudent, who presumably accepts wise guidance, is said to 'understand his steps', which makes his moral rectitude not a matter of desire or external authority but a matter of knowledge. Proverbs pertinent to the moral ambiguity of 14.12 target various loci of moral failure, and although that larger problem calls upon the agent's desires, knowledge, and adherence to authority, the issue of moral ambiguity centres upon one's intellectual perception. Again, as will be argued, that perception sees clearest when wise teachers are heeded, God feared, and desires rightly directed, and yet the evidence relevant to moral ambiguity, as presented here, exhibits that problem as an issue of knowledge.

greater amount of material and resists cognition-affection-adherence distinctions. For in Proverbs as a whole, knowing good is not always a sufficient condition for doing good; its depiction of moral agency, as I argue elsewhere, is more Aristotelian than it is Socratic. See Arthur Keefer, *The Book of Proverbs and Virtue Ethics: Integrating the Biblical and Philosophical Traditions* (Cambridge: Cambridge University Press, forthcoming).

87. Passages relevant to moral ambiguity include Prov. 11.22; 12.15; 13.19; 14.8, 12-13; 15.21; 16.21, 24-25; 17.4, 8, 28; 18.16, 24; 20.6, 17; 21.14; 26.22-26; 29.5; 30.20-23; cf. 17.24; 27.7. Of these, only Prov. 13.19 and 15.21 make the problem one of desire (cf. 20.17; 27.7). If the use of bribes aroused affective confusion in those subject to moral ambiguity, which it probably did, that would then incorporate 17.8 and 18.16. Proverbs 10.23 is often translated with affective terms, not supplied by the MT, making the role of desire unclear: 'Doing wrong is like a joke to a fool, but wisdom is pleasure to a man of understanding'. The second line reads, וחכמה לאיש תבונה.

Two proverbs regarding moral ambiguity will be examined in this section: 'The words of a whisperer are like tasty morsels, they go down into the chambers of the belly' (18.8); 'There is a way that is straight before a man; but its end is the way of death' (14.12). These passages disclose concord between Aletti's interpretation of Proverbs 1–9 and the moral world of 10–29, and will demonstrate the didactic function of 1–9 as it prepares the interpreter not only to expect moral ambiguity but also to find its solution.

3.2.2.1. *Proverbs 18.8*

Proverbs 18.8 discloses moral ambiguity in a way slightly different to what has been expressed by other passages from Proverbs 10–29. It says,[88]

דברי נרגן כמתלהמים	18.8	The words of a whisperer are like tasty morsels,
והם ירדו חדרי־בטן		they go down into the chambers of the belly.

The other texts from Proverbs 10–29 show evil characters as morally distorted, confusing good and bad, such as the one who 'lacks sense' and finds 'folly a joy' instead of adhering to the good way of the wise man (15.21). But this is not what we see in Prov. 18.8. The proverb does not depict evil people who stray from wisdom's way and treat evil as if it is good, like those bad and morally confused characters of Proverbs 1–9. Proverbs 18.8 instead exhibits the problem of moral ignorance, which Aletti himself observed.

> le seul reproche qu'on puisse faire aux méchants est d'être des in-sensés, des sots, d'une sottise et d'une ignorance coupable.... L'idiot est justement celui qui ne sait ni ne veut prendre du temps pour discerner, dans le discours d'autrui, le vrai du faux.[89]

The person who lacks sense in Prov. 15.21 and calls folly a joy may very well align with the person described here by Aletti. The point is that this character has made a confused decision about something's moral quality, which is a problem distinct from the moral ambiguity of that thing or ambiguity within the world itself, as is displayed by 18.8. Proverbs 15.21 displays a moral agent gone wrong; Prov. 18.8 displays an object in moral ambiguity, akin to what appears in Proverbs 1–9.

---

88. The LXX reads, ὀκνηροὺς καταβάλλει φόβος ψυχαὶ δὲ ἀνδρογύνων πεινάσουσιν ('Fear throws down the lazy, and the souls of the effeminate shall hunger').
89. Aletti, 'Seduction', 140.

3. *Educational Goals*

Proverbs 18.8 employs distinctive language to describe 'the words of a whisperer', as the four occurrences of נרגן within the OT appear only in Proverbs (16.28; 18.8; 26.20, 22) and derivatives of the root in Deut. 1.27; Isa. 29.24; and Ps. 106.25 to describe those who 'murmur' as opposed to accepting instruction. The 'whisperer' may slander or grumble, and although he seems to speak in a bad way, the evil quality of speech is not as obvious as the one who reviles or scoffs or utters falsehood (19.29; 21.24; 24.9; 30.10). Elsewhere in Proverbs, the whisperer 'separates close friends' (16.28) and breeds a quarrel (26.20), the evidence altogether suggesting that נרגן connotes something subtler than blatant wrongdoing.

In 18.8, his words liken to 'morsels' (מתלהמים), a *hapax legomenon* (par. 26.22) that, based on the Arabic cognate *lahima*, may connote a delicious flavour so that someone is 'wolfing down gossip like food'.[90] Finally, these morsels descend into the חדרי בטן ('inner parts of the body'), a phrase that occurs only in Proverbs (20.27, 30; par. 26.22) and stems from the Egyptian 'casket of the belly' (*hnw n ḫ.t*).[91] Both phrases indicate the belly as a 'dwelling place for words' and, when joined to the rest of the language from Prov. 18.8, display its distinctive nature and connection with Egyptian instructions.[92] 'The words of a whisperer are like tasty morsels, they go down into the chambers of the belly.' Although 18.8 continues to show itself as a fit example for the current topic, it remains to be seen if the other Egyptian and OT resources resolve the interpretive issue at hand.

Other proverbs that mention the whisperer identify the troublemaking consequences of his words – estranging friends (16.28) and contributing to quarrels (26.20) – and suggest a disapproval of the character in 18.8. Similarly, 18.7 says that 'A fool's mouth is his ruin, and his lips are a snare to his soul', portraying a speech problem from the speaker's perspective. It is the one who uses words in these sayings that has the problem. In contrast to these passages, 18.8 focuses on the listener, mentioning the attractiveness of the speaker's words to inform an audience who might devour them. That is, the problem in 18.8 lies with the one who hears. If we consider words from the listener's point of view, then other proverbs in chapters 10–29, such as 16.21, 23-24, compound the moral ambiguity.

---

90. Fox, *Proverbs 10–31*, 641. So Whybray, *Proverbs*, 267.
91. Shupak, *Where Can Wisdom Be Found?*, 291–7.
92. Shupak, *Where Can Wisdom Be Found?*, 292.

> The wise of heart is called discerning,
>   and sweetness of lips increases persuasiveness.[93]
> The heart of the wise makes his mouth prudent
>   and adds persuasiveness to his lips.
> Pleasant speech is honey of the comb,
>   sweetness to the soul and health to the bone.

According to these statements, a wise mind increases the persuasiveness of speech, and pleasant words are likened to honey that is sweet and gives health to the hearer. Proverbs 16.21 makes a similar point, showing that the speech of a good person tastes good, which suggests that wise words are delicious like the words of the whisperer. How, then, can one tell the difference? In Proverbs 10–29, both wise instruction and murmured gossip taste good to the hearer, constructing a morally ambiguous world where good and bad conflict, leaving the listener at a loss for how to discern what not only tastes good but is good.[94]

Egyptian texts leave a similar impression. *Ani* 7.9-10 says 'A man's belly is wider than a granary, and full of all kinds of answers; Choose the good one and say it, while the bad is shut in your belly'.[95] The speaker contains good and evil, and he must choose the good, yet how so? *Ani* 7.9-10 simply says 'choose the good one', but leaves one wondering, how do I discern the good from the bad in order to choose the better part? *Ani* 7.4-5 lends a bit of clarity: 'One will do all you say if you are versed in the writings; Study the writings, put them in your heart, then all your words will be effective'.[96] While this passage offers suggestions for the speaker, it is of limited help for our question. For the moral ambiguity in *Ani* stems from the speaker and is not portrayed from the perspective of the listener. Therefore, the problem of discerning what is heard remains unaddressed and perhaps remains a problem distinct to Proverbs.[97] In view of the relevant evidence in Proverbs 10–29, Prov. 18.8 leaves the interpreter with a moral ambiguity, portraying a world where bad words taste good. Since no solution readily arises from plausible interpretive resources to resolve the ambiguity, I will suggest that Proverbs 1–9 provides insight into this interpretive challenge, after first consulting another proverb.

---

93. For this sense of לקח, see Prov. 7.21 and Keefer, 'A Shift', 113–14.
94. Meinhold (*Sprüche*, 300) finds 'an especially close parallel' in Jer. 15.16, which recounts the joyful outcome of Jeremiah tasting God's words.
95. *AEL* 2:140.
96. *AEL* 2:140.
97. Other passages about the 'belly' also maintain the speaker's perspective (Shupak, *Where Can Wisdom Be Found?*, 291–7).

3.2.2.2. *Proverbs 14.12*

An interpretive situation similar to the one found with Prov. 18.8 occurs with 14.12.

יש דרך ישר לפני־איש ואחריתה דרכי־מות	14.12	There is a way that is straight before a man, but its end is the way(s) of death.

The saying describes a moral ambiguity at best and moral confusion at worst. In short, a person sees his way as 'straight', connotative of the right way (12.15; 14.2; 21.8), but what he sees turns out to be wrong. What looks good is actually bad and the person in this scenario fails to realize it. The proverb portrays a person morally confused, and it prompts the interpreter to wonder whether he or she views life in this way. Harbouring an interpretive challenge so similar to Prov. 18.8, yet in different language and from a slightly different perspective, 14.12 requires a less lengthy treatment and will add clarity and strength to the ongoing argument. The problem in 14.12 is one of moral ambiguity.

Proverbs in the vicinity of 14.12 suggest that 'prudent' (ערום) people understand their ways, in contrast to the simpleton and fool. 'The wisdom of the prudent is to discern (*hiphil* בין) his way, but the folly of fools is deceit' (14.8). 'The simpleton believes every word, but the prudent understands (*qal* בין) his steps' (14.15). The prudent person somehow understands and discerns his way, and does not, it seems, believe every word he hears as the simpleton would (14.15a), or associate himself with deceit in the ways that fools do (14.8b). If these character terms are imported into Prov. 14.12, so that the prudent or simpleton are somehow aligned with the moral possibilities in 14.12, then we return to issues dealt with in Chapter 2, where the identity and function of character terms are aided by Proverbs 1–9.[98] Since that is not the interest of this chapter, and 14.12 itself does not include character terms, considering this saying from the angle of moral ambiguity as depicted in Proverbs 1–9 remains the focus. In support of treating 14.12 alone, notice its replicate in 16.25, which lacks a character-driven literary context like 14.12's (e.g. 14.8, 15). Proverbs 16.25 says that 'the violent man entices his neighbour and leads him in a way not good', ensuring that bad people may persuade to bad ends but all the while fortifying the point made in 14.12 – a bad way might look good, that is, enticing. For a violent person to persuade someone towards a bad path, that someone would most likely need to perceive

---

98. For connections between verses in this section of Proverbs 14, see Knut M. Heim, *Like Grapes of Gold Set in Silver: An Interpretation of Proverbial Clusters in Proverbs 10.1–22.16*, BZAW 273 (Berlin: de Gruyter, 2001), 178–9.

the bad path as actually good. The point prompts the question that arose with Prov. 18.8 – how does someone determine the right path from the apparently right path? How might a neighbour know if he or she is being enticed down a way of evil rather than a way of peace? Some interpreters, such as Waltke, offer a theological answer to the question:

> The house of the wicked is annihilated because it is built on the flimsy foundation of human epistemology, the relative truth accessible to human sight. Only the omniscient, omnipotent God knows the true road that leads to life, reality as it actually is. Truth is beyond the reach of finite humanity; the Lord himself must reveal the right way through his inspired sage, and the disciple must accept that revelation by faith.[99]

Waltke argues that God's revelation provides insight for the human, and in support he cites Prov. 3.7 and 30.1-6. In contrast to such an optimistic proposal, Whybray says

> there is no suggestion here of the making of a choice between good and evil or between wisdom and folly. The proverb simply states that life contains hidden snares: the road ahead may seem to lead straight...to the desired goal, but there may be...hidden and fatal dangers further on.[100]

Whybray too appeals to Proverbs 1–9, yet it seems to bring no interpretive import to 14.12, which stands alone and indicates that 'there is a way that is straight before a man, but its end it the way of death', with 'no suggestion here of the making of a choice'.[101] In view of Whybray's interpretation and its disregard for 1–9, Prov. 14.12 contains no warning but only a matter of fact: bad things look good, or at least ישר. I hope to develop these allusions to Proverbs 1–9 by affixing the insights established earlier in this section to the interpretive question from 14.12.

The interpretive challenges and the potential solutions for two sayings in Proverbs 10–29 have been set out, prompted by their correspondence with Proverbs 1–9 and its mission to delineate the moral ambiguity of the world. The connections between Proverbs 1–9 and 10–29 do not simply attest to coherence or disparity, as Whybray suggests, but rather set up a

---

99. Waltke, *Proverbs 1–15*, 592. Also, Wildeboer, *Sprüche*, 42. Plöger (*Sprüche*, 171–2) remarks that the warnings of the wisdom teacher are missing in 14.12 but that the pupil possesses the principles to fight apathy.

100. Whybray, *Proverbs*, 215.

101. Similarly, Sæbø (*Sprüche*, 205) connects Prov. 14.11-12 with Eccl. 8.8-10 and 9.2-6, as instances of 'unexplainable phenomena' (so Scherer, *Das weise Wort*, 149).

relationship with which to test the long-voiced claim that Proverbs 1–9 functions as an introduction to the rest of Proverbs. This function so far seems 'didactic', providing a framework that lends interpretive insights for particular passages in Proverbs 10–31, and it remains to be seen if the connection of 1–9 with 14.12 and 18.8 bolsters this argument.

3.2.3. *The Function of Proverbs 1–9 for Proverbs 18.8 and 14.12*

As argued earlier, Proverbs 1–9 displays a world of moral ambiguity similar to what appears in passages from Proverbs 10–29, where good and bad words taste delicious. Likewise, Wisdom and Folly both appear attractive to their audiences, who remain ignorant of the true nature of this persuasion when not tutored by the father. However, although Proverbs 1–9 and 10–29 share this moral vision, the former displays it within the context of prolonged poems and the father's commentary. These features create a framework for the moral situation unavailable in Proverbs 10–29, an awareness, diagnosis and solution regarding moral ambiguity that shed light on 18.8 and 14.12.

Proverbs 1–9 instils three points that frame the interpretation of Prov. 18.8, which likens 'The words of a whisperer' to 'tasty morsels, they go down into the chambers of the belly'. First, the father draws attention to the superiority of his words by attesting to their source in tradition (4.1-13), labelling his precepts as 'good' and locating their origin in family transmission. Second, this teaching leads to Wisdom, for embracing her constitutes the central facet of the father's teaching (4.7): 'The beginning of wisdom – acquire wisdom!' Additionally, Wisdom bestows a bounty (4.8-9) and leads one on the way of life, as opposed to the way of folly, which is followed unto destruction. Such is the point of the 'two ways' poems in Prov. 4.10-27, wherein the boy should 'Keep hold of instruction and do not let go; protect her, for she is your life' (4.13). Third, as Aletti points out, the father roots wisdom's eminence and his own words in their divine origin (2.6; Prov. 8): 'la parole du sage est une parole *transmise* (iv 1-4). Le discours du sage et celui des insensés (y compris la femme adultère) diffèrent par leur *origine*. Le discours du sage est un don de Yahweh.'[102] The divine origin, culminating in Proverbs 8, leaves the solution to moral ambiguity clear: 'Tout l'effort rhétorique des chapitres précédents visait à démasquer cette faculté que l'homme a'.[103] Aletti perhaps overstates the significance of 'order' in answering the interpretive

---

102. Aletti, 'Seduction', 141. These aspects of wisdom's superiority all touch on the more fundamental question of wisdom's authority and how the biblical material, as well as other ancient Near Eastern texts, authorized wisdom.

103. Aletti, 'Seduction', 143.

question of moral ambiguity, an emphasis that, as will be argued in the next chapter, should be placed more on a wisdom-mediated relationship with the Lord, but for the present issue, a solution becomes clear.

This solution regards the problem observed above, where sayings like 16.21 and 18.8 liken speech to tasty food, and yet suggest that both wise instruction and murmured gossip taste good to the hearer, constructing a morally ambiguous world where good and bad conflict and leaving the listener at a loss for how to discern what not only tastes good but is good. When read in light of the joint observations gathered from Proverbs 1–9 and the network of goals from the previous section, the solution to the morally ambiguous world encountered in 10–29 lies in the character of the listener who must embrace wisdom in relationship to the Lord and under the teacher's tutelage, and thereby nurture the skill of discernment to ascertain the true quality of speech. Proverbs 1–9, then, shows that only by discernment, a quality of wise character, can someone resist the tasty morsels of the whisperer (18.8) and devour the instruction of the wise (16.23-24). In this way, Collection I functions didactically.

Like Prov. 18.8, Prov. 14.12 portrays a morally ambiguous world where bad things look good: 'there is a way that is straight before a man, but its end is the way of death'. A person sees his way as right and follows it to death, unaware of its true quality. How, then, can the truly right path be determined? Proverbs 14.8 and 14.15 suggest that 'prudent' people can discern the right way, but the sayings do not explain how such discernment functions or where it comes from.[104] I contend that Proverbs 1–9 offers insight into this dilemma: the discernment necessary to know the truly ישר way from the falsely ישר way begins with the father's instruction and the fear of the Lord, leading to the acquisition of wisdom and growth in wise character that she facilitates with the Lord's help. Such human character harbours the moral wherewithal to determine right from wrong, good words from bad, a straight path from an allusion. Proverbs 1–9 supplies an interpretive frame of goals and a solution to moral ambiguity that offer a dynamically coherent reading of sayings like Prov. 14.12 and 18.8.

3.2.4. Conclusion and Implications

Aletti provided an alternative interpretation of Proverbs 1–9 that accounts for its rhetorical aims and dovetails neatly with my earlier section on the aims, values, and educational construct of 1–9. Distinctly, this section of my study used 1–9 as its starting point, and, in the case of this chapter as

---

104. Meinhold (*Sprüche*, 235) remarks that 14.12 'can hardly be squared' with the conception of the two paths in Proverbs 1–9.

3. *Educational Goals*

a whole, the two methods of approaching Proverbs enriched each other. Approaching 10.1–22.16 first, extracting its interpretive questions, and consulting 1–9 as a resource for those questions proved fruitful; likewise, starting with 1–9 and determining its own priorities without the concerns of 10.1–22.16 uncovered unforeseen connections with 10.1–22.16 to expose the didactic function of Proverbs 1–9. Both methods treated themes of rhetoric in Proverbs – how and what it persuades towards – and revolved around its educational goals. My initial interests and argument on these topics show concord with Aletti's interpretation of Proverbs 1–9, all of which have now been integrated and extended to the rest of the book of Proverbs.

Four cases in particular demonstrated the didactic function of Proverbs 1–9 in the realm of educational goals. Proverbs 16.16 and 22.1 confront the interpreter with a choice between values and an unqualified concept of 'fame/reputation' that are respectively organized and deciphered when interpreted in light of Proverbs 2 and 7–8. If forced to choose between wisdom (16.16) and fame (22.1), pick wisdom. As for the neutral repute denoted by שׁם, Proverbs 1–9 qualifies the concept as renown derived from wise character. The next interpretive challenge, found in Prov. 30.1-9, stems from Agur's lament that he has failed to learn wisdom, but it is not clear why this constitutes a problem. Proverbs 1–9 constructs a frame of educational goals that explains Agur's problem by locating it within an overarching aim of the book. Agur bemoans a lack of understanding, not in and of itself but because it attests to his incomplete education in the school of wisdom, echoing the now unfulfilled objectives of 1.2-7. The final two examples, Prov. 14.2 and 18.8, portray the world as morally ambiguous, a characteristic observed first in the poems of Proverbs 1–9, where bad things, especially, can look good. What the sayings in Proverbs 10–30 do not provide, however, is a solution. How do I distinguish the good from the bad when wise instruction and gossip taste delicious (18.8)? And how do I know if the way that, in my eyes, lies 'straight' ahead leads to death instead of life (14.2)? Proverbs 1–9 supplies an answer, instructing the interpreter that only discernment – a part of wise character developed through embracing wisdom with the help of the Lord and the father's teaching – will enable the interpreter to rightly evaluate moral ambiguity.

Proverbs 1–9 continues to function didactically by providing a framework of educational goals and a moral vision of the world that provide interpretive insight for material in Proverbs 10–31. This function is demonstrable when approaching the book of Proverbs from two directions: starting with 10.1–22.16, the primary mode of this study, but also by starting with Proverbs 1–9, methodologies that complement each other and corroborate a consistent relationship for 1–9 and the rest of the book. Moving away from educational goals and moral ambiguity, the next chapter accounts in full for a figure so far mentioned in part: יהוה. By examining the references to him throughout Proverbs, the function of Proverbs 1–9 can be determined from a theological perspective.

4

THEOLOGICAL CONTEXT

The 'Lord' has come up at certain points in this study, but to say that my argument has dealt with the theological context of Proverbs would be an overstatement. In this chapter, I give concentrated attention to the material in Proverbs that mentions the 'Lord' or 'God' and examine the scope of his activity. As with the literary features of Proverbs and the relationships between the book's major sections, the theological material of Proverbs has been considered one of the book's contexts, through which other content can be understood. For some interpreters, this material is explained as a final redactional layer of sayings in the book, and for others one of its constitutive elements, firmly united to 'non-theological' sayings and providing such sayings with a theological colouring.[1] These ongoing debates feature the theological references of Proverbs – namely references to the Lord – as one of the book's many contexts, and the first question that one faces when considering those passages is how they are best approached and organized. Of the 375 proverbs in Prov. 10.1–22.16, fifty-seven refer to the Lord or God, and I suggest that they organize quite neatly into three categories: human postures towards the Lord; the supremacy of his wisdom and sovereignty; and the Lord's affection and assessment.[2]

---

1. See McKane, *Proverbs*, 10, 413–14; Heim, *Grapes*, 316; Katharine Dell, *The Book of Proverbs in Social and Theological Context* (Cambridge: Cambridge University Press, 2006), 108–9.

2. In linear fashion: 10.3, 22, 27, 29; 11.1, 20; 12.2, 22; 14.2, 26, 27, 31; 15.3, 8, 9, 11; 15.16, 25, 26, 29, 33; 16.1-7, 9, 11, 20, 33; 17.3, 5, 15; 18.10, 22; 19.3, 14, 17, 21, 23; 20.10, 12, 22-24, 27; 21.1-3, 30, 31; 22.2, 4, 12, 14. I exclude 21.12, which refers to the 'righteous one', because it may indicate simply a human. If it does refer to the Lord, it would fit in with the Lord's affection and assessment. To Whybray's count of 55 references, I add those that mention the 'Maker' (עשׂה) (14.31; 17.5). For

Human Postures towards the Lord

The Fear of the Lord	15.33; 16.6	10.27; 14.2, 26, 27; 15.16; 19.23; 22.4
Positive and Negative Postures	16.3	10.29; 14.31; 16.20; 17.5; 18.10; 19.3, 17; 20.22

Supremacy of the Lord's Wisdom and Sovereignty

Wisdom	16.1, 9	15.3; 19.21; 20.24, 27; 21.30; 22.12
Sovereignty	16.4	10.3, 22; 15.25; 16.11, 33; 19.14; 20.12; 21.1, 31; 22.2

The Lord's Affection and Assessment

Abomination of the Lord	16.5	11.1, 20; 12.22; 15.8, 9, 26; 17.15; 20.10, 23
General Affection and Assessment	16.2, 7	12.2; 15.11, 29; 17.3; 18.22; 21.2, 3; 22.14

The first set of passages feature human postures towards the Lord, which include references to the 'fear of the Lord', and the attitudes and actions of humans. Postures may be positive, such as those who commit to him (16.3) or wait for him (20.22), or negative, like those who rage against (19.3) or insult the Lord (14.31; 17.5).[3] The second group of texts suggests that the Lord's wisdom and power supersede those of humankind. By wisdom, he keeps omnicompetent watch over people and situations (15.3; 22.12), and he plans with superior skill and insight (e.g. 16.1, 9; 20.24). With supreme sovereignty, he controls or holds the final say in matters of justice (16.11), war (21.13), and daily life (10.3), also operating as an omnipotent creator (16.4; 22.2). Passages in the third group underscore the Lord's emotional posture towards humans or his penetrating evaluation of them, in other words, his affection and assessment. This final category represents all references to the Lord's 'abomination', as well as his favour (12.2; 18.22), acceptance (21.3), anger (22.14), or powers of perception (15.11; 16.2) and its consequences (16.2b; 17.3).

Each of these three categories is represented in a single passage containing the highest concentration of references to the Lord in 10.1–22.16,

---

those who account for the majority of verses with breakdowns slightly different than my own, see Gramberg, *Das Buch*, 2–16; André Lelièvre, *La sagesse des Proverbes: Une leçon de tolérance* (Genève: Labor et Fides, 1993); John W. Miller, *Proverbs* (Scottdale, PA: Herald Press, 2004), 206–17.

3. I include Prov. 10.29, because 'the way of the Lord' and 'refuge' denote the subject's behaviour and trust in the Lord.

what has been called a theological 'kernel': Prov. 15.33–16.9.⁴ The Lord appears in every verse of 15.33–16.9, except for verse 8, which, nevertheless, comfortably integrates into the passage's theological schema. From this kernel I examine three sayings in turn: 16.3 pertains to human postures towards the Lord; 16.9 concerns the supremacy of the Lord's wisdom and sovereignty, to which 22.19 is added in order to extend conclusions beyond 10.1–22.16; and 16.2 deals with the Lord's affection and assessment. As exhibited in previous chapters, the texts of 10.1–22.16 present interpretive challenges and consequently supply interpretive questions that are then posed to Proverbs 1–9. In this section, it will be shown that Proverbs 1–9 furnishes interpretive insight for the theological framework of Proverbs 10–29 and in this way functions didactically. But it will also become clear that this introductory role, in the theological context at least, operates with certain qualifications; the limits of its boundaries will be pushed. Proverbs 1–9 does not answer every question about Proverbs, and even when it does answer questions, which I will argue remain distinctive, other portions of the OT interject.

4.1. *Human Postures towards the Lord*

4.1.1. *Human Postures towards the Lord in Proverbs 16.3*

גל אל־יהוה מעשׂיך	16.3	Commit your works to the Lord
ויכנו מחשבתיך		and your plans will be established.

Like a number of other passages pertaining to human postures towards the Lord (10.29; 18.10; 20.22), Prov. 16.3 baldly commands the interpreter to commit one's works to him. It woodenly reads, 'Roll (*qal* גלל) your works to the Lord', using a verb that clearly connotes 'trust' (Ps. 37.5; cf. 22.8-10) and when negated means 'take away' (Josh. 5.9).⁵ The verse exhorts one to 'roll upon', 'entrust', or 'commit' works to the Lord. These works probably represent all human actions, since within the local literary context they parallel 'plans' and appear with a series of כל in

---

4. Scherer (*Das weise Wort*, 190) notices that the eight occurrences of יהוה in Prov. 15.33–16.7 are not only Collection II's highest concentration of divine references but are 'die längste stichwortbedingte Spruchkette der ganzen Sammlung'.

5. The term גלל need not be emended to גלע (Meinhold, *Sprüche*, 266), and the evidence does not permit us to say that גלל means 'to make one's plans congruent with God's will' (Fox, *Proverbs 10–31*, 609).

16.2, 4-5, suggesting a comprehensive scope.⁶ '*All* the ways of a human are pure in his eyes' (16.2a); 'the Lord made *everything* for its answer' (16.4a); '*everyone* haughty in heart is an abomination to the Lord' (16.5a). Proverbs 16.3 quite plausibly implies, 'Commit *all* your works to the Lord'.⁷ While the verses surrounding 16.3 feature the Lord's supremacy – he seems to make, know and oversee everything – Prov. 16.3 itself, especially its initial injunction, emphasizes the posture of humans towards the Lord. For they should entrust all matters to him, matters he will indeed establish.

The primary interpretive challenge of this saying stems not from what it denotes – the semantic features come across clearly – but rather from what it connotes, implies, or assumes. By commanding humans to trust the Lord, Prov. 16.3 assumes that the Lord is worthy of human trust, a presupposition evident in other references to the Lord in 10.1–22.16, which liken the Lord to a stronghold (10.29; 18.10) or commend interpreters to 'wait for the Lord', who will assuredly 'help' them (20.22). A number of other explanations for why the Lord might deserve trust also appear in Collection II: the Lord is wise and in control (16.1, 9); he dispenses hatred and favour and punishment to humans (16.5; 12.2; 21.3); perhaps most plainly, and economically, he will 'establish your plans' (16.3b).⁸ These texts establish a notably affective and transcendent God, yet, outside of his bald power and recompense, they offer little incentive to trust him. The assumption of God's trustworthiness might be explained by the identity of the text's historical audience, if it includes those of the covenant community who could have drawn upon additional theological knowledge to ground their trust in the Lord. The proverb's ties with other OT texts support the possibility, that one might trust the Lord due to a broad conception of his theological might.

Within the OT and outside of Prov. 16.3, the lexeme גלל occurs in the imperative *qal* five times, twice commanding people to 'roll' a large stone (Josh. 10.18; 1 Sam. 14.33) and three times in Psalms, one of which requests that God would 'take away from me' (גל מעלי) the scorn and contempt of insolent people (119.22). The two remaining uses of גלל in

---

6. Heim, *Grapes*, 209; Delitzsch, *Proverbs*, 1:336. For 'plans' and 'establish' see Prov. 16.9 in section 4.2.1.

7. Scherer (*Das weise Wort*, 194) rightly notes the phonic pattern created by the repeated כל in 16.2-5 to which גל contributes.

8. The 'steadfast love and faithfulness' in Prov. 16.6, which could be the Lord's and thereby incentives to trust him, remain too ambiguous to offer authoritative help with addressing the question of 16.3.

Psalms resemble its use in Prov. 16.3. In Ps. 22.9[8] the psalmist recalls the taunts of others who say 'Trust (גל) in the Lord; let Him deliver him; let Him rescue him; for He delights in him'. The jeers imply that the psalmist might trust the Lord because of the Lord's ability to rescue him and delight in him. One wonders whether these jeers reflect grounds with which the psalmist would agree or grounds misapplied by his enemies. It seems that the jeers most likely represent the psalmist's beliefs, albeit those he currently struggles to believe, which are then deployed by his enemies as ammunition for mockery.[9] Elsewhere in the psalm, the psalmist appeals to the trust that his ancestors had in the Lord and the consequent salvation that God performed for them (22.5-6[4-5]), while he later bids that the congregation fear and praise the Lord on grounds that the Lord did not hide his face from the psalmist but responded to his cry (22.24-25[23-24]).

The *qal* imperative of גלל also occurs in Ps. 37.5, where the psalmist enjoins the congregation to trust the Lord rather than envy wrongdoers. The psalm contains significant lexical links with language prominent in Proverbs: 'your way', דרכך (v. 5); the 'wicked' and 'righteous', צדיק/רשע (v. 12); the righteous speaking 'wisdom', חכמה (v. 30); and the 'upright', ישר (v. 37).[10] The grounds for the imperative 'Commit your way to the Lord' in Ps. 37.5a seems to be that God will indeed act, as the following line says: 'Trust (בטח) in him and he will act'. He will also make the vindication of those who trust in him brilliant (v. 6) and, as other parts of the psalm indicate, he knows the days of the blameless (v. 18) and will rescue those who take refuge in him (v. 40).[11] If posed with the question, 'why trust the Lord?', the author(s) of Psalms 22 and 37 may, in summary, reply, 'because he responds with salvation; he hears his people in whom he delights, and he acts for them'.

It would be inappropriate to evaluate the sufficiency of these reasons for trusting the Lord, but it is not out of place to say that they offer an alternative perspective to the transcendent, albeit emotional, God of Prov. 10.1–22.16. In Psalms he is powerful, knowledgeable and ready for

---

9. John Goldingay, *Psalms*. Vol. 1, *Psalms 1–41*, BCOT (Grand Rapids, MI: Baker Academic, 2006), 330.

10. Cf. Ps. 37.6, 28-29 and Prov. 2.21-22; 4.18.

11. For a maximal interpretation of Psalm 37 as a psalm concerned with wisdom, see Simon Cheung (*Wisdom Intoned: A Reappraisal of the Genre 'Wisdom Psalms'*, LHBOTS 613 [London: Bloomsbury T&T Clark, 2015], 53–78, esp. 70–1), who reasonably holds that the theme of trusting the Lord features in Ps. 37.1-6 and that the clauses in verses 4b and 6 undergird the call to trust him in verse 5.

action.¹² On initial evaluation, the lexical and thematic links with Psalm 37 do inform the interpretation of 16.3, and they establish a potentially significant connection for an intertextual study of Proverbs and the OT. We could also move beyond the particular lexical link of גלל and consider the question – why trust the Lord? – based on all lexemes for 'trust' or on other pertinent evidence in the OT that offers an answer to this question. Although that would be a valid way to go about answering the question, and may produce a result just as good as Proverbs 1–9, Proverbs 1–9 must still be accounted for. The interpretive challenge of 16.3 remains, and so I turn now to Proverbs 1–9 to examine its reasons for trusting the Lord.

4.1.2. *Human Postures towards the Lord in Proverbs 1–9*

Proverbs 1–9 is averse neither to the concept of God nor to the act of trusting him. Each chapter, except for Proverbs 4 and 7, mentions 'the Lord' or 'God' at least once, with the references totalling 22.¹³ A particularly good example arises in Prov. 3.1-12, when, in 3.5, the Proverbial father says to his son, 'Trust (בטח) in the Lord with all your heart, and on your own understanding do not lean'. The command arrives within a lecture about the relationship between the son and the Lord that begins with a call to cherish the father's instructions (3.1-3) and notice their consequences: 'So you will find favour and good success in the eyes of God and humankind' (3.4). This initial mention of God (אלהים) transitions to a series of references to the Lord (יהוה) at 3.5 and follows with seven direct or indirect references to him in 3.6-12. In summary: the son will find favour in the eyes of God (3.4); he should 'trust in the Lord' (3.5), acknowledge him (3.6a), and the Lord will make straight his paths (3.6b). The Lord is to be feared (3.7) and honoured (3.8); he disciplines, reproves, loves and delights in the son (3.11-12).

---

12. Scherer's (*Das weise Wort*, 194) observation about the phonic connections in Prov. 16.2-5, noted earlier, support the possibility that גל was selected for 16.3 because of its phonic qualities, which, from a diachronic perspective, would possibly lessen its connection with Psalm 37 for those arguing that this portion of Proverbs developed later. However, placing the lexeme after the first use of כל, instead of in verse 4 or 5 after the pattern establishes itself, weakens the explanation that the lexeme appears for phonological reasons (see Keefer, 'Sound Patterns', 35–49; Thomas McCreesh, *Biblical Sound and Sense: Poetic Sound Patterns in Proverbs 10–29* [Sheffield: JSOT Press, 1991], 34). Cf. another rare lexeme in Ps 37.4 (ענג) and Job 22.26; 27.10.

13. Proverbs 1.7, 29; 2.5-6, 17; 3.4-5, 7, 9, 11-12, 19, 26, 32-33; 5.21; 6.16; 8.13, 22, 35; 9.10.

When posed with the question, why trust in the Lord?, Prov. 3.5-12 discloses answers that resemble those found in Prov. 10.1–22.16.[14] The Lord deserves trust because of his supreme wisdom, given the fact that the son should neither rely on his own insight (בינה; 3.5b) nor be wise in his own eyes (היה חכם; 3.7a) but rather trust the Lord and fear him (3.5a, 7b). The Lord also deserves trust because of his supreme control over situations, since he can straighten the son's paths (3.6b).[15] Finally, the Lord deserves trust because of the consequences of relying upon him, since, by implication he heals the son (3.8) and supplies him with abundant resources (3.9-10). The incentives to trust the Lord in 3.5-10 add little to the incentives brought forward by 10.1–22.16, not least 15.33–16.9 itself, which mentions supreme wisdom, superior control, and favourable consequences. However, 3.1-12 supplies something that the other portions of Proverbs and the Psalms mentioned above do not, and it appears in its concluding verses:

מוסר יהוה בני אל־תמאס	3.11	My son, do not reject the Lord's discipline,
ואל־תקץ בתוכחתו		and do not loathe his reproof.
כי את אשר יאהב יהוה יוכיח	3.12	For the one whom the Lord loves, he reproves,
וכאב את־בן ירצה		like a father the son in whom he delights.

The passage reiterates the address to 'my son' (בני; v. 11), which began Proverbs 3 (v. 1), and encourages him to not despise the Lord's reproof. To encourage the boy amidst such discipline, the father underscores the Lord's love and likens it to a father's, 'for the one whom the Lord loves, he reproves, like a father the son in whom he delights' (v. 12).[16] The

---

14. Proverbs 3.21-26 mentions security and the Lord. I only briefly note that at the end of the pericope in 3.26a, the emphatic position of the Lord (כי יהוה יהיה בכסלך) indicates that he is the pinnacle of confidence. Due to the positive language of security and contrasting fear of the storm, the only alternative is to trust him. These features corroborate a didactic intent of the theological context in Proverbs 3.

15. This is reflected in Proverbs 2, where the reasons to pursue wisdom (2.6) include that the Lord gives wisdom (2.6) and stores it (2.7a); he is a shield (2.7b) and guards both paths and people (2.8), protecting his people from the evil way, evil men and women (2.12, 16).

16. Proverbs 3.1-12 forms a separate section because of the distribution of בן (vv. 1, 11, 12), the concentration of references to the Lord, and the independence of 3.13-18, based on אשר (vv. 13, 18) and its topic of Wisdom. Though occupied with redactional issues, Schäfer (*Die Poesie*, 78–90) sees 3.5-12 as unfolding a theological dimension of the 'steadfast love and faithfulness' of 3.3.

son should trust the Lord, not least during difficulty, because the Lord loves and cares for him, like a father who delights in his child.[17] In Louis Derousseaux's words, this is 'la pedagogie divine paternalle',[18] and the divine fatherhood here does not spotlight transcendence or power, nor even simply historical activity, but rather the affective, familial care of a father for his son. When Prov. 3.1-12 is read as a frame for 16.3, it incorporates these paternal incentives to 'commit' one's works to the Lord with those supplied by 10.1–22.16, not only cohering with the Lord's supreme wisdom and knowledge and his dispensation of consequences, but adding to these. 'Commit your works to the Lord' (16.3a), not only because the Lord is omnipotent and omniscient but also because he cares about those who trust him. Proverbs 1–9 supplements the reasons to trust the Lord found elsewhere by incorporating God's love as a motivator. By implication, the 'plans' that 'will be established' in 16.3b, most likely by the Lord, include not only the sensible and certain scenarios that flow from a wise and powerful God, but also benevolent plans of the sort that a happy father might envision for his son.

Psalm 16.3 occurs within the theological 'kernel' of Prov. 10.1–22.16 and instates a bald command to 'trust the Lord'. The verse's local and wider literary contexts offer certain incentives to trust, reasons based on what might be labelled God's 'transcendent' nature, and such reasons are matched by Prov. 3.1-12, which contains a high concentration of references to God and also affirms his transcendence. However, 3.1-12 also supplies reasons to trust God based on his more 'immanent' characteristics, namely, his love and delight for humans as conveyed through a familial metaphor.[19] In the Psalms, too, we are told that the Lord is worthy of trust because he is the sort of God who saves his people and acts on their behalf, being holy and the one to whom kingship belongs. None of these descriptors arises in Proverbs 1–9, and each of them plausibly contributes to the interpretation of Prov. 16.3. But Proverbs 1–9 still retains something that these relevant

---

17. Proverbs 3.11-12 recalls Job 5.17, and aside from issues of date or influence, Job's theological point supports the conclusion that even without explicit disobedience to God, his people suffer under his fatherly love. While possibly stated at an inopportune time, Eliphaz tells Job that 'blessed is the one whom God corrects' (Job 5.17). Elsewhere, as a father, God corrects the king as son, a trying process but not without sustained steadfast love to his people and purpose (2 Sam. 7.14-16).

18. Louis Derousseaux, *La crainte de Dieu dans l'Ancien Testament: royauté, alliance, sagesse dans les royaumes d'Israël et de Juda* (Paris: Éditions du Cerf, 1970), 328.

19. Perhaps this insight offers evidence in favour of reading the 'steadfast love and faithfulness' in Prov. 16.6 as qualities of the Lord.

Psalms do not – paternal imagery for an adoring Lord – and consequently makes a distinctive deposit to the meaning of the proverb. Proverbs 1–9, therefore, gives the interpreter theological categories both coherent with and supplementary to 10.1–22.16, offering a new way of interpreting 16.3 and proverbs like it. For, as an introduction, those chapters portray the Lord in a way that might spur readers on to seize him as a stronghold (10.29), trust him (16.20), find asylum in him as a strong tower (18.10), and wait patiently for his deliverance (20.22).

4.2. *The Supremacy of the Lord's Wisdom and Sovereignty*

The previous section considered a single interpretive question from a single proverb that represents one of three theological categories in Proverbs: human postures towards the Lord. Proverbs 16.3, taken from Collection II's theological 'kernel' (15.33–16.9), demonstrated the didactic function of Proverbs 1–9 for this theological category. The current section explores another category of theological sayings in 10.1–22.16 and again uses a representative example – Prov. 16.9 – for the group, which contains proverbs that pertain to God's wisdom and sovereignty.

4.2.1. *Wisdom and Sovereignty in Proverbs 16.9*

| לב אדם יחשב דרכו | 16.9 | The heart of man plans his way |
| ויהוה יכין צעדו | | while the Lord establishes his steps |

Proverbs 16.9 relays the supremacy of God's wisdom and sovereignty, a supremacy, that is, relative to a human's: 'The heart of man plans his way, while the Lord establishes his steps'. With *piel* חשב, the first line conveys a primarily cognitive notion of human planning that often indicates evil scheming (e.g. Prov. 24.8; Nah. 1.9; Dan. 11.24). These problematic instances, though, are often grammatically qualified by a preposition to designate that a human schemes 'against' someone else, as Prov. 24.8 similarly states, 'Whoever plans to do evil (מחשב להרע), he will be called a schemer' (so Hos. 7.15). More broadly, and most likely in Prov. 16.9, the verb means 'consider/think' or 'plan', without a positive or negative connotation, such as when the psalmist 'thinks about' his ways (119.59) or 'considers the days of old' (Ps. 77.6[5]; cf. Pss 73.16; 144.3). The *piel* חשב in Prov. 16.9 portrays a human thinking about, possibly planning, his way in life, not necessarily with malicious or autonomous intent, but certainly by exerting the knowledge that he possesses: 'the heart of man plans his way'.

The second line says that 'the Lord establishes his steps'. When the Lord 'establishes' (*hiphil* כון) something, he arranges and sets it in place (Prov. 8.27; Ps. 65.6), prepares it (Zeph. 1.7; cf. Prov. 6.8; 24.27), and sometimes morally fortifies the ways of his followers (Ps. 119.133; cf. Ps. 10.17). All senses carry a notion of permanence, and the sense of 'arrange' probably fits best with the context of human plans in 16.9.[20] So the Lord permanently arranges someone's steps while the human thinks about or plans them. Although most of the semantics of this proverb are clear, a few observations and interpretive challenges remain. First, Prov. 16.9 combines both features of its theological category (wisdom and sovereignty), incorporating human knowledge (i.e. 'wisdom') and divine control, a control that, it seems, exceeds the human's and also entails divine knowledge. If the Lord 'arranges' the ways of humankind by his supreme power, he surely possesses the cognitive wherewithal to do so. Given the fact that the human in 16.9 'considers' his own way, the proverb presumes that the Lord considers it even more and thereby incorporates divine wisdom and sovereignty.

Second, while Prov. 16.9 contains discernible lexemes and exemplifies the Lord's wisdom and sovereignty, it also offers an interpretive challenge, one that arises from the relationship of its lines, manifesting a significant theological question. The question is exemplified in, though not reducible to, the interpretation of the *waw* that joins the two lines, which may translate as 'but' or 'and' or 'while', the latter of which would capture both 'but/and' senses. The *waw* may render, 'The heart of man plans his way *but* the Lord establishes his steps', indicating a disjunction between human plans and divine arrangement. Yet the *waw* may render, 'The heart of man plans his way *and* the Lord establishes his steps', conveying a complementary relationship between human plans and divine arrangement. Both remain open possibilities if the passage is interpreted as '*while* the Lord establishes his steps' and highlight the primary issue at hand, which is one of theological ambiguity. The passages surrounding Prov. 16.9 offer little clarification on the ambiguous nature of how its lines relate. The content of 15.32 indicates that two lines may unmistakably contrast, as ignoring instruction and despising oneself clearly oppose the image of one listening to reproof and acquiring intelligence. 'The one who ignores instruction despises himself, but the one who listens to reproof acquires intelligence'. Other proverbs use the second line to affirm the first, for committing one's works to the Lord results in one's plans being established (16.3; so 16.6). Finally, many lines reflect the ambiguity of

---

20. See Elmer Martens, 'כון', *NIDOTTE* 1:615–17. In Prov. 16.9, a man's 'way' parallels his 'steps', suggesting that the latter is a manner of life or course of action.

16.9. 'The plans of the heart belong to a man, *while* from the Lord is the answer of the tongue. All the ways of a man are pure in his eyes, *while* the Lord weighs spirits' (16.1-2). These proverbs suggest at least a contrast between God and humans, and the syntactical priority of 'from the Lord' in 16.1 suggests that God is ultimately authoritative, and yet they remain ambiguous as to whether the relationship is one of harmony or discord, with the grammatical features and surrounding passages offering little clarity on the issue.[21]

Claus Westermann discusses many of the sayings that comprise this category, which I have called 'The Supremacy of the Lord's Wisdom and Sovereignty', a title he would probably replace with 'Gott und sein Wirken als Grenze menschlicher Möglichkeiten', with which he heads his section on these passages.[22] His title summarizes his theological point – these proverbs address human limitations in view of God's capabilities – and unsurprisingly leads him to interpret the lines of 16.9 as a contrast ('but/aber'), for at least two reasons.[23] First, Westermann seems to assume a negative view of humanity, underscoring not only their 'limitations' but also implying a misguided response to those limitations, concluding that 'Alle diese Sprüche wurden je in besondere Situationen hinein gesprochen, in denen es notwendig war, dies auszusprechen an die Adresse eines, der gerade diese Grenze zu vergessen oder zu mißachten im Begriff war'.[24] Such a negative interpretation of human limitations also stems from Westermann's emphasis on God's role as creator. Referring to Prov. 15.11, he asserts that such statements can be made, 'weil Jahwe

---

21. Proverbs 16.1 reads, לאדם מערכי־לב ומיהוה מענה לשון. Scherer (*Das weise Wort*, 196), for instance, identifying links between 16.9 and 16.1-3, asserts that an antithetic structure is recognizable in 16.1-2 and 16.9. While I find the case more complicated as argued above, Scherer (202–5) rightly argues against Thomas Pola, who proposes a connection between Psalm 132 and Prov. 16.1-15 (see Thomas Pola, 'Die Struktur von Proverbia 16,1-15', *Biblische Notizen* 80 [1995]: 47–72). Meinhold (*Sprüche*, 266) identifies an interpretive issue in Prov. 16.3 similar to what I have observed in 16.9.

22. Westermann, *Wurzeln*, 137.

23. Westermann, *Wurzeln*, 137. He says, 'einem Tatbestand oder einer Absicht aufseiten des Menschen steht ein „Aber" Gottes entgegen. Dieses „Aber" weist auf die Grenzen, die dem Menschen gesetzt sind.'

24. Westermann, *Wurzeln*, 138. In this vein, Meinhold (*Sprüche*, 269) cites *Ani* 8.9-10 and *Amenemope* XIX.16-17. Gerhard von Rad's (*Wisdom in Israel*, trans. James Martin [London: SCM Press, 1972], 97–106) interpretation of 16.9 and related sayings entails a similar pessimism but underscores the incomprehensibility of God's ways rather than what humans do not know, ought to know or could know. Such sayings imply that humans ought to remain 'open to the activity of God' (101).

der Schöpfer des Menschen ebenso wie der Schöpfer des Alls ist'.[25] Westermann's strictly pessimistic view of the contrast in 16.9 arises in part from his assumptions about human limitations and the proverbs that address them, yet also from theological views presumably based on proverbs about God's role as creator.

I do not question the place of human 'limitations' in these proverbs, as my title for this section suggests; the Lord's supremacy in wisdom and sovereignty implies an inferiority in human wisdom and power. However, I do question Westermann's anthropological conclusion, that these proverbs address 'someone who was about to forget this boundary or limitation', which justifies a contrast ('but') in the lines of 16.9. Might the ambiguity of the lines' relationship, which may in fact render the observation that humans plan their ways *and* the Lord establishes their steps, provide an alternative to Westermann's interpretation? Perhaps Prov. 16.9 indicates that humans consider their lives in accordance with God, who thereby arranges and establishes their plans. These possibilities reveal the more fundamental interpretive challenge of 16.9, that is, what is the relationship between human wisdom and power, and divine wisdom and power? The preceding discussion shows that they may be at odds with or complement each other, and either option leaves much about the relationship unclear. Other sayings that champion the Lord's wisdom and sovereignty only compound the issue: in Prov. 21.30, 'There is no wisdom, no understanding, no counsel against the Lord', and 20.24 nearly states the question for us: 'A man's steps are from the Lord; but a man, how can he understand his way?' What is the relationship of humans and the Lord with respect to the main topics of this section: wisdom and sovereignty? Proverbs 1–9 offers some intriguing insights into the question.

4.2.2. *Wisdom and Sovereignty in Proverbs 1–9*

Before examining the Lord's wisdom and sovereignty in Proverbs 1–9, we should consider the nature of wisdom itself in 1–9, particularly whether or not any other types of wisdom, such as human wisdom or 'Wisdom's' wisdom, appear in these chapters and how they relate to the Lord's. According to Collection I, the Lord possesses wisdom, gives (2.6) and originates it (8.22-31), even, it seems, making 'wisdom' exclusively his own: 'for the Lord gives wisdom, and, from his mouth, knowledge and understanding' (2.6). The author of this passage does not pit divine wisdom over and against human wisdom but knows only one, a position consistent with the rest of Proverbs 1–9. Proverbs 5.1 mentions 'my

---

25. Westermann, *Wurzeln*, 138. Proverbs 15.11 says, 'Sheol and Abaddon lie open before the Lord; how much more the hearts of the children of man!' (ESV).

wisdom' and 'my understanding' to refer to the father's teachings, which are not contrasted to God's wisdom but equated to it (2.1-2). In Prov. 8.9, Wisdom claims her words are 'right to him who understands', implying a knowledge that precedes wisdom and might rival the wisdom of God, but the 'one who understands' in 8.9 refers to one already wise and so perceptive of Wisdom's words.[26] Proverbs 1–9, therefore, does not distinguish two different forms of wisdom (or understanding); one type is maintained, and only wickedness and foolishness stand as alternatives.

Proverbs 1–9 does acknowledge limits to human knowledge, namely, normal, creaturely limitations, such as the inability to know what happens during sleep (3.24), but otherwise, these chapters emphasize that humans limit their knowledge due to arrogance. In 3.5b and 3.7a, for example, the father forbids that the son put his own wisdom in place of God's. The son ought to trust the Lord's understanding instead of arrogantly trusting his own. Along with arrogance, humans limit their knowledge by inattention and thereby fail to acquire God's wisdom, as 5.13-14 indicates: 'I did not listen to the voice of my teachers or incline my ear to my instructors. I was quickly in all evil, in the midst of the assembly and congregation.'[27] To the interpretive question under consideration – how does Proverbs 1–9 view the supremacy of the Lord's wisdom and the place of humankind's? – these passages offer the initial answer: God's wisdom constitutes the only wisdom of Proverbs 1–9, and it supersedes the knowledge of humans, who limit their acquisition of it through arrogance and inattention.

Honing an answer to the interpretive question of Prov. 16.9, Proverbs 1–9 underscores the Lord's sovereignty in primarily two passages: 3.19-20 and 8.22-31. The first, 3.19-20, presents God's wisdom and sovereignty together to forward its central point: wisdom is an instrument of God's creative and sovereign activity.[28]

יהוה בחכמה יסד־ארץ	3.19	The Lord, by wisdom, founded the earth;
כונן שמים בתבונה		he established the heavens by understanding.
בדעתו תהומות נבקעו	3.20	By his knowledge the deeps were split;
ושחקים ירעפו־טל		and the clouds dropped dew.

26. Fox, *Proverbs 1–9*, 190.

27. The lexeme כמעט often means 'almost', but here, as in Pss. 2.12 and 81.15[14], it means 'quickly/soon' (Fox, *Proverbs 1–9*, 198; Fox also cites Isa. 1.9 for support, but 'few' seems to better suit the passage unless the *atnach* is moved back to שׂריד).

28. Sæbø (*Sprüche*, 69–71) argues that all four instructions of Proverbs 3 converge on the emphasis of the Lord's sovereignty and primacy, with wisdom and human belief as main themes.

The repetitive *by* (ב) wisdom signals an instrumental sense, where wisdom operates as the means or aid that facilitates God's creative work. As an instrument, wisdom is a point of connection between God and his creation. This portrayal of divine wisdom in 3.19-20 is followed in 3.21-26 with implications for the proverbial son: 'keep sound wisdom and discretion' (3.21b).[29] The father, in this passage, does not bid the son to trust the Lord or acknowledge him as the source of prosperity like he did in 3.1-12.[30] Instead, he bids his boy to heed wisdom and goes on to portray her steadfast advantages, saying that if he will keep wisdom 'then you will walk on your way securely, and your foot will not stumble' (3.23). Wisdom will protect the son and keep him safe (3.24). A similar promise of security appears in the next verses, when the father tells his son not to fear sudden trouble (3.25): 'For the Lord will be your confidence, and he will keep your foot from capture' (3.26). In this verse, it is no longer wisdom but the Lord who protects the son, affirming that wisdom and the Lord complement each other with parallel roles.

Objecting to the complementary roles of wisdom and the Lord in Prov. 3.21-26, Whybray argues that wisdom will 'infallibly protect' the son and that God's protection marks an unrelated alternative:

> These verses [3.25-26] form a kind of appendix to vv. 21-4, but one which is somewhat at variance with their message. In v. 25 panic (*paḥad*) clearly picks up the verb (*pāḥad*) of v. 24a; but since the pupil or reader has already been assured that constant attention to 'sound wisdom and discretion' will infallibly preserve him from such fear, this additional admonition is redundant. Then in v. 26 Yahweh is suddenly and belatedly introduced as providing an alternative reason for confidence, with no attempt to indicate that he is in any way connected with the above 'sound wisdom'.[31]

Rather than the incoherence proposed by Whybray, I would argue that the passage conveys that as the Lord protects, so God-given wisdom

---

29. Schäfer (*Die Poesie*, 93–6) links Prov. 3.19-20 more closely with 3.13-18. While these texts do share themes and lexemes related to creation, Prov. 3.13-18 nevertheless corroborates my point for wisdom as a mediator (e.g. Fox [*Proverbs 1–9*, 160] labels vv. 13-18 as the usefulness of wisdom for man, and vv. 19-20 as the usefulness of wisdom for God). I focus on 3.21-26 because of its imperative mood, which aims to instil the preceding reflections didactically, and its climactic nature, as it completes a logical progression from vv. 13-18 and vv. 19-20, especially evident in the verbs of vv. 13, 18, and 21 (see Waltke, *Proverbs 1–15*, 255–6).

30. See section 4.1.

31. Whybray, *Proverbs*, 71.

constitutes a means of protection. Wisdom cooperates with the Lord, as she did at creation (3.19-20), and serves as the connective tissue for God and humanity.[32]

This description hints at what some interpreters, as early as the 1920s, have called the 'mediating' role of wisdom in Proverbs 1–9, exhibited most clearly through Wisdom's appearance in Proverbs 8, the second text that addresses the interpretive question under discussion.[33] In Prov. 8.22-31, Wisdom speaks about God creating the earth and about how she fitted into that activity. She accentuates her antiquity (vv. 22-29) and also her affections: she was God's 'delight' everyday and 'rejoiced' in the world and humankind (vv. 30-31).[34] This passage garners most attention, especially recently, due to its significance for a 'creation order', which interpreters often attempt to align with a moral order.[35] Accounting for the ordering activities of God, Aletti nevertheless argues that the passage focuses on wisdom and her role for humankind, concluding that it enforces 'la mediation de la sagesse', as she functions as the mediator between God and humans.[36]

---

32. Étienne-Noël Bassoumboul (*Des sagesses à la sagesse: Étude de l'unité sapientielle en Pr 1–9* [Paris: J. Gabalda, 2008], 166) affirms the instrumental sense of ב and the section's purpose (Prov. 3.13-20) to underscore the preferability of wisdom. From a direction different than mine, Bassoumboul argues that 3.11-20 produces a hierarchy of humans, wisdom and the Lord, where the Lord's correction begets wisdom, which functions as his instrument of creation and as inseparable from human life, so that, in brief, 'la sagesse conduit à YHWH' (167; see also 161–7). Cf. Roland E. Murphy ('Wisdom and Creation', *JBL* 104 [1985]: 9) who follows von Rad.

33. For a review of the discussion, see Gerlinde Baumann, *Die Weisheitsgestalt in Proverbien 1–9: Traditionsgeschichtliche und Theologische Studien* (Tübingen: J. C. B. Mohr, 1996), 42–3, 50–4, also 291–4. Since Heinrich in the 1920s, the discussion has focused on the literary aspects of Prov. 8.22-31 (e.g. Aletti; Yee; see below), the significance of Wisdom's image for the historical context of Proverbs (Camp, *Wisdom*, 272–82), and notions of creation and social order (Dell, *Proverbs*, 139–46). However, it remains to be seen how Wisdom as mediator might inform the interpretation of the book of Proverbs.

34. Proverbs 8.30a may add that she was God's 'workman' (for discussion, see Loader, *Proverbs 1–9*, 356–60).

35. See Lennart Boström, *The God of the Sages: The Portrayal of God in the Book of Proverbs* (Stockholm: Almqvist & Wiksell International, 1990), 53; Waltke, *Proverbs 1–15*, 414–15; cf. Weeks, *Introduction*, 112–13.

36. Jean-Nöel Aletti, 'Proverbes 8, 22-31. Étude de structure', *Biblica* 57 (1976): 25–37; 'the mediation of wisdom'.

I set aside notions of order and pick up the concept of mediator observed here, because it seems to better reflect the concerns of the author(s) of Proverbs. The author of Proverbs 8 does not broach the concept of sovereignty to acclaim God as creative orderer but rather to extol wisdom, as Fox writes, 'Everything in the chapter serves the rhetorical goal of influencing the reader to desire wisdom.... The description of creation, which is just an elaboration of v 22, adds no new information. Its purpose is to heighten Wisdom's grandeur by describing the glorious works *to which God gave her precedence.*'[37] According to Fox, humans ought to desire and attain Wisdom, who is sovereignly and creatively used by God. She is also, I would add, the mediator between humanity and God himself. Before and after 8.22-31, Wisdom calls her audience to grasp her, as the supplier of life's good gifts (8.18-21) and again aligned with the Lord.[38] Proverbs 8.35 even says that the one who finds her 'finds life and obtains favour from the Lord'. In other words, come to Wisdom and receive from God; for she mediates divine blessing.

4.2.3. *The Function of Proverbs 1–9 for 16.9*

I have not been attempting to drive a wedge between God and humanity or to divorce any notion of order from Proverbs 1–9, rather I have been attempting to locate the author's primary concerns about the relationship between God and humans within passages that feature the Lord's supreme sovereignty. These passages, Prov. 3.19-26 and 8.22-36, intimate that between God and humanity stands wisdom, or, more accurately, that God and humanity share a close proximity but their relationship is facilitated by wisdom. Like God, she protects humankind and bestows blessings, and humans who approach her tend to find the Lord. In summary, Proverbs 1–9 presents God's wisdom as the only wisdom, with folly, arrogance, and inattention as its only alternatives. Consequently, the Lord's sovereignty

---

37. Fox, *Proverbs 1–9*, 289, 293. So Weeks, *Instruction*, 101, 123. Cf. Leo G. Perdue, *Wisdom & Creation: The Theology of Wisdom Literature* (Nashville, TN: Abingdon Press, 1994), 84; Gilbert, *L'Antique sagesse*, 206.

38. The Lord and wisdom also combine under the guise of sovereignty in Proverbs 2, aligned here as protectors. God is 'a shield for those who walk in integrity' (2.7b, see vv. 6-8), yet 'discretion will watch over you, understanding will guard you' (2.11, see vv. 10-12). Likewise, in Prov. 3.19-20 as the Lord protects, so God-given wisdom constitutes a means of protection, and in 3.11-12 when the blessings of wisdom do not appear as they should, humans can rely on the Lord (see Plöger, *Sprüche*, 39–40). Proverbs 2, 3 and 8 incorporate God's sovereignty to esteem wisdom's worth and parallel it with the Lord's role as protector.

is abler than humankind's to navigate life, so the greatest responsibility lies on humans to listen to, embrace, and use wisdom while trusting God's superior control and understanding. Wisdom functions in tandem with the Lord to protect humans and guide their way, yet she functions as a divine partner so accessible to human beings, the mediator between God and humankind.

That formulation from Proverbs 1–9 should not be understated. For it is not so readily or specifically articulable based on Proverbs 10–29, and it supports the case that Proverbs 1–9 supplies interpretive insight into 16.9, which is representative of close to twenty proverbs from 10.1–22.16 that feature the supremacy of the Lord's wisdom and sovereignty but do not expound upon how these qualities relate to their human counterparts. The problem was manifested in, though not restricted to, an ambiguous relation of lines in 16.9, namely, 'The heart of man plans his way *while* the Lord establishes his steps', leaving open the possibilities that human plans counter the Lord's or accord with them. Westermann opts for the former, presuming a depraved view of humankind, who tend to overestimate their capabilities. His interpretation requires all proverbs relevant to the subject to be spoken 'to someone who was about to forget or disregard this boundary/limit [Grenze]'. Does reading Proverbs 1–9 as an interpretive framework cohere with such a conclusion? It does, in part, by suggesting that humans may reject the Lord's wisdom in preference of their own 'wisdom' and thereby need to hear 16.9 as a warning: the Lord 'establishes man's steps', and he overrides arrogant or ungodly humans who 'plan their own ways'. However, complementing the need for humility because of God's supreme wisdom and sovereignty, Proverbs 1–9 also portrays a positive relationship between God's governance and his gift of wisdom. Wisdom, as a mediator, enables humans to plan their ways in cooperation with the Lord. Consequently, Prov. 16.9 would actually boost confidence for humans who consider their plans with God-given wisdom, plans which the Lord himself may establish. 'The heart of man plans his way [with wisdom] *and* the Lord establishes his steps.'

Proverbs 1–9 substantiates both interpretations, a conclusion that may seem to offer nothing near a profound interpretive insight. For, in previous examples, Proverbs 1–9 seems to point towards one of several possible interpretations raised by 10–29, supplying interpretive insight by decisively directing readers towards the most plausible hermeneutical option. But in this case, Proverbs 1–9 seems to confirm ambiguity, to point fingers in two directions rather than one and to offer no real help at all for better understanding Prov. 16.9. That apparent concern, though, is no real problem. First, it is important to clarify that, in this case, Proverbs 1–9 is not introducing ambiguity; the proverb is already ambiguous and 1–9 at most coheres with that ambiguity. Second, in corroborating the ambiguity of 16.9, Proverbs 1–9 (a) displays its theological coherence with other portions of Proverbs and (b) manifests a limitation in its introductory role. It does not answer each and every hermeneutical question raised by 10–29, and by selecting this example I hope to ensure that that point is made.

Third, despite the fact that 1–9 confirms one aspect of ambiguity in 16.9 and pushes the boundaries of its introductory function, it nonetheless offers a distinctive insight into the saying and removes one of its obscurities, namely, the unspecified relationship between humans and God. For what has become clear and incredibly interesting is the degree of insight that 1–9 gives into the theological backcloth of the two possible interpretations of 16.9. In this way it 'fills the gaps' of sayings that state terse observations about human beings and the supreme capabilities of God. When the 'plans of the heart belong to a man' (16.1) or 'the heart of man plans his way' (16.9), someone may be planning life based on his or her own wisdom instead of the Lord's and thereby confront the oppositional plans of God who establishes his own way. As specified in 1–9, the 'wisdom' that might counter God's is one's own, and in those chapters one is deterred from planning life based upon it. But when humans plan based on God-given wisdom, then the human–divine relationship becomes one of concord. That possibility is ambiguously stated in 10–29 and emphatically detailed in 1–9; Wisdom mediates between humans and God for those who embrace her. It seems that God's wisdom, rather than soaring over the capacities of human beings, fills these gaps and facilitates interaction between God and humankind.

4.2.4. *Summary of Proverbs 16.3 and 16.9*

Two passages from Prov. 10.1–22.16 representative of its references to the Lord have been interpreted in light of Proverbs 1–9 to demonstrate its didactic function. The first section showed how 16.3 baldly commands the interpreter to commit one's works to the Lord and, like other sayings that portray human postures towards the Lord, thereby assumes that the Lord is trustworthy. Proverbs 3.1-12 reveals that the Lord deserves trust because of his supreme wisdom, his control over situations, and the consequences of relying on him, all factors that appear in 15.33–16.9 not to mention 10.1–22.16 as a whole. Proverbs 3.1-12, however, features something that Collection II does not: the Lord's loving, fatherly character and the offer of reliable wisdom, which humans cannot attain independently. Proverbs 1–9 instils in the interpreter a confidence in the Lord who protects and a confidence in the Lord's wisdom that enables security in life, so that when approaching 16.3 the interpreter has more than omnipotent and omnicompetent incentives to trust.

Proverbs 16.9 also harbours these assumptions, evident in its stark juxtaposition of human and divine wisdom and control: 'The heart of man plans his way while the Lord establishes his steps'. The proverb, and others like it, leaves a 'gap' in the details of how these two sides of wisdom and control relate, but Proverbs 1–9 provides a means of reconciliation. Proverbs 3.19-26 and 8.22-36 portray the Lord's superior sovereignty and, within this context, align him with wisdom, specifying her as the mediator between God and humans. Wisdom protects like God and bridges the gulf between anthropological striving and planning, and the Lord's supreme knowledge and actions. As mediator, Wisdom may lead humans to adjust their thoughts and plans to God's or may assure them that these plans indeed agree and that their realization lies within the Lord's security. In short, Proverbs 1–9 functions didactically by providing a framework of reasons to trust the Lord and a conception of wisdom as mediator between God and humans.

4.2.5. *The Function of Proverbs 1–9 for Human Postures and the Lord's Supremacy in Proverbs 22.17-21*

Having concentrated on the material in Prov. 10.1–22.16, it remains to be seen how Proverbs 1–9 functions for 22.17–29.27. Both of the insights established in this chapter – human postures, and the Lord's wisdom and sovereignty – extend to this remaining material, with 22.19 being a particularly illustrative example. Proverbs 22.17–29.27 directly refers to the 'Lord' or 'God' twelve times, and these theological references make up less than 6 percent of the material.[39] The contrast in frequency with 10.1–22.16 is immediately noticeable, as over 15 percent of 10.1–22.16 includes a reference to the Lord or God, with a number of these appearing in the 'theological kernel' (15.33–16.9), a dense series of theological proverbs not present in 22.17–29.27. The first reference to the Lord in 22.17–29.27 arises in its third verse, Prov. 22.19, which forms part of a five-verse section:

---

39. Proverbs 22.19, 23; 23.17; 24.18, 21; 25.2, 22; 28.5, 25; 29.13, 25-26 (of the 220 verses in 22.17–29.27). These advocate trust in or fear of the Lord, and portray his sovereign and king-like behaviours.

הט אזנך ושמע דברי חכמים	22.17	Incline your ear and hear the words of the wise;
ולבך תשית לדעתי		apply your heart to my knowledge
כי־נעים כי־תשמרם בבטנך	22.18	For [it will be] pleasant if you keep them within you,
יכנו יחדו על־שפתיך		if, together, they are ready on your lips
להיות ביהוה מבטחך	22.19	That your trust might be in the Lord,
הודעתיך היום אף־אתה		I make you know,[40] today, even you.
הלא כתבתי לך [שלשים] במועצת ודעת	22.20	Have I not written for you thirty [sayings][41] in counsel and knowledge,
להודיעך קשט אמרי אמת להשיב אמרים אמת לשלחיך	22.21	to make you know the truest words of truth,[42] to give true answers to those who send you?

The passage begins with its primary exhortation to action – 'incline your ear and hear the words of the wise; apply your heart to my knowledge' (v. 17) – and follows with reasons – 'for [it will be] pleasant if you keep them within you, if, together, they are ready on your lips' (v. 18). To this exhortation and its grounds, the verse under consideration adds a purpose: 'that your trust might be in the Lord, I make you know, today, even you' (v. 19). This statement most likely contributes to the motivating reasons to 'hear' given in verse 18, so that listening (v. 17) begets pleasant results (v. 18) and at the same time trust in the Lord (v. 19).[43] One question arises immediately: how does listening to these instructions lead to trusting God? According to Longman,

> It is not made explicit how the teaching will increase trust, and so we are left to speculate. Perhaps the idea is that as the advice works in life, then it breeds confidence in its ultimate author. Or perhaps it is calling on trust in Yahweh as the first step toward implementing the advice found here. As one practices trust by following the advice…then one grows in trust as the unexpected consequences come.[44]

---

40. The performative perfective, which signals that the action occurs simultaneously with speaking, suits the context (see *IBHS*, 489, P. 30.5.1d).

41. Neither the *Ketiv* ('formerly'; שלשום) nor the *Qere* ('noble things'; שלישים) make sense here. The emendation to שלשים (thirty) is widely accepted based on the reference in *Amenemope*.

42. The superlative rendering finds support in Eccl. 12.10: דברי אמת ישר. For the absolute form of קשט see Ps. 60.6[4].

43. Sæbø, *Sprüche*, 280.

44. Longman, *Proverbs*, 416.

The challenge distils to one of relating human teaching to trusting the Lord, which is best left for later while I instead consider the second challenge of the passage, a question identical to the one derived from Prov. 16.3 – why trust the Lord? Although 22.19 views trust from a different perspective – 16.3 commends trust in God while 22.19 promises to produce trust in God – the sayings share a fundamental assumption: the Lord is trustworthy. So, again, why trust the Lord? We must consult evidence outside of Proverbs 1–9 for an answer to these questions before turning to 1–9 itself.

Proverbs 22.17–29.27 contains eleven other references to the Lord, and three of these inform the Lord's trustworthiness. Proverbs 28.25 says 'A greedy man stirs up strife, but the one who trusts in the Lord is enriched', and Prov. 29.25 reads, 'Trembling before man lays a snare, but the one who trusts in the Lord is set on high'.[45] Both passages positively portray trust in God and indicate that such trust leads to 'enrichment' and security, promises that plausibly motivate trust in the Lord but at the same time leave the content of that motivation vague.[46] They imply that the Lord can and will supply protection and enrichment. The third passage (23.17-18) does not use language of 'trust', but it does say, 'Do not let your heart envy sinners, but rather, continue fear of the Lord all the day. Surely there is a future and your hope will not be cut off'. A 'future' and 'hope', then, supply the grounds for trust given by Prov. 23.17-18, while enrichment and protection appear in 28.25 and 29.25. These reasons for trust resemble those of 10.1–22.16, especially the favourable consequences of relying on God. Therefore, in its assumptions and interpretive resources, Prov. 22.19 differs little from sayings of the same family in 10.1–22.16.

Proverbs 22.19 sits within a part of Proverbs that calls upon an additional resource for its interpretation: the *Instruction of Amenemope*. The Egyptian text contains clear parallels with Prov. 22.17–23.11, including thematic and linguistic similarities that indicate that Proverbs likely drew from *Amenemope*, albeit for its own purposes as seen in its arrangement and modifications.[47] The surrounding verses among which Prov. 22.19 appears

---

45. Often translated 'greedy man/Habgieriger' (e.g. ESV; NASB; Meinhold, *Sprüche*, 473), רחב נפש in Prov. 28.25 refers to one with a 'wide appetite'. Being 'enriched' may more specifically refer to being 'fattened'.

46. In Prov. 29.25, the phrase 'set on high', from *pual* שׂגב, connotes security. The phrase 'trembling before man' (חרדת אדם) is often translated 'fear of man' (ESV; NASB).

47. On the connection of these texts, see below and, among others, Nili Shupak, 'The Instruction of Amenemope and Proverbs 22.17–24.22 from the Perspective of Contemporary Research', in Troxel et al., *Seeking out the Wisdom*, 203–20; Fox, *Proverbs 10–31*, 753–67.

(22.17-21) all correspond to passages from *Amenemope*, but 22.19 itself discloses no direct attachment to the Egyptian instructions.[48] Although the proverbial text distinctly includes יהוה, *Amenemope* does include references to Egyptian gods that may offer reasons for trusting them. Fox says that 'Although 22.19a is not verbally dependent on *Amenemope*, it is very much in line with the spirit of his teachings, the only real difference being that it uses the name of Israel's God'.[49] The passages from *Amenemope* that most directly address the quest for trusting a deity or most closely resemble Prov. 22.19 include X.12-15, which reads,

> You shall pray to the Aten when he rises,
> Saying: 'Grant me well-being and health';
> He will give you your needs for this life,
> And you will be safe from fear.[50]

These lines appear in *Amenemope*'s seventh chapter (IX.10–X.15). The first two lines (X.12-13) offer what Vincent Laisney calls the 'raisons religieuses' for the whole chapter, and the second two (X.14-15) name the promises that stem from heeding the religious exhortations. 'Pray to the Aten' and 'he will give you your needs for this life, and you will be safe from fear'. According to Laisney, 'Ils énumèrent aussi les biens que l'on peut demander et espérer légitimement du dieu'.[51]

Amenemope motivates action in the world and prayers to the Aten based on the consequences that these behaviours produce, a driver concordant with the proverbs from 22.17–29.27 mentioned earlier that hold out hope, security, and enrichment for those who trust the Lord. The affinities of the Proverbial text and *Amenemope* extend to other teleological aspects, as both identify prosperity as the aim of instruction (III.17–IV.2; Prov. 22.18). Despite these similarities, *Amenemope* offers no additional grounds for trusting the Lord, and the divine name itself utterly differentiates these texts, as both references to the 'Lord' in 22.17–23.11 find no partner in *Amenemope* (22.19, 23).[52] Furthermore, Prov. 22.19 states the

---

48. Diethard Römheld, *Wege der Weisheit: Die Lehren Amenemopes und Proverbien 22,17–24,22*, BZAW 184 (Berlin: de Gruyter, 1989), 151, see also 13–26; Vincent Pierre-Michel Laisney, *L'Enseignement d'Aménémopé*, Studia Pohl: Series Maior 19 (Rome: Pontificio Istituto Biblico, 2007), 239–46.

49. Fox, *Proverbs 10–31*, 709.

50. *AEL* 2:153.

51. Laisney, *L'Enseignement*, 111. *Amenemope* VII.7-10 reflects a perspective similar to X.12-15.

52. Laisney, *L'Enseignement*, 240. Cf. Römheld, *Wege*, 151–2.

aim of instruction with crystal clarity – to trust the Lord – in contrast to the implied notions of trust in *Amenemope*. The Egyptian text, despite its influence on the author of Prov. 22.17–23.11, offers no distinctive answer to the theological question produced by Prov. 22.19 – why trust the Lord? *Amenemope* proffers a reason that resembles those of Prov. 22.17–29.27, even 10.1–22.16 – namely, trust the Lord because of the beneficial consequences – but offers little more in terms of interpretive resources for 22.19. Hence, the interpretive journey arrives at a place very similar to Prov. 16.3, namely, wondering if Proverbs 1–9 may supply grounds for trusting God. Again, there are reasons to think it does.

A number of linguistic connections appear in Prov. 22.17-21 and Proverbs 1–9, including 'incline your ear' (4.20; 5.1, 13) and 'hear' (1.8; 4.1), with additional links in 22.17b-18 and 2.2b; 4.21; 6.21; 7.3.[53] Proverbs 22.17-21 does not consequently function just like Proverbs 1–9, but its five verses do recall some of the central features of Proverbs 1–9 and warrant an investigation into how these two portions of material relate. As to the question about why to trust the Lord, recall the insights drawn from 3.1-12, where the author outlines incentives for his exhortation to 'trust in the Lord' (3.5), including God's superior wisdom, his supreme control over situations, and, like Prov. 22.17–29.27 and *Amenemope*, the beneficial consequences of trusting him. But Prov. 3.11-12 supplemented this set of reasons with the Lord's fatherly care: 'My son, do not reject the Lord's discipline and do not loathe his reproof. For the one whom the Lord loves, he reproves, like a father the son in whom he delights.' The Lord's love for the Proverbial pupil, like a father's love for his son, receives no parallel testimony elsewhere in Proverbs, and these personal, affective grounds offer a distinctive motivation for obeying 22.17 – 'incline your ear and hear the words of the wise; apply your heart to my knowledge' – and subsequently for trusting the Lord of 22.19. Proverbs 3.1-12, therefore, offers an interpretive framework that lends insights into 22.17–29.27 and its references to the Lord, particularly human postures towards him.

This example resembles Prov. 16.3, yet it is also similar to another category of theological sayings from Collection II: those that depict the supremacy of the Lord's wisdom and sovereignty. Proverbs 22.19 couples human trust in the Lord with teaching without explaining the nature of the connection. Hearing the words of the wise (22.17) supposedly facilitates

---

53. Ansberry, *Be Wise*, 120 n. 169. See also Whybray, *Proverbs*, 326. Plöger (*Sprüche*, 267) says that Prov. 22.19 supplies a function ('Zweckbestimmung') for the collection of proverbs that follow, like 1.2-6 does for the whole book.

trust in the Lord (22.19), but, as mentioned earlier, 'It is not made explicit how the teaching will increase trust, and so we are left to speculate'.[54] How does heeding the 'words of the wise' and the teacher's knowledge lead to trust in the Lord?

Already directing this question towards Proverbs 1–9, Fox has suggested that 22.19 states a purpose that matches 1.1-7 and 2.1-22 (esp. 2.5). According to him,

> [22.19] asserts that the purpose of the teachings of Part III is to inculcate trust in God. This is the promise also of the Prologue (1.1-7) and Lecture II (2.1-22), especially 2.5. Yet few of the maxims teach this directly. (Prov. 23.4 and 23.17 imply it.) It is an axiom for this author that all wisdom leads to trust in God. When one learns the right modes of behavior and their consequences, in the practical as well as moral realms, one comes to view the world as an orderly, just system and comes to trust its ruler.[55]

These comments seem to pick up on something that I explicated in the earlier discussion on Prov. 16.9 – that Proverbs 1–9 portrays wisdom as the mediator between God and humans, and that she particularly functions like the Lord in bestowing blessings on people and protecting them. Proverbs 3.19-26 and much of Proverbs 8 exemplified these characteristics. However, I am not sure that wisdom's motivational role leads to emphasizing 'the world as an orderly, just system' as described by Fox, and it certainly deters from interpreting her as a dispensable means to God. Proverbs 1–9 portrays the search for wisdom leading to God (2.1-5) who then dispenses wisdom to humans (2.6) and relates to them through her (2.7-11). Consequently, Proverbs 1–9 encourages interpreters to see that behind 22.17-19 lies not a system of order, whether moral or religious, but a dynamic, mediated relationship with the Lord that is propelled by the instructions within 22.17–23.11 and elsewhere in Proverbs. The statements in 22.17 and 22.19 may convey that between listening to instruction and living a wise life lies the Lord, who gives such wisdom and enables humans to live in accordance with her.

With the example of Prov. 22.19, I have extended the conclusions of Proverbs 1–9's didactic function beyond 10.1–22.16 and into another section of Proverbs. Interpretive challenges similar to those in 16.3 and 16.9 appear in 22.19, given its reference to the Lord, human posture towards him, and relationship to wisdom, which produces questions

---

54. Longman, *Proverbs*, 416.
55. Fox, *Proverbs 10–31*, 708.

about reasons for trusting the Lord and the place of wisdom in that trust. Proverbs 1–9 again offers a framework that other portions of Proverbs and resources of plausible benefit do not dispose. By supplying this theological framework, Proverbs 1–9 functions didactically for the interpretation of Proverbs 10–31.

4.2.6. Conclusion

There is one final section that will bring this chapter to a close, but so far it has been seen that 16.9 and the discussion about God's superior wisdom and sovereignty complement the previous section on human postures towards the Lord. As with 16.3, Prov. 16.9 starkly juxtaposes a statement about God and humanity: humans plan their way; God establishes it. God may endorse the life course envisioned by humans or he might override their schemes. However, two passages in Proverbs 1–9 (3.19-26; 8.22-36) emphasize the Lord's sovereignty and so happen to place these remarks within a context that both underscores the role of wisdom for humans and incorporates the activity of the Lord. Wisdom, it seems, functions as a mediator between God and humanity, quite a distinctive role when Proverbs is viewed within the OT as a whole and a role that offers helpful insights on Prov. 10.1–22.16. Furthermore, the sort of planning that might oppose her is one's very own 'wisdom', which is also described and denounced in Proverbs 1–9. The arguments from the previous two sections – human postures towards the Lord (16.3) and the supremacy of his wisdom and sovereignty (16.9) – apply to Prov. 22.19, which discloses interpretive challenges similar to but distinct from the earlier texts. For Prov. 22.19 assumes that the Lord is trustworthy and presupposes a relationship between him and humanity. This example solidifies the didactic function of Proverbs 1–9 and extends its domain to passages outside of 10.1–22.16.

4.3. *The Lord's Affection and Assessment*

The previous two sections accounted for passages in Prov. 10.1–22.16 that refer to the Lord and portray human postures toward him or feature his wisdom and sovereignty. The final theological category, also based on material in 10.1–22.16 that mentions 'the Lord' or 'God', incorporates proverbs that portray the Lord's affection and assessment, referring to his emotional posture towards people and actions, or his awareness and evaluation of them. Sayings like Prov. 16.5, for instance, which predicates a haughty heart as an 'abomination to the Lord', appear in this category, as do sayings about God's anger, favour, and perceptive powers. In this section, one passage representative of the current theological category is again selected, one that also belongs to the theological 'kernel' of Collection II (15.33–16.9): Prov. 16.2.

4.3.1. *The Lord's Affection and Assessment in Proverbs 16.2*

	16.2	All the ways of a man are pure in his eyes,
כל־דרכי־איש זך בעיניו		
ותכן רוחות יהוה		while the Lord weighs spirits.

Proverbs 16.2 represents the category of theological sayings that address the Lord's affection and assessment, declaring that 'All the ways of a man are pure in his eyes, while the Lord weighs spirits'. The lexeme for 'pure' (זך) describes oil and ritual objects as free from impurities (Exod. 27.20; 30.34; Lev. 24.2, 7) or, in an ethical sense, is used for doctrine (Job 11.4) and prayers (Job 16.17). In Proverbs, זך qualifies 'conduct' (פעל; 20.11; 21.8), conveying a sense of moral uprightness attested also in Job (8.6; 33.9), which suggests that 'pure conduct' in this case means purity from iniquity and transgression (33.9).[56] A saying nearly identical to Prov. 16.2 alters only this one lexeme (זך) to replace it with ישר ('upright'; 21.2), confirming that זך most plausibly refers to moral purity in 16.2. The interpretive challenge of 16.2 derives from this lexeme for 'pure', as it prompts the question, 'what is impure?', that is, what is the human problem within Prov. 16.2? The problem is most likely an ethical issue, and it seems to be latent within the proverb's context. If 'all the ways of a man are pure in his eyes', then what in particular is he pure from and what could be the problem?

On the surface, it appears that Prov. 16.2 holds little interest in a human problem, and that it rather aims to observe that humans judge their ways as 'pure' – we can say 'morally right' for now – and that God operates as the ultimate evaluator. P. Mommer states a stark version of this interpretation: Prov. 16.2 'declares that what matters is not the private judgment of a human being but the incorruptible and certain judgment of Yahweh… [H]e determines whether the individual is acting properly'.[57] Although it is questionable to say that a human's private judgment does not matter, Mommer may accurately represent what 16.2 observes, namely, God's determinative ethical appraisal. However, the language of the saying suggests that it implies more about the human–divine situation than a juxtaposition of moral judgments.

---

56. The context of the Job passages implies that Job's very claim to 'pure' status is 'impure', at least according to his friends.

57. P. Mommer, 'תכן *tkn*', *TDOT* 15:664.

The phrase 'in [someone's] eyes' refers, basically, to their opinion or judgment and in Proverbs characterizes how the fool views his own uprightness (12.15) or wisdom (26.5, 12; cf. 28.11): 'The way of a fool is right [ישר] in his own eyes' (12.15).[58] These sayings indicate that considering one's ways as 'pure' may resemble the opinion of a fool, but none of them offers evidence regarding what is wrong with such an opinion – except that it may be false – or why such an opinion arises. Furthermore, these sayings do not place the Lord, not to mention his affection and assessment, within their sights, which draws attention to the distinctive feature of Prov. 16.2.[59] Not only does it contain a distinct term (זך), it also joins human moral evaluation with the Lord's, a combination that adds a theological element to my primary question – what is the human problem? – and, after searching Proverbs 10–31, leaves us wanting for an answer.

Other pertinent texts include Ps. 119.9 and its use of זכה, where the psalmist wonders 'How can a young man make [or keep] his way pure?' and then implies that impurity would entail straying from the Lord's commands or sinning (119.10-11). In Isa. 5.20-21, the prophet accuses those 'wise in their own eyes' of confusing good and evil, calling evil good and good evil. The prophet declares that this angers the Lord (5.25), but, like other passages with a connection to Prov. 16.2, leaves us wondering about the nature of the human problem therein. Psalm 119.9 and Isa. 5.20-21 begin to compile a catalogue of possible resolutions to the problem, and yet we must also account for the second line of Prov. 16.2.

The second line of Prov. 16.2 offers insight into our question, as it reads, 'while the Lord weighs spirits'. The lexeme for 'weigh' (תכן), like זך, occurs infrequently in the OT (the root, 13×) and attests to the distinctive nature of Prov. 16.2. It does appear in Prov. 24.12, where it contributes to a rhetorical question that refers to the Lord: 'does not *he who weighs the heart* perceive it?' The rhetorical question addresses the 'problem' of this passage, that humans have been ignorant of a local crime or at least used ignorance as an excuse for inaction and, after someone receives a death sentence, say, 'Behold, we did not know this'. To this statement, the proverbial author responds, does not God weigh and perceive the heart?, implying that God sees their inner world, regardless of the sincerity of their ignorance. Based on 24.12, ignorance might constitute the human problem

---

58. Carl Schultz, 'עין *('ayin)'*, *TWOT* 1612a. For a helpful compendium of this idiom in the OT, see F. J. Stendeback, 'עין *'ayin'*, *TDOT* 11:28-44, esp. 36–8.

59. Two other proverbs assert that the 'eyes of the Lord' are in all places (15.3) and watch knowledge (22.12).

underlying Prov. 16.2. However, another occurrence of תכן (1 Sam. 2.3) suggests an additional possibility – arrogant human talk – and, finally, there is the evidence from one other proverb.

Proverbs 20.9 uses the verbal form of זך to ask, 'Who can say, "I have made my heart pure (זכיתי); I am clean from my sin (טהרתי מחטאתי)"?' In this passage, purity aligns with a lack of 'sin', pointing towards another lexical resource that might aid the current question. The lexeme חטאת refers to 'sin' and in several cases acquires a definition: it is juxtaposed to righteousness (13.6; 14.34), predicated to 'haughty eyes and a proud heart' (21.4), and likened to 'devising folly' (24.9). However, it in no case occurs with the Lord's evaluation, and in several passages it is used without a particular denotation: 'the gain of the wicked leads to sin' (10.16b); 'sin overthrows the wicked' (13.6b); 'sin is a disgrace to a people' (14.34b).[60] These passages offer an insight into the question at hand akin to that of the passages mentioned earlier, which form a collection of possible connotations for 'impurity', but lack the context of the Lord's evaluation. The same could be said of the various statements in Prov. 15.31–16.8, which imply that 'purity' may look like one or all of many things: receiving instruction (15.31-33), committing one's work to the Lord (16.3), not being arrogant (16.5), fearing the Lord and pleasing him (16.6-7), and being righteous (16.8).

Similarly, evidence from the OT bearing firm lexical or conceptual links with Prov. 16.2 presents a collage of answers to the current interpretive question and, when 16.2 is read within that context, displays a picture of how one might feel self-assuredly 'pure'.[61] The image is ample: sinful

---

60. Proverbs 14.12 and 30.12 lend similarly limited insights to the question (cf. Plöger, *Sprüche*, 189). Aside from debates about whose 'steadfast love and faithfulness' appear in Prov. 16.6, the point that 'iniquity is atoned for' (יכפר עון) indicates that the solution to iniquity includes the Lord's atonement and that this proverb itself harbours assumptions that warrant the help of other biblical material (see, e.g., Mark Boda, *A Severe Mercy: Sin and Its Remedy in the Old Testament*, Siphrut 1 [Winona Lake: Eisenbrauns, 2009], 374–5). A. Negoiţă and H. Ringgren ('זָכָה *zākhāh*', *TDOT* 4:62–4) assert that the adjectival use of זכה (i.e. זך) connotes the notion of צדק, which may suit Job 8.6 and Ps. 51.6[4] but not necessarily the passages in Proverbs.

61. Hartmut Gese (*Lehre und Wirklichkeit in der alten Weisheit: Studien zu den Sprüchen Salomos und zu dem Buche Hiob* [Tübingen: Mohr, 1958], 45–50) differentiates proverbial sayings like 16.9 from ancient Egyptian instructions due to their views on the 'determination of hearts'. In Egypt, the determination arises from a more metaphysically grounded determination; in Israel, the Lord can act independently of human action. Gese contrasts the biblical proverbs that show the Lord acting against

uncleanliness, intellectual disposition, human autonomy, revolt against God, blindness to injustice As a result, it is safe to say that for the scope of evaluation, 'Ausschlaggend sind dabei nicht nur die Taten, sondern auch die ihnen zugrundeliegenden Qualitäten, Motive und Absichten'.[62] The problem likely entails the whole person, more than just their actions, and the texts above indicate wrongdoing especially towards the Lord. These answers are intriguing and feasible, whether they represent notions of impurity based on a Bible-wide scope of interpretation or they hint at a stock of knowledge that was common to many ancient readers of Proverbs. But we cannot overlook the fact that they leave us a little uncertain as to which one pertains most to Prov. 16.2, though perhaps they can all apply, and, more importantly, they are missing a clear connection to the second line of that proverb, namely, the Lord's assessment of human beings. For one not only feels 'pure in his own eyes' but is also told that God is the one who 'weighs spirits', and in that regard one final piece of relevant evidence from Proverbs commends itself: Prov. 5.21-23. First, Prov. 5.21 depicts the Lord's assessment of human ways: 'For a man's ways are before the eyes of the Lord, and he observes all his pathways'. Second, 5.22-23 propounds a human problem, using lexemes related to זך: 'His iniquities (עֲוֺנוֺתָיו) will ensnare him, and he will be held fast in the cords of his sin (חטאתו)' (5.22). Third, 5.21-23 occurs within Proverbs and notably within Proverbs 1–9, which, I have been arguing, stands at a place within the book that warrants the interpreter's attention and functions in a way that has so far offered an interpretive framework for understanding Prov. 10.1–22.16. The question derived from 16.2 – what is the nature of the human problem? – is now posed to Proverbs 1–9.

4.3.2. The Lord's Affection and Assessment in Proverbs 1–9
Proverbs 1–9 presents the Lord's affection and assessment in three primary perspectives: (1) he assesses all the ways of humankind (5.21); (2) he bestows favour upon certain people (3.4, 34; 8.35); (3) he 'hates' or abhors certain people and actions (3.32; 6.16). Of these references to God's affection and assessment, Prov. 3.31-32 and 5.21-23 are focused on in this section, as they detail, respectively, ethical instructions and a series

---

human plans (e.g. 16.1) with texts like *Amenemope* XX.3-6 and *Ptahhotep* 115-116, 548-552 (*AEL* 2:158; 1:65, 74). Cf. Erik Hornung, *Conceptions of God in Ancient Egypt: The One and the Many*, trans. J. Baines (London: Routledge & Kegan Paul, 1983), 210–11.
  62. Meinhold, *Sprüche*, 266.

of warnings about sexual relations while underscoring the affections or assessments of the Lord and humans. Through the combination of these elements, these passages acutely address the interpretive question from 16.2.

The first passage (3.31-32) lies after a list of prohibitions about social relations (3.27-30), like 'Do not devise evil against your neighbour who lives trustingly with you' (v. 29). The prohibitions end in verse 31 with a final order: 'Do not envy a man of violence, and do not choose any of his ways'. The imperatives leading up to this verse dictate actions – do not withhold, or say, or plan or quarrel – and, with the exception of 'devising evil' against a neighbour (v. 29), the instructions do not explicitly target the emotions of the audience. In other words, the attention of these prohibitions is on personal behaviour rather than personal affections. However, the focus in 3.31 momentarily shifts from behaviour to attitude when it enjoins – 'do not envy' – and then forbids the audience from choosing the ways of violence. '*Do not envy* a man of violence, and do not choose any of his ways.'

Verse 31's interest in affection continues in verse 32, which states 'For the devious person is an abomination to the Lord but with the upright is his counsel'. The 'abomination to/of the Lord' crops up throughout Proverbs as a judgment against what the Lord hates, landing primarily upon wicked people and wicked actions. Like the Lord's abomination, 'envy' also reappears in Proverbs in warnings similar to 3.21. Proverbs 24.1, for instance, accentuates an affective focus: 'Do not *envy* the wicked or *desire* to be with them'. Envy, in Proverbs 10–31, relates to human emotions, indicates that such emotions are prone to problems, and suggests that Proverbs aims to redirect them. Hence, do not envy or desire to be with the wicked (24.1); 'do not let your heart envy sinners but continue in the fear of the Lord' (23.17); a calm heart gives life, but envy rots the bones (14.30). Proverbs 3.31-32, though, incorporates the Lord's affections into its comments about human emotion. The sharp juxtaposition of human 'envy' and divine abhorrence in 3.31-32 suggests that the author intends to facilitate an exchange in emotions. He mirrors someone who might 'envy a violent man' with the Lord abhorring such perverse men.[63] He replaces the affections of envy with affections of hatred and goes on to propound

---

63. Though overlooking the significance of the remarks about affections and focusing instead on the ideal social behaviours espoused by Prov. 3.21-35, Bassoumboul (*Das sagesses*, 167–70) concludes that 'Il souligne que la mesure de cet idéal est YHWH'. He explains that 3.31 intends to keep the son away from imitating 'the methods' of the violent man, a purpose of the passage that I contend depends upon certain affections.

a set of divine affections in verses 33-35, wherein the Lord curses, scorns and disgraces wicked character types, and blesses, favours and honours righteous types. Who would envy such targets of God's curse?[64]

Divine affection and human emotion appear not only in biblical instructional literature. Two passages in the *Instruction of Amenemope* use the Egyptian version of תועבת יהוה ('abomination of the Lord') as grounds for admonitions against false speech and action:[65]

> Do not speak falsely to a man,
> The god abhors it;
> Do not sever your heart from your tongue.
> That all your strivings may succeed.
> You will be weighty before the others,
> And secure in the hand of the god.
> God hates the falsifier of words,
> He greatly abhors the dissembler. (XIII.15–XIV.3)
>
> Do not cheat a man (through) pen on scroll,
> The god abhors it. (XV.20-21)

In these passages, perhaps composed during the height of 'personal piety' in ancient Egypt, the instructions 'do not speak falsely' and 'do not cheat a man', plus the reiteration of divine affection in XIV.2-3, resemble the tone of Prov. 3.28-32. Hence, 'Do not speak falsely to a man; the god abhors it.... God hates the falsifier of words, He greatly abhors the dissembler' (XIII.15-16; XIV.2-3). However, these instructions do not address human affections, either positively or negatively, or propound the audience with an inventory of divine attitudes towards good and evil as in Prov. 3.33-35.[66] Therefore, by juxtaposing prohibitions with the god's affections, the Egyptian material encourages attention towards the Lord's affection and assessment in Proverbs, but in Proverbs it nevertheless seems that something innovative is occurring.

---

64. Being in God's 'counsel' (סוד; 3.32b) may involve communication between those involved (Ps. 25.14; as 'council', see Jer. 23.18, 22).

65. See *AEL* 2:154–5. Cf. *Amenemope* V.8-9; XVIII.8–XIX.1.

66. The theological framework that lies below the surface of a text like *Amenemope*, based on the bulk of evidence from ancient Egypt, differs substantially from the image of God portrayed in the OT (see Hornung, *Conceptions*, 186–216, esp. 195–6, 201–2, 212). Though unconvincingly arguing for a monotheistic conception of Egyptian *ntr*, Joseph Vergote ('La Notion de Dieu dans les Livres de Sagesse Égyptiens', in *Les Sagesses du Proche-Orient Ancien: Colloque de Strasbourg 17–19 mai 1962* [Paris: Presses Universitaires de France, 1963], 170–86) provides a thorough list of references and quotations for Egyptian instructional texts that mention 'god'.

The human affective problem and the solution of acquiring divine affections finds support in another passage of the OT that joins language of human desire and the Lord's abomination: Deut. 7.25-26.

> The images of their gods you shall burn with fire. You shall not covet the silver or gold that is upon them or take it for yourselves, lest you be ensnared by it, for it is an abomination to the Lord your God. And you shall not bring an abomination into your house and become devoted to destruction (חרם) like it. You shall utterly detest it and utterly abhor it, for it is devoted to destruction.

Notice how the author of the passage prohibits humans from coveting and grounds the prohibition in the Lord's alternative affections: 'Do not covet the silver or gold that is on [the images of foreign gods] and take it for yourself...for it is an abomination to the Lord your God'. Yet the passage moves beyond a juxtaposition and into prescriptive, emotional guidance. For the people 'must utterly detest and utterly abhor' the silver and gold. Using forceful language (שקץ ותשקצנו ותעב תתעבנו), Deut. 7.26 enjoins its audience to feel how God feels; as he abhors the idol-related substances of foreign nations, so you, Israel, shall abhor them. The behavioural instruction offered in Deut. 7.25-26 incorporates emotional obedience, grounded upon the emotions of the Lord who then serves as the model for how his people should feel.

A similar exchange, I contend, occurs in Prov. 3.31-32, which condemns misguided human emotions and follows with an alternative, divine emotion that redirects the audience's affections, a strategy absent from Proverbs 10–31.[67] Proverbs 3.31-32 viewed within 3.28-35 suggests that when Proverbs 1–9 mentions the affections of the Lord, it aims to commend these affections to humans. Inversely, it indicates that the human problem includes the failure to share God's feelings towards

---

67. Proverbs 23.17 offers no instruction for how to feel about wickedness, though it corroborates the point that humans should feel how God does: 'Your heart shall not envy sinners but rather be in the fear of the Lord all the day' (see also 10.3; 12.12; 24.1, 19; cf. 1.22; 6.25). On implicit views of desire and desire as such throughout Proverbs, see Stewart, *Poetic Ethics*, 130-69. Following Lyu, Stewart's treatment of desire in Proverbs is bound up with character types and their 'poetic' features, which I address in Chapter 2. She also acknowledges that 'The patterning of desire in Proverbs is developed to the most elaborate extent in chapters 1–9' (147), which, for her, form character 'in the likeness of wisdom' (162). Forming desire in the likeness of the Lord remains unaddressed, and Stewart's examples show how the sayings in Proverbs 10–29 hold no explicit theological aspect (e.g. 12.1; 13.5; 18.2; 21.15; 24.13-14).

wickedness.⁶⁸ As we investigate an answer to the question of what constitutes the human problem, the Proverbs 3 passage is only one portion of the evidence in 1–9 regarding the Lord's affection and assessment. As mentioned at the end of section 4.3.1, due to a pair of terms for 'sin' and 'iniquity', the second passage in Proverbs 1–9 pertinent to the current question arises in Proverbs 5.

כי נכח עיני יהוה דרכי־איש	5.21	For a man's ways are before the eyes of the Lord,
וכל־מעגלתיו מפלס		and he observes all his paths.

Proverbs 5.21 baldly states 'For a man's ways are before the eyes of the Lord, and he observes all his paths'. This verse inaugurates the conclusion of Proverbs 5 (5.22-23), which summarizes an ethical evaluation of the preceding story, wherein the father again commends his teaching (vv. 1-2) only to present an exposé of a temptress (vv. 3-6), the man seduced by her (vv. 7-14), and the proper context of sexual activity (vv. 15-20). The story portrays what happens to men who succumb to the temptations of a dangerous female by outlining the consequences for the man's honour, time (5.9), possessions, and energy (5.10): he loses all of them. These losses culminate in a realization of his foolish behaviour and a confession of what went wrong: 'How I hated discipline, and my heart despised reproof! I did not listen to the voice of my teacher or incline my ear to my instructors' (5.12-13). He 'hated' discipline and 'despised' reproof, language that attests to a problem of affection; he harboured the wrong feelings toward pedagogical instruction.

The Lord's evaluation does not appear in the confession of 5.12-14 but arises instead seven verses later, at the end of the chapter in 5.21. The verse says that the Lord sees and examines all the ways of humans, not least of this man, and proceeds to offer another appraisal of those lured by the Proverbial temptress:

For a man's ways are before the eyes of the Lord,
    and he observes all his paths.
His iniquities will ensnare him,
    and he will be held fast in the cords of his sin.
He will die by a lack of discipline,
    and by his great folly he strays. (5.21-23)

---

68. Based on a brisk study of sin and its solution in Proverbs 1–9, without focusing on the texts in question, Boda (*Severe Mercy*, 374; see 359–76) concludes that wisdom in Collection I 'entails turning away and rejecting evil and turning to and embracing righteousness, both in the affections as well as in practice'.

In short, these verses explain the reasons for the man's behaviour in 5.3-14 – iniquity, sin, folly, and a lack of discipline. Based on the lightbulb scenario of 5.11-12, where at the end of his life this man realizes the source of his former problems, it seems that ignorance may have been his greatest fault. In his latter days he suddenly realizes his former attitude. But his admission of conscious, negative postures toward instruction, and the explanation in 5.22, particularly the 'sin' and 'iniquity' that spurred his downfall, indicate that perhaps 'ignorance' does not best capture the problem. As Christl Maier concludes, based on the generalized nature of the terms for wrongdoing in 5.22, 'Dabei ist es unerheblich, ob diese wissentlich oder unwissentlich geschehen sind'.[69]

What, then, is the problem in Proverbs 5? As 5.21 wants us to know, God certainly sees it. It may include the broad scope of iniquity and sin conveyed by עָוֹן and חטא in 5.22.[70] However, the confession in verses 12-13 suggests an affective problem, one more directly related to the 'lack of discipline' and the 'folly' mentioned in 5.23. The man hated discipline and reproof and did not desire to listen to his teachers. Might it be accurate to say that he was right 'in his own eyes', at least until old age, and that God sees not only an illicit tryst but also the improper affections of a sinful man? He wrongly hated and despised the instruments of instruction that would have led him aright earlier in life. This passage does not, like 3.31-32, suggest that the audience align their affections with the Lord's, but it does show the nature of the human problem when the Lord is watching. His affection (3.31-32) and assessment (5.21) occur within Proverbs 1–9 in contexts quite concerned with the affections of humans, to show that one way humans go wrong is by failing to feel how God feels.

Before returning to Prov. 16.2, consider two more observations about the Lord's affection and assessment from Proverbs 1–9. In the first place, none of the passages that mention or depict these concepts provides a background or justification for the Lord's affection; they assume the Lord's moral standards as categorical.[71] For example, certain things are an abomination to the Lord, full stop. In the second place, Collection I is not interested to explain why the Lord hates such activity but is concerned with clarifying what he hates, that is, the purview of his abomination, such

---

69. Maier, *Die 'fremde Frau'*, 125.

70. On the use of these lexemes elsewhere, especially in the book of Psalms, see below. 'Transgression' (פשׁע) in Proverbs seems to refer to wrongdoing against other humans rather than God (e.g. 19.11; 28.24).

71. Against the possibility that the negative consequences of such behaviour, perhaps generalized as 'social disorder', constitute the grounds for the Lord's stance, see Boström, *God*, 202.

as the characters, actions, and, as explored in this section, the misguided affections of human beings. Both of these points are affirmed by 6.12-19, which portrays the bad behaviour of certain people and critiques it with a simple appeal to the Lord's hatred for them. While the wicked person and man with crooked speech will come to ruin, they likewise meet the disfavour of the Lord, who hates and finds as abhorrent haughty eyes, lying tongues, and hands that shed innocent blood. In summary, the Lord sets the standard for the moral judgment of humans, and Proverbs 1–9 attempts to align the interpreter's affections and assessment with the Lord's. The core problem, then, for humans is their failure to approach and respond to good and evil in the way that God does.

4.3.3. *The Function of Proverbs 1–9 for 16.2*

Having posed the interpretive question of this section about Proverbs' theology to Proverbs 1–9, I now return to the source of the question: Prov. 16.2. Representative of several sayings in 10.1–22.16 about the Lord's affection and assessment, Prov. 16.2 remarks that 'All the ways of a man are pure in his eyes, while the Lord weighs spirits'. The quite distinct language for 'pure' (זך) refers to moral uprightness and joined with 'in his eyes' conveys that humans hold an opinion about their ways, judging them to be morally right. Following this judgment, the second line of 16.2 states that the Lord 'weighs spirits' to indicate that he knows and assesses the hearts of those humans who see their ways as pure. The challenge of this proverb comes not so much from its language of the Lord 'weighing' hearts or from what exactly it means by being pure 'in one's eyes'. It is the distinctive language of 'pure' in 16.2 that prompts an intriguing enquiry into what constitutes 'impurity' in the view of this saying and the book of Proverbs. That is, what is the nature of the human problem? Other material in Prov. 10.1–22.16, while provoking similar questions, offers several possible answers to the question, as do other passages from the OT with conceptual or lexical links to Prov. 16.2. These resources suggest promising resolutions, particularly attractive in their scope and for those reading Proverbs with an extensive knowledge of the OT. But the distinctive contribution of Proverbs 1–9 is evident, as it combines what none of these other materials do, namely, the anthropological and theological perspectives contained in Prov. 16.2.[72] Proverbs 3.31-32 and

---

72. Deuteronomy 7.25-26 informs Prov. 5.31-32 more than Prov. 16.2 because of its direct links to the former (i.e. 'abomination of the Lord'). Had the phrase appeared in Prov. 16.2, then that would broach a possibly more significant interpretive relation between Prov. 10.1–22.16 and Deuteronomy, one worth exploring for other passages, given the presence of the Lord's abomination in Proverbs.

5.21-23, as well as 6.12-19, are reliable resources for this interpretive challenge, addressing human problems in the context of divine affection and assessment.

Proverbs 3.31-32 and the whole of Proverbs 5 show that the Lord sets the standard for the moral outlook of human beings, and that Proverbs 1–9 attempts to align the interpreter's affections and assessment with this standard. To pose the question of Prov. 16.2 – what is the human problem? – to Proverbs 1–9, the core problem is the failure to approach and respond to good and evil in the way that God does. Proverbs 1–9 affirms that humans have a penchant for evil, or at least find it attractive, and therefore provides a framework to see that, on the one hand, 16.2 connotes a problematic human ethical judgment. That is, 'all the ways of a man are pure in his own eyes', even though none of his ways actually are pure. Such interpretations find approval from some commentators, such as Waltke, who in 16.2 sees people who 'justify "all their actions"' and enter into conflict with the Lord's true evaluation.[73] But Proverbs 1–9 supports the voices of those like Fox, who contend that Prov. 16.2, on the other hand, 'does not mean that all people are inevitably self-righteous. Proverbs nowhere displays such a jaundiced view of humanity'.[74] Proverbs 16.2 may connote that 'all the ways of a man are pure in his own eyes' and are nevertheless sometimes in line with the Lord's standard.

These interpretive positions recall the debate that surrounds Prov. 16.9 and whether it connotes a positive or negative view of humanity. In section 4.2, Proverbs 1–9 imposed a framework upon these options, not so much to decide between options or to refute an interpretation, but to add a subtlety and nuance often unrecognized. Likewise, for Prov. 16.2, Proverbs 1–9 reorients discussions and invites attention to the human imitation of God, in its efforts to portray the human problem as one of failure to feel how God feels, especially about evil, and assess it according to his standards. According to Mommer, 'what matters is not the private judgment of a human being but the incorruptible and certain judgment of Yahweh'.[75] According to Proverbs 1–9, the human judgment does matter, not in that it determines good and evil, but in that Proverbs envisions a people with moral judgments that should align with God's. Lastly, how might this alignment be achieved? Proverbs 5 indicates that in order to acquire God's affection and assessment, to the extent that it is possible, humans must listen to the teachings of authorized instructors. The man

---

73. Waltke, *Proverbs 15–31*, 10.
74. Fox, *Proverbs 10–31*, 608.
75. Mommer, *TDOT* 15:664.

in Proverbs 5 bemoans his recalcitrance, and it seems the author himself forwards this man as an example to show that God feels and thinks otherwise, and to inspire his audience to follow suit. For, as Proverbs 1–9 makes clear, the Lord sets the moral standard, and, with this insight as well as its conception of affection and assessment, functions didactically by providing an interpretive framework for Prov. 10.1–22.16. So, despite the subtlety of certain functions of Proverbs 1–9 here, its chapters offer clear and distinctive insights into the theological questions of Proverbs 10–29 and in that way functions as an introduction.

4.3.4. The Qualifications and Context of Proverbs 1–9 as an Introduction
Proverbs 16.2 and the discussion about God's affection and assessment completes my deliberate venture into the theological world of Proverbs. Despite selecting only three of the fifty-seven sayings that mention 'the Lord' or 'God' in Prov. 10.1–22.16 (16.2, 3, 9), this selection represents the variety of theological perspectives in the collection and demonstrates how Proverbs 1–9 functions didactically with respect to each. Proverbs 16.3 broaches issues of how humans posture themselves toward God – especially the question of why to trust him – and 3.1-12 discloses that God deserves trust because of his supreme wisdom, superior control, favourable consequences, and most distinctly his love and delight for people. Within the context of the Lord's wisdom and sovereignty, Prov. 16.9 starkly juxtaposes a statement about God and humanity. Humans plan their way; God establishes it. For such an ambiguous relation, two passages in Proverbs 1–9 (3.19-26; 8.22-36) demonstrate that divine wisdom functions as a mediator between God and humanity, bridging the gap in sayings like Prov. 16.9. Gathering the conclusions of the first two sections, I applied these insights to 22.17-21, a passage that also presumes the Lord as worthy of trust and details little about the relation of humans and God. Consequently, Proverbs 1–9 offers insight beyond 10.1–22.16, perhaps functioning as an introduction for 10–31 as a whole. Lastly, Prov. 16.2 presents the interpreter with the challenge of discerning the human problem in Proverbs, derived from remarks about human morality and the Lord's affection and assessment. Proverbs 3.31-32 and Proverbs 5 and 6.12-19 show that the Lord norms the moral world for humans who struggle to align their affections and their appraisal of good and evil with the Lord's. All of these examples show how Proverbs 1–9 functions didactically by supplying an interpretive framework for Proverbs 10–31, not necessarily imposing a single reading upon proverbs that reference the Lord, but nuancing and enhancing the interpretation of those passages.

4.3.5. Conclusion

Proverbs 16.2 was the final example in my study because it introduces significant qualifications to and implications for what it means to call Proverbs 1–9 an 'introduction'. As mentioned, while Proverbs 1–9 does operate as an introduction for 16.2 in the way that I have been maintaining, it also harbours its own assumptions on the topic of divine affection and assessment. It gives no justification for why the Lord feels the way he does about human wrongdoing; nor does it explain why his feelings are ethically authoritative. Other passages in the OT provide cogent contributions to the interpretation of 16.2, offering several human problems that may answer the question of what makes someone 'impure': sinful uncleanliness, intellectual disposition, human autonomy, revolt against God, and blindness to injustice. To my mind, these are all understandably biblical ways that someone might not be as 'pure' in one's own eyes as one thinks.

Furthermore, in Deut. 7.25-26 too we see human impurity, and yet a solution is also offered that resembles what we find in Prov. 3.31-32. Theologically and anthropologically, these two passages make similar suggestions: that one should feel as the Lord feels about wrongdoing; for he abhors it. Proverbs 5, though, does forward a distinctive diagnosis for the problem of being 'pure in one's own eyes' – a hatred for discipline and reproof, the failure to heed one's teachers, and an ignorance of God's assessment of the situation – and therefore it should not be discredited in its introductory function for Proverbs 10–29. Holding that conclusion in place, there is a sense in which the interpretive challenges of 16.2 push the boundaries of how Proverbs 1–9 functions as an introduction. For the plethora of explanations for 16.2 found within the OT itself dovetails with the nature of the explanation given by Proverbs 1–9 and likewise coheres with the theological assumptions within it.

That becomes even clearer in view of two lexemes used by Proverbs 1–9: חטא and עון. These terms for 'sin' and 'iniquity', associated with 16.2's notion of 'purity', brand what the man in Proverbs 5 got wrong, and yet they, in one case, rarely occur in Proverbs (i.e. עון) and, in the other, presume quite a bit of conceptual stock (i.e. חטא). Forms of חטא can refer to 'sinner(s)', to the activity of 'missing' something, or to 'sin' in the abstract.[76] As mentioned, the lexeme's sense of 'sin' is juxtaposed to righteousness (13.6; 14.34), predicated to 'haughty eyes and a proud

---

76. For 'sinner(s)' (חטאים/חוטא), see Prov. 1.10; 11.31; 13.21-22; 14.21; 23.17. For 'miss', see 8.36; 19.2; cf. 20.2. For 'sin' (חטאת), see 10.16; 13.6; 14.34; 20.9; 21.4; 24.9.

heart' (21.4), and likened to 'devising folly' (24.9), and is otherwise used without explicit definition. עון occurs only in Prov. 5.22 and 16.6, with the latter occurrence having a meaning that the passage itself does not clarify: 'by steadfast love and faithfulness *iniquity* is atoned for'. עון occurs in the book of Psalms 31 times, and Koch concludes that 'Just which transgressions or crimes actually lead to *'āwōn* is not explicated', citing Ps. 89.32-33[31-32] as the exception, which, nevertheless, refers to the king's children transgressing guidelines normative for royalty, rather than all the people of Israel transgressing the Mosaic law.[77] In Psalms, these lexemes often appear clustered together, as in 32 and 51, and seem to 'express the totality and immensity of culpability' rather than indicating the measure of the offence or its precise nature.[78] Clearly, the lexemes in Prov. 5.22 connote wrongdoing against God and fellow humans, but what else might lurk behind this 'sin' and 'iniquity'? Can we know more about the ethical standard in Proverbs, aside from the premise that God determines it and that 'sin' has a close relation to pride and folly?

These questions dovetail with the remarks of Wildeboer, who, in his comments on Prov. 5.21-22, says that God punishes 'wenn nun der Mensch Gottes Gesetz übertritt', and that Prov. 16.2 prompts the audience to adopt God's law as his moral will and standard.[79] The law, for Wildeboer, marks the key to understanding moral wrong in these passages, suggesting that one human problem in Proverbs, one I would consider major based on these texts, is lawlessness. Humans transgress the law of God, and God, who assesses all humans, feels certain ways about it. In short, certain challenges in Prov. 16.2 are softened thanks to Proverbs 1–9, and yet other challenges in 16.2 spawn even more puzzles within Proverbs 1–9 itself, suggesting that 1–9 makes assumptions about certain topics, not least theological, and thereby requires its own resources for interpretation. These assumptions do not compromise its didactic role; they reveal its limitations, along with a starting point for how Proverbs might integrate with other portions of the OT and its ancient context. Similarly, given the subtlety and nuance surrounding the examples of 16.2 and 16.9, one wonders if the introductory function of Proverbs 1–9 is more difficult to see than it is helpful. But the nuance of its role does not necessarily mean that that role is obscure; it only seems so because the process of explaining its function – that function itself being in some ways simple – is a complex task.

77. K. Koch, 'עון, *'āwōn'*, *TDOT* 10:553.
78. Boda, *Severe Mercy*, 446.
79. Wildeboer, *Sprüche*, 16; see also 47–8.

By reading back and forth between the theological content of Proverbs 10.1–22.16 and 1–9, the book of Proverbs is still shown to have an introduction, its first nine chapters orienting the reader to a certain theological context that clears up certain challenges in the sayings material. But what is striking about the examples of 16.2 and 16.9 is that they represent a mode of theological thought not necessarily distinct to Proverbs. Assertions of the Lord's superior wisdom and sovereignty, and the moral authority of his affections and assessment crop up in many OT texts, albeit in their own distinctive ways, all of which suggests a common set of theological beliefs. Other topics explored in this study – character types, moral ambiguity, and the aims of Proverbs – are, by comparison, somewhat characteristic of the book and specific to it. For the volume and clarity with which these elements occur in Proverbs overshadow their presence elsewhere in the OT, and that may suggest that the readers of Proverbs had incongruous stores of knowledge. They seem to have possessed a foundation of theological knowledge in a way that they did not for these other interpretive topics. Hence, for aspects of the Lord's wisdom, sovereignty, affection and assessment we see less didacticism from Proverbs 1–9 and more straightforward coherence in its relation to Proverbs 10–29, though, again, not without significant contributions to interpretation. Therefore, the, in some ways, unremarkable insights that Proverbs 1–9 offers 16.2 and 16.9 do not jeopardize its function as an introduction. It actually makes good sense in light of the alternative sources of information that an original reader would have plausibly held. What is remarkable is that Proverbs 1–9 ties up these basic theological beliefs with the figure of Wisdom, and that its elaboration on how she relates to those beliefs has implications for how 16.2 and 16.9 are understood.

That is only a brief look down one of many promising avenues that can now be pursued with the introductory function of Proverbs 1–9 in place. These chapters, standing at the outset of the book of Proverbs, have long been called a 'prologue' or 'introduction', and I have argued that in both the detail and the 'big picture' of the book, Proverbs 1–9 functions didactically by supplying interpretive frameworks for chapters 10–31. It teaches interpretive skills that help the interpreter to understand and explicate material in 10–31, within literary, rhetorical, and theological contexts. By functioning in this didactic way, Proverbs 1–9 fulfils the promises of Prov. 1.1-7, which claims that the interpreter will 'understand' Proverbs (1.2) and 'explicate' its material (1.6). The issues that need explicating arise from the 'assumptions' in Prov. 10.1–22.16, that is, the information and skills that are required for interpreting the proverbs. As a primary part of its didactic function, Proverbs 1–9 informs the particular interpretive challenges that arise from these assumptions and does so in a way that is coherent with 10–31 and distinctive, sometimes more so than alternative sources of information, such as other ancient Near Eastern texts, OT passages, and intellectual or experiential knowledge demonstrably possessed by the ancient audiences of Proverbs. Specifically, Proverbs 1–9 establishes the literary identity and rhetorical function of the characters of Proverbs; it creates a network of aims and values by establishing particular educational goals that organize certain statements in Proverbs 10–31; and it substantiates the role of the Lord and his relationship to humanity for sayings that only briefly mention him. In each of these ways, Proverbs 1–9 forms an interpretive framework to explain much of what is latent and unstated by the proverbial material.

Bibliography

Adams, Samuel L. 'The Social Location of the Scribe in the Second Temple Period'. In *Sibyls, Scriptures, and Scrolls: John Collins at Seventy*, edited by Joel Baden, Hindy Najman, and Eibert J. C. Tigchelaar, 22–37. JSJSup 175. Leiden: Brill, 2016.
———. *Wisdom in Transition: Act and Consequence in Second Temple Instructions*. JSJSup 125. Leiden: Brill, 2008.
Aitken, Kenneth. *Proverbs*. Philadelphia, PA: Westminster Press, 1986.
Aletti, Jean-Noël. 'Proverbes 8, 22-31. Étude De Structure'. *Biblica* (1976): 25–37.
———. 'Seduction et Parole en Proverbs I–IX'. *VT* 27 (1977): 129–44.
Alster, Bendt. *The Instructions of Suruppak: A Sumerian Proverb Collection*. Mesopotamia: Copenhagen Studies in Assyriology 2. Copenhagen: Akademisk Forlag, 1974.
———. *Proverbs of Ancient Sumer: The World's Earliest Proverb Collections*. Bethesda, MD: CDL, 1997.
Ansberry, Christopher B. *Be Wise, My Son, and Make My Heart Glad: An Exploration of the Courtly Nature of the Book of Proverbs*. BZAW 422. Berlin: de Gruyter, 2011.
Askin, Lindsay. *Scribal Culture in Ben Sira*. JSJSup 184. Leiden: Brill, 2018.
Balentine, Samuel Eugene. *Job*. Macon, GA: Smyth & Helwys, 2006.
Bartholomew, Craig G. *Ecclesiastes*. BCOT. Grand Rapids: Baker Academic, 2009.
Barucq, André. *Le Livre des Proverbes*. Paris: J. Gabalda, 1964.
Bassoumboul, Étienne-Noël. *Des sagesses à la sagesse: Étude de l'unité sapientielle en Pr 1–9*. Paris: J. Gabalda, 2008.
Baumann, Gerlinde. *Die Weisheitsgestalt in Proverbien 1–9: Traditionsgeschichtliche und Theologische Studien*. Tübingen: J. C. B. Mohr, 1996.
Bertheau, Ernst. *Die Sprüche Salomo's*. Leipzig: Weidmann, 1847.
Bland, Dave. 'Formation of Character in the Book of Proverbs'. *Restoration Quarterly* 40 (1998): 221–38.
Bleek, Friedrich. *An Introduction to the Old Testament*, edited by Johannes Friedrich Bleek and Adolf Kamphausen. London: Bell & Daldy, 1869.
Boda, Mark. *A Severe Mercy: Sin and Its Remedy in the Old Testament*. Siphrut: Literature and Theology of the Hebrew Scriptures 1. Winona Lake, IN: Eisenbrauns, 2009.
Boström, Lennart. *The God of the Sages: The Portrayal of God in the Book of Proverbs*. Stockholm: Almqvist & Wiksell International, 1990.
Bridges, Charles. *An Exposition of the Book of Proverbs*. London: Seeley, 1847.
Brown, William P. *Wisdom's Wonder: Character, Creation, and Crisis in the Bible's Wisdom Literature*. Grand Rapids, MI: Eerdmans, 2014.
Byargeon, Rick. 'The Structure and Significance of Prov 9:7-12'. *JETS* 40 (1997): 367–72.
Camp, Claudia V. *Wisdom and the Feminine in the Book of Proverbs*. Decatur, GA: Almond Press, 1985.

Carr, David McLain. *The Formation of the Hebrew Bible: A New Reconstruction.* New York: Oxford University Press, 2011.
Cheung, Simon. *Wisdom Intoned: A Reappraisal of the Genre 'Wisdom Psalms'.* LHBOTS 613. London: Bloomsbury T&T Clark, 2015.
Clifford, Richard. *Proverbs: A Commentary.* Louisville, KY: Westminster John Knox Press, 1999.
———. 'Reading Proverbs 10–22'. *Interpretation* 63 (2009): 242–53.
Clines, David. *Job 1–20.* WBC 17. Dallas, TX: Word Books, 1989.
Cohen, A. *Proverbs: Hebrew Text and English Translation with Introduction and Commentary.* London: Soncino, 1945.
Cook, Johann. *The Septuagint of Proverbs: Jewish and/or Hellenistic Proverbs? Concerning the Hellenistic Colouring of LXX Proverbs.* VTSup 69. Leiden: Brill, 1997.
Corley, T. J. J. 'An Intertextual Study of Proverbs and Ben Sira'. In *Intertextual Studies in Ben Sira and Tobit: Essays in Honor of Alexander A. Di Lella, O.F.M,* 155–82. CBQMS 38. Washington. D.C.: Catholic Biblical Association of America, 2004.
Cornill, Carl. *Einleitung in das Alte Testament.* Freiburg: J. C. B. Mohr, 1892.
Crenshaw, James. 'Sirach'. *NIB* 5.
Davison, W. T. *The Wisdom-Literature of the Old Testament.* London: Charles H. Kelly, 1900.
Delitzsch, Franz. *Biblical Commentary on the Proverbs of Solomon.* 2 vols. Translated by M. G. Easton. Edinburgh: T. & T. Clark, 1880.
Dell, Katharine. *The Book of Proverbs in Social and Theological Context.* Cambridge: Cambridge University Press, 2006.
Derousseaux, Louis. *La crainte de Dieu dans l'Ancien Testament: royauté, alliance, sagesse dans les royaumes d'Israël et de Juda.* Paris: Éditions du Cerf, 1970.
Dick, Michael. 'The Legal Metaphor in Job 31'. *CBQ* 41 (1979): 37–50.
Estes, Daniel J. *Hear, My Son: Teaching and Learning in Proverbs 1–9.* New Studies in Biblical Theology 4. Leicester: Apollos, 1997.
Ewald, Heinrich. *Die Poetischen Bücher des alten Bundes.* Gottingen: Vandenhoeck & Ruprecht, 1837.
Fleming, James. 'Some Aspects of the Religion of Proverbs'. *JBL* 51 (1932): 31–9.
Fox, Michael V. *Ecclesiastes: The Traditional Hebrew Text with the New JPS Translation.* Philadelphia: Jewish Publication Society, 2004.
———. 'Frame-narrative and Composition in the Book of Qohelet'. *Hebrew Union College Annual* (1977): 83–106.
———. *Proverbs 1–9: A New Translation with Introduction and Commentary.* AB 18A. New York: Doubleday, 2000.
———. *Proverbs 10–31: A New Translation with Introduction and Commentary.* AB 18B. New Haven: Yale University Press, 2009.
———. 'Words for Folly'. *Zeitschrift für Althebraistik* 10 (1997): 4–17.
———. 'Words for Wisdom'. *Zeitschrift für Althebraistik* 6 (1993): 149–65.
Frahm, Eckart. *Babylonian and Assyrian Text Commentaries: Origins of Interpretation,* Guides to the Mesopotamian Textual Record 5. Münster: Ugarit Verlag, 2011.
Frankenberg, W. 'Ueber Abfassungs-Ort und-Zeit, Sowie Art und Inhalt von Prov. I–IX'. *ZAW* 15 (1895): 104–32.
Fredericks, Daniel. *Ecclesiastes & the Song of Songs.* AOTC. Downers Grove, IL: InterVarsity Press, 2010.

Freuling, Georg. *'Wer eine Grube gräbt...': Der Tun-Ergehen-Zusammenhang und sein Wandel in der alttestamentlichen Weisheitsliteratur.* Neukirchen-Vluyn: Neukirchener Verlag, 2004.

Fuhs, Hans. *Sprichwörter.* Würzburg: Echter Verlag, 2001.

Gemser, Berend. 'The Instructions of 'Onchsheshonqy and Biblical Wisdom Literature'. In *Studies in Ancient Israelite Wisdom*, edited by James Crenshaw, 134–60. New York: KTAV, 1976.

Gerstenberger, Erhard. *Psalms: Part I: With an Introduction to Cultic Poetry.* Grand Rapids, MI: Eerdmans, 1988.

Gese, Hartmut. *Lehre und Wirklichkeit in der alten Weisheit: Studien zu den Sprüchen Salomos und zu dem Buche Hiob.* Tübingen: Mohr, 1958.

Gilbert, Maurice. *L'Antique sagesse d'Israël: Études sur Proverbes, Job, Qohélet et leurs prolongements.* Etudes Bibliques. Pendé, France: Gabalda, 2015.

Gilchrist, Margaret Odell. 'Proverbs 1–9: Instruction or Riddle'. *Proceedings, Eastern Great Lakes & Midwest Bible Society* (1984): 131–45.

Goldingay, John. 'The Arrangement of Sayings in Proverbs 10–15'. *JSOT* 19 (1994): 75–83.

———. *Psalms: Volume 1, Psalms 1–41.* BCOT. Grand Rapids: Baker Academic, 2006.

Gramberg, Karl. *Das Buch der Sprüche Salomo's neu übersetzt.* Leipzig: J. A. G. Weigel, 1828.

Habel, Norman. *The Book of Job: A Commentary.* OTL. London: SCM Press, 1985.

Hammond, Henry. *A Paraphrase and Annotations Upon the Books of the Psalms.* London: Royston, 1659.

Hausmann, Jutta. *Studien zum Menschenbild der älteren Weisheit (Spr 10ff.).* FAT 7. Tübingen: Mohr Siebeck, 1995.

Heim, Knut M. 'Coreferentiality, Structure and Context in Proverbs 10:1-5'. *Journal of Translation and Textlinguistics* 6 (1993): 183–209.

———. *Like Grapes of Gold Set in Silver: An Interpretation of Proverbial Clusters in Proverbs 10:1–22:16.* BZAW 273. Berlin: de Gruyter, 2001.

———. *Poetic Imagination in Proverbs: Variant Repetitions and the Nature of Poetry.* Winona Lake, IN: Eisenbrauns, 2013.

Herbert, A. S. 'The "Parable" (MĀŠĀL) in the Old Testament'. *Scottish Journal of Theology* 7 (1954): 180–96.

Hermisson, Hans-Jürgen. *Studien zur israelitischen Spruchweisheit.* Neukirchen-Vluyn: Neukirchener Verlag des Erziehungsvereins, 1968.

Hitzig, F. *Die Sprüche Salomo's.* Zürich: Orell, Füssli und Comp., 1858.

Hoglund, Kenneth. 'The Fool and the Wise in Dialogue: Proverbs 26:4-5'. In *Learning from the Sages: Selected Studies on the Book of Proverbs*, edited by Roy Zuck, 339–52. Grand Rapids, MI: Baker Books, 1995.

Hornung, Erik. *Conceptions of God in Ancient Egypt: The One and the Many.* Translated by J. Baines. London: Routledge & Kegan Paul, 1983.

Horst, Friedrich. *Hiob.* BKAT 16/1. Neukirchen-Vluyn: Neukirchener, 1968.

Jones, Edgar. *Proverbs and Ecclesiastes: Introduction and Commentary.* Torch Bible Commentaries. London: SCM Press, 1961.

Jones, Scott C. 'Wisdom's Pedagogy: A Comparison of Proverbs VII and 4Q184'. *VT* 53 (2003): 65–80.

Kayatz, Christa. *Studien zu Proverbien 1–9.* Neukirchen-Vluyn: Neukirchener Verlag, 1966.

Keefer, Arthur. *The Book of Proverbs and Virtue Ethics: Integrating the Biblical and Philosophical Traditions*. Cambridge: Cambridge University Press, forthcoming.

———. 'A Shift in Perspective: The Intended Audience and a Coherent Reading of Proverbs 1:1-7'. *JBL* 136 (2017): 103–16.

———. 'Sound Patterns as Motivation for Rare Words in Proverbs 1–9'. *JNSL* 43 (2017): 35–49.

Keil, Carl Friedrich, George C. M. Douglas, and Friedrich Bleek. *Manual of Historico-Critical Introduction to the Canonical Scriptures of the Old Testament*. 2 vols. Edinburgh: T. & T. Clark, 1869.

Kidner, Derek. *Psalms 1–72: An Introduction and Commentary on Books I and II of the Psalms*. TOTC. London: Inter-Varsity Press, 1973.

Kim, Hee Suk. 'Proverbs 1–9: A Hermeneutical Introduction to the Book of Proverbs'. PhD dissertation, Trinity International University, 2010.

King, Philip J., and Lawrence E. Stager. *Life in Biblical Israel*. Louisville, KY: Westminster John Knox Press, 2001.

Kitchen, Kenneth A. 'Biblical Instructional Wisdom: The Decisive Voice of the Ancient Near East'. In *Boundaries of the Ancient Near Eastern World: A Tribute to Cyrus H. Gordon*, edited by Meir Lubetski, Claire Gottlieb and Sharon R. Keller, 346–63. Sheffield: Sheffield Academic Press, 1998.

———. 'Proverbs and Wisdom Books of the Ancient Near East: The Factual History of a Literary Form'. *Tyndale Bulletin* 28 (1977): 69–114.

Kovacs, Brian W. 'Is There a Class-Ethic in Proverbs?' In *Essays in Old Testament Ethics*, edited by John Willis and James Crenshaw, 173–89. New York: KTAV, 1974.

Kynes, Will. *My Psalm Has Turned into Weeping: Job's Dialogue with the Psalms*. BZAW 437. Berlin: de Gruyter, 2012.

Laisney, Vincent Pierre-Michel. *L'Enseignement d'Aménémopé*. Studia Pohl: Series Maior 19. Roma: Pontificio Istituto Biblico, 2007.

Lang, Bernhard. *Wisdom and the Book of Proverbs: A Hebrew Goddess Redefined*. New York: Pilgrim Press, 1986.

Lelièvre, André. *La sagesse des Proverbes: Une leçon de tolérance*. Geneva: Labor et Fides, 1993.

Lichtheim, Miriam. *Late Egyptian Wisdom Literature in the International Context: A Study of Demotic Instructions*. OBO 52. Göttingen: Vandenhoeck & Ruprecht, 1983.

———. *Moral Values in Ancient Egypt*. OBO 155. Göttingen: Vandenhoeck & Ruprecht, 1997.

———. 'Observations on Papyrus Insinger'. In *Studien zu altägyptischen Lebenslehren*, edited by Erik Hornung and Othmar Keel, 283–306. Freiburg: Universitätsverlag, 1979.

Loader, James A. *Proverbs 1–9*. HCOT. Leuven: Peeters, 2014.

Longman III, Tremper. *Job*. Grand Rapids: Baker Academic, 2012.

———. *Proverbs*. BCOT. Grand Rapids, MI: Baker Academic, 2006.

Lyu, Sun Myung. *Righteousness in the Book of Proverbs*. FAT II/55. Tübingen: Mohr Siebeck, 2012.

Maier, Christl. *Die 'fremde Frau' in Proverbien 1–9: Eine exegetische und sozialgeschichtliche Studie*. Freiburg: Vandenhoeck & Ruprecht, 1995.

Mäkipelto, Ville. *Uncovering Ancient Editing: Documented Evidence of Changes in Joshua 24 and Related Texts*. BZAW 513. Berlin: de Gruyter, 2018.

McCreesh, Thomas P. *Biblical Sound and Sense: Poetic Sound Patterns in Proverbs 10–29*. Sheffield: JSOT Press, 1991.

McKane, William. 'Functions of Language and Objectives of Discourse According to Proverbs 10–30'. *La sagesse de l'Ancien Testament* (1979): 166–85.

———. *Proverbs: A New Approach.* OTL. London: SCM Press, 1970.

Meinhold, Arndt. *Die Sprüche.* Zürcher Bibelkommentare: Altes Testament 16. Zurich: Theologischer Verlag, 1991.

Miles, Johnny E. *Wise King – Royal Fool: Semiotics, Satire and Proverbs 1–9.* JSOTSup 399. London: T&T Clark, 2004.

Miller, John W. *Proverbs.* Scottdale, PA: Herald Press, 2004.

Milstein, Sara J. 'Reworking Ancient Texts: Revision through Introduction in Biblical and Mesopotamian Literature'. PhD dissertation, New York University, 2010.

———. *Tracking the Master Scribe: Revision through Introduction in Biblical and Mesopotamian Literature.* New York: Oxford University Press, 2016.

Moore, Rick D. 'A Home for the Alien: Worldly Wisdom and Covenantal Confession in Proverbs 30,1-9'. *ZAW* 106 (1994): 96–107.

Muntinghe, Hermann. *Die Sprüche Salomo's.* Frankfurt: Jäger, 1800.

Murphy, Roland E. *The Tree of Life: An Exploration of Biblical Wisdom Literature.* New York: Doubleday, 2002.

———. 'Wisdom and Creation'. *JBL* 104 (1985): 3–11.

Müller, Achim. *Proverbien 1–9: Der Weisheit Neue Kleider.* BZAW 291. Berlin: de Gruyter, 2000.

Müller, Reinhard, Juha Pakkala and R. B. ter Haar Romeny. *Evidence of Editing: Growth and Change of Texts in the Hebrew Bible.* Atlanta, GA: SBL, 2014.

Nel, Philip Johannes. *The Structure and Ethos of the Wisdom Admonitions in Proverbs.* Berlin: de Gruyter, 1982.

Newsom, Carol A. 'Models of the Moral Self: Hebrew Bible and Second Temple Judaism'. *JBL* 131 (2012): 5–25.

Owens, Daniel C. *Portraits of the Righteous in the Psalms: An Exploration of the Ethics of Book 1.* Eugene, OR: Pickwick, 2013.

Parkinson, R. B. *Poetry and Culture in Middle Kingdom Egypt: A Dark Side to Perfection.* London: Continuum, 2002.

Pemberton, Glenn D. 'The Rhetoric of the Father in Proverbs 1–9'. *JSOT* 30 (2005): 63–82.

Perdue, Leo G. *Proverbs.* Interpretation. Louisville, KY: John Knox Press, 2000.

———. *The Sword and the Stylus: An Introduction to Wisdom in the Age of Empires.* Grand Rapids, MI: Eerdmans, 2008.

———. *Wisdom & Creation: The Theology of Wisdom Literature.* Nashville, TN: Abingdon Press, 1994.

———. *Wisdom Literature: A Theological History.* Louisville, KY: Westminster John Knox Press, 2007.

Plöger, Otto. *Sprüche Salomos (Proverbia).* BKAT 17. Neukirchen-Vluyn: Neukirchener Verlag, 1984.

Pola, Thomas. 'Die Struktur von Proverbia 16,1-15'. *Biblische Notizen* 80 (1995): 47–72.

Poole, Matthew. *Annotations upon the Holy Bible.* New York: Robert Carter & Brothers, 1696.

Preuss, Horst Dietrich. *Einführung in die alttestamentliche Weisheitsliteratur.* Stuttgart: W. Kohlhammer, 1987.

Rad, Gerhard von. *Wisdom in Israel.* Trans. James Martin. London: SCM, 1972.

Richter, Hans-Friedemann. 'Hielt Agur sich für den Dümmsten aller Menschen? (Zu Prov 30,1-4)'. *ZAW* 113 (2001): 419–21.

Ringgren, Helmer. *Sprüche*. Göttingen: Vandenhoeck & Ruprecht, 1962.
Römheld, Diethard. *Wege der Weisheit: die Lehren Amenemopes und Proverbien 22,17–24,22*. BZAW 184. Berlin: de Gruyter, 1989.
Sæbø, Magne. 'From Collections to Book – A New Approach to the History of Tradition and Redaction of the Book of Proverbs'. In *Proceedings of the Ninth World Congress of Jewish Studies*, edited by Moshe Goshen-Gottstein and David Assaf, 99–106. Jerusalem: World Union of Jewish Studies, 1986.
———. *Sprüche*. Das Alte Testament Deutsch 16. Göttingen: Vandenhoeck & Ruprecht, 2012.
Sandoval, Timothy. *The Discourse of Wealth and Poverty in the Book of Proverbs*. Leiden: Brill, 2006.
———. 'Revisiting the Prologue of Proverbs'. *JBL* 126 (2007): 455–73.
Sasson, Ilana. 'The Book of Proverbs Between Saadia and Yefet'. *Intellectual History of the Islamic World* 1 (2013): 159–78.
Saur, Markus. 'Die Literarische Funktion und die Theologische Intention der Weisheitsreden des Sprüchebuches'. *VT* 61 (2011): 447–60.
Schäfer, Rolf. *Die Poesie der Weisen: Dichotomie als Grundstruktur der Lehr- und Weisheitsgedichte in Proverbien 1–9*. Neukirchen-Vluyn: Neukirchener Verlag, 1999.
Scherer, Andreas. *Das weise Wort und seine Wirkung: Eine Untersuchung zur Komposition und Redaktion von Proverbia 10,1–22,16*. Neukirchen-Vluyn: Neukirchener Verlag, 1999.
Schipper, Bernd. *Hermeneutik der Tora: Studien zur Traditionsgeschichte von Prov 2 und zur Komposition von Prov 1–9*. BZAW 432. Berlin: de Gruyter, 2012.
Schroer, Silvia. *Wisdom Has Built Her House: Studies on the Figure of Sophia in the Bible*. Collegeville, MN: Liturgical Press, 2000.
Schwab, Zoltan. *Toward an Interpretation of the Book of Proverbs: Selfishness and Secularity Reconsidered*. JTISup 7. Winona Lake, IN: Eisenbrauns, 2013.
Scoralick, Ruth. *Einzelspruch und Sammlung: Komposition im Buch der Sprichwörter Kapitel 10–15*. Berlin: de Gruyter, 1995.
Seidl, Theodore. 'Who Stands Behind the RSH' in Psalm 50:16A? The Ethical Testimony of Psalm 50:16-22'. In *Psalmody and Poetry in Old Testament Ethics*, edited by Dirk J. Human, 76–92. New York: T&T Clark, 2012.
Seow, Choon-Leong. *Ecclesiastes: A New Translation with Introduction and Commentary*. AB 18C. New York: Doubleday, 1997.
Shead, Andrew G. 'Ecclesiastes from the Outside In'. *Reformed Theological Review* 55 (1996): 24–37.
Shields, Martin A. 'Malevolent or Mysterious? God's Character in the Prologue of Job'. *Tyndale Bulletin* 61 (2010): 255–70.
Shupak, Nili. 'The Instruction of Amenemope and Proverbs 22:17–24:22 from the Perspective of Contemporary Research'. In *Seeking out the Wisdom of the Ancients: Essays Offered to Honor Michael V. Fox on the Occasion of His Sixty-Fifth Birthday*, edited by Ronald L. Troxel, Kelvin G. Friebel and Dennis R. Magary, 203–20. Winona Lake, IN: Eisenbrauns, 2005.
———. 'Positive and Negative Human Types in the Egyptian Wisdom Literature'. In *Homeland and Exile: Biblical and Ancient Near Eastern Studies in Honour of Bustenay Oded*, edited by Gershon Galil, Mark Geller and Alan Millard, 245–60. VTSup 130. Leiden: Brill, 2009.
———. *Where Can Wisdom Be Found? The Sage's Language in the Bible and in Ancient Egyptian Literature*. OBO 130. Fribourg: Academic Press Fribourg, 1993.

Sinnott, Alice M. *The Personification of Wisdom*. Aldershot, UK: Ashgate, 2005.
Sneed, Mark. 'White Trash Wisdom: Proverbs 9 Deconstructed'. *JHS* 7 (2007): 1–10.
Steinmann, Andrew E. 'The Structure and Message of the Book of Job'. *VT* 46 (1996): 85–100.
Stewart, Anne. *Poetic Ethics in Proverbs: Wisdom Literature and the Shaping of the Moral Self*. New York: Cambridge University Press, 2016.
Stuart, Moses. *A Commentary on the Book of Proverbs*. New York: M. W. Dodd, 1852.
Toy, C. H. *A Critical and Exegetical Commentary on the Book of Proverbs*. ICC. Edinburgh: T. & T. Clark, 1904.
Umbreit, Friedrich Wilhelm Carl. *Commentar über die Sprüche Salomo's*. Heidelberg: J. C. B. Mohr, 1826.
Van Leeuwen, Raymond C. 'The Background to Proverbs 30:4aα'. In *Wisdom, You Are My Sister: Studies in Honor of Roland E. Murphy, O.Carm., on the Occasion of His Eightieth Birthday*, edited by Michael L. Barré, 102–21. CBQMS 29. Washington, DC: Catholic Biblical Association of America, 1997.
———. 'The Book of Proverbs'. *NIB* 5.
Vergote, Joseph. 'La Notion de Dieu dans les Livres de Sagesse Égyptiens'. In *Les Sagesses du Proche-Orient Ancien: Colloque de Strasbourg 17–19 mai 1962*, 159–90. Paris: Presses Universitaires de France, 1963.
Viviers, Hennie. 'The "Body" and Lady Wisdom (Proverbs 1–9)'. *OTE* 18 (2005): 879–90.
Waltke, Bruce K. *The Book of Proverbs: Chapters 1–15*. NICOT. Grand Rapids, MI: Eerdmans, 2004.
———. *The Book of Proverbs: Chapters 15–31*. NICOT. Grand Rapids. MI: Eerdmans, 2005.
Weeks, Stuart. *Instruction and Imagery in Proverbs 1–9*. Oxford: Oxford University Press, 2007.
———. *An Introduction to the Study of Wisdom Literature*. London: T&T Clark, 2010.
Westermann, Claus. *Wurzeln der Weisheit: die ältesten Sprüche Israels und anderer Völker*. Göttingen: Vandenhoeck & Ruprecht, 1990.
Whybray, R. N. *The Composition of the Book of Proverbs*. Sheffield: Sheffield Academic Press, 1994.
———. *Proverbs*. London: Marshall Pickering, 1994.
———. *Wealth and Poverty in the Book of Proverbs*. JSOTSup 99. Sheffield: Sheffield Academic Press, 1990.
———. *Wisdom in Proverbs: The Concept of Wisdom in Proverbs 1–9*. London: SCM Press, 1965.
Wilbanks, Pete F. 'Non-proverb Proverbial Bookends: A Possible Lens for Viewing the Book of Proverbs'. Paper presented at the Southwest Regional Meeting of the ETS. New Orleans, LA, 26 March 2000.
Wildeboer, G. *Die Sprüche*. Freiburg: J. C. B. Mohr, 1897.
Yee, Gale. 'I Have Perfumed My Bed with Myrrh: The Foreign Woman *('issâ zarâ)* in Proverbs 1–9'. *JSOT* 43 (1989): 53–68.
Yoder, Christine. 'Forming 'Fearers of Yahweh': Repetition and Contradiction as Pedagogy in Proverbs'. In *Seeking out the Wisdom of the Ancients: Essays Offered to Honor Michael V. Fox on the Occasion of His Sixty-Fifth Birthday*, edited by Ronald L. Troxel, Kelvin G. Friebel and Dennis R. Magary, 167–83. Winona Lake, IN: Eisenbrauns, 2005.

———. 'The Objects of Our Affections: Emotions and the Moral Life in Proverbs 1–9'. In *Shaking Heaven and Earth: Essays in Honor of Walter Brueggemann and Charles B. Cousar*, edited by Kathleen O'Conner, E. Elizabeth Johnson, Christine Elizabeth Yoder and Stanley Saunders, 73–88. Louisville, KY: Westminster John Knox Press, 2005.

———. *Proverbs*. Abingdon Old Testament Commentaries. Nashville, TN: Abingdon Press, 2009.

Zabán, Bálint Károly. *The Pillar Function of the Speeches of Wisdom: Proverbs 1:20-33, 8:1-36, and 9:1-6 in the Structural Framework of Proverbs 1–9*. BZAW 429. Berlin: de Gruyter, 2012.

Zimmerli, Walther. 'Zur Struktur der Alttestamentlichen Weisheit'. *ZAW* 51 (1933): 177–204.

Index of References

Hebrew Bible/ Old Testament

Genesis
9.21	82
16.9	70
30.35	70
32.29	82
27.20	168
30.34	168

Exodus
21.20-27	89
23.5	89

Leviticus
19.17-18	89
24.2	168
24.7	168

Numbers
12.8	5
16	98
16.2	98, 115
16.35	98
24.3	117
24.15	117

Deuteronomy
1.27	135
4	37
4.1	121
4.6	121
7.25-26	174, 177, 180
7.26	174
8	37
8.5	23
8.12-14	121
9.9	23
11.2	23
19.11	89
26.19	98
28	37
30.11-14	121
33.8	58

Joshua
5.9	145
10.18	146

Judges
1–9	12
5.6	62
8.3	87
14.12-19	5

1 Samuel
2.3	170
2.9	58
14.33	146

2 Samuel
6	4
7.14-16	150
23	98
23.1	117
23.2	117
23.18	98
23.19	98

1 Kings
3.9	4
3.11	4
4.31	98, 99
6–7	4
10.1	5

1 Chronicles
5.24	98

2 Chronicles
9.1	5

Nehemiah
1	12
6.13	99
8.2-3	4
8.7	4
8.8	4
8.9	4

Job
1–2	8, 9
1.1-5	8
1.6–2.13	8
2.11-13	8
3–42	8
3.1–42.6	8
3.17	66
5.8	9
5.17	9, 150
6.8-10	119
6.13-15	9
6.24-25	119
6.24	4
6.30	119
7.11	87
7.17-21	119
8.3-6	9
8.6	168, 170
8.20	9
9.16	119
9.21-24	119
9.22	66
11	120

11.4	168	19	26	119	26
11.6	120	22	147	119.9	169
11.7-11	120	22.4-5	147	119.10-11	169
11.7	120	22.5-6	147	119.22	146
13.1-3	119	22.8-10	145	119.26	151
13.4-12	119	22.8	147	119.34	4
15.4-6	9	22.9	147	119.130	4
15.9-10	9	22.23-24	147	119.144	4
16.2-4	119	22.24-25	147	119.169	4
16.17	119, 168	24	66	139	120, 121
17.9	66	25.14	173	139.19-24	121
17.10	119	26	66	144.3	151
19.25-27	119	30.3	124		
21.7	119	32	181	*Proverbs*	
21.34	119	34	66	1–9	1, 3, 4, 7,
22.5	9	35.19	124		10–52,
22.21	9	37	26, 66,		55–7,
22.26	148		147, 148		59–64, 67,
23.11-12	119	37.1-6	147		68–76, 79,
27.5-6	119	37.4	147		82–4, 86,
27.10	148	37.5	145, 147		87, 89–92,
28	120	37.6	147		94, 96, 97,
28.12	120	37.7	66		100–103,
28.15-19	96	37.9	66		106, 107,
28.23	120	37.12	147		109, 111–
28.28	120	37.18	147		17, 121–
31.35-37	119	37.28-29	147		32, 134,
33.9	168	37.30	147		136–42,
34.34	52	37.40	147		145, 148,
38–39	119	50.16	66		150, 151,
40.2	119	51	181		160, 161,
40.7-8	119	51.4	170		163, 165–
42.7-17	8	51.6	170		7, 171,
		60.4	162		174–83
Psalms		60.6	162	1–5	63
1	12	68.13	96	1–2	60, 62
1.1	56	68.14	96	1	40, 42, 57,
1.2	82	73	121		59, 61–3
1.6	56	73.16	151	1.1–24.22	32
2	12	77.5	151	1.1–22.16	50, 51
3.7	73	77.6	87, 151	1.1-14	58
3.8	73	77.7	87	1.1-11	7
9.18	124	78.2	5	1.1-7	2–4, 6, 15,
9.19	124	89.31-32	181		16, 27–9,
15	66	89.32-33	181		59, 79, 80,
15.1-2	66	92	121		82, 123,
16.10	58	106.25	135		166, 182

Proverbs (cont.)		1.19	59–61, 70	2.7-9	56
1.1-6	6, 17	1.20-33	40, 57, 62,	2.7-8	58
1.1-2	7		79–82, 91,	2.7	122, 149
1.1	16, 29		102	2.8	62, 110,
1.2-7	19, 29, 59,	1.20-22	79		149
	123, 141	1.22-33	22, 129	2.9-11	109
1.2-6	19, 59,	1.22-27	80	2.9	58, 62,
	165	1.22-24	130		107
1.2-3	59	1.22	61, 80, 81,	2.10-11	107
1.2	2–7, 19,		174	2.11	83, 108
	123, 182	1.23	81, 87	2.12-19	107, 108
1.3-11	7	1.24	80, 81	2.12-15	62, 110
1.3	4, 7, 19,	1.25	80	2.12	56, 58, 66,
	59	1.26-28	82		108, 149
1.4-11	7	1.28-31	80	2.13-15	56, 58
1.4	6, 59, 79	1.28	80	2.13	62
1.5-6	59	1.29	80, 148	2.14	58
1.5	6, 59, 79,	1.30	80	2.15-16	58
	81	1.31	62	2.15	56, 62
1.6	2–7, 16,	1.32	61, 62, 80	2.16-19	58, 110
	19, 182	1.33	61, 81	2.16	108, 149
1.7-8	51	2–9	64	2.17-19	166
1.7	32, 59, 61,	2	26, 37, 39,	2.17	148
	80, 81,		42, 58, 59,	2.18-20	62
	110, 130,		62, 63, 68,	2.18	62
	148		102, 103,	2.19	56
1.8–9.18	29		106–11,	2.20-22	56, 61,
1.8	130, 165		122–5,		107–9
1.10–2.22	59		127, 141,	2.20	58, 62, 66,
1.10-19	39, 57,		149		108, 109
	59–61, 68,	2.1-22	166	2.21-22	18, 58,
	70, 80, 82,	2.1-11	108		108–10,
	90, 91	2.1-7	122		127, 147
1.10-14	62	2.1-5	109, 122,	2.21	109
1.10	57, 61,		166	3	26, 39, 68,
	180	2.1-4	107		149, 175
1.11	57	2.1	110	3.1-12	44, 148–
1.12	7	2.2-3	83		50, 160,
1.13-14	57	2.2	165		165, 179
1.13	57, 59,	2.4-5	110	3.1-4	98, 100
	129	2.5-6	148	3.1-3	148
1.14	59	2.5	107, 166	3.1	149
1.15	62	2.6-8	107	3.2	67
1.16-19	62	2.6	110, 123,	3.3-8	67
1.16	60, 130		139, 149,	3.3	23, 149
1.17	18		166	3.4-5	148
1.18	61	2.7-11	166	3.4	148, 171

3.5-12	149	3.32-33	148	5.21-23	171, 175,
3.5-10	149	3.32	171-73		178
3.5-9	19	3.33-35	18, 173	5.21-22	181
3.5-7	125	3.34	56, 171	5.21	62, 148,
3.5	148, 149,	4	11, 148		171, 175,
	165	4.1-13	139		176
3.6-12	148	4.1-9	130	5.22-23	59, 130,
3.6	63, 148,	4.1-4	139		171, 175
	149	4.1	165	5.22	171, 176,
3.7	138, 148,	4.2	130		181
	149	4.3-4	130	5.23	176
3.8	148, 149	4.5-6	130	5.31-32	177
3.9-10	149	4.7	139	6	26, 64
3.9	148	4.8-9	139	6.1-19	23, 29, 30,
3.11-12	44, 148,	4.10-27	139		39, 60, 90
	165	4.10-19	56, 59, 63	6.1-5	60
3.11	23, 149	4.11	62, 63	6.1	56
3.12	23, 149	4.13	130, 139	6.6-11	29, 60, 70,
3.13-18	149	4.14-19	60		71
3.13	56, 83,	4.14	60, 61	6.6	55, 62
	149	4.16-17	56	6.9	55
3.14	100	4.16	60	6.10-11	70
3.15	114	4.17	60	6.12-19	45, 60,
3.17	63	4.18-19	63		177–9
3.18	19, 32,	4.18	147	6.12-15	29
	149	4.20	165	6.14	56
3.19-26	44, 161,	4.21	165	6.16	148, 171
	166, 167,	4.26-27	63	6.17-19	60
	179	5	29, 45, 59,	6.17	56, 60
3.19-20	123		175, 176,	6.18	130
3.19	148		178–80	6.19	56
3.21-35	172	5.1-2	175	6.21	165
3.21-30	61	5.1	83, 165	6.25	174
3.21-26	149	5.3-14	176	6.29	56
3.21	172	5.3-6	175	6.34	56
3.23	63	5.5-6	62, 63	7–9	63
3.26	148, 149	5.7-14	175	7–8	19, 41, 42,
3.27-30	172	5.9	175		102, 103,
3.28-35	174	5.10	175		107, 108,
3.28-32	173	5.11-12	176		110, 111,
3.29	56, 172	5.12-14	175		127, 128,
3.31-35	39, 61	5.12-13	175, 176		141
3.31-32	45, 61,	5.13	165	7	11, 26, 43,
	171, 172,	5.15-20	175		103, 104,
	174, 176–	5.19	129		130, 148
	8, 180	5.20	32	7.1-3	103
3.31	63, 172			7.3	23, 165

Proverbs (cont.)		8.20	62, 105			102, 111–
7.4-5	103	8.21	105, 129			17, 125–8,
7.4	103, 104	8.22-36	161, 167,			131, 132,
7.5	103, 104		179			134–6,
7.6-23	103	8.22-31	11, 44,			138, 140,
7.7	61		105			145, 160,
7.8-23	61	8.22	148			174, 179,
7.8	62	8.23	105			180, 182
7.12-13	104	8.30	105	10–22	3	
7.13-20	104	8.32-36	56, 106	10–15	47, 48, 50,	
7.16-18	104	8.32	106, 107		51, 53, 55	
7.18	129	8.33	106, 107	10–11	47	
7.19	62	8.34-35	106	10	16, 55	
7.21-23	130	8.34	106	10.1–22.16	1–3, 5,	
7.21	104, 136	8.35	106, 148,		15–17,	
7.22-23	130		171		19, 23–5,	
7.24	103	8.36	104, 180		27–9, 31,	
7.25-27	103	9	29, 102,		33, 35–40,	
7.25	103		104, 129		42–4,	
7.26-27	104	9.4	22, 129		46–52,	
7.27	104	9.7-12	29		54–7, 59,	
8	26, 104,	9.7-9	18, 61		62, 64, 67,	
	106, 110,	9.7	56		69, 71–9,	
	139	9.10	32, 124,		82, 84, 87,	
8.1-21	105		148		92, 94–7,	
8.1-3	104	9.12	32		100, 101,	
8.1	104	9.16	22, 129		116, 128,	
8.2-3	104	10–31	3, 7, 18,		129, 141,	
8.3-4	104		19, 25–8,		143–7,	
8.5	4, 61		33, 35–8,		149–51,	
8.6-9	105		40, 43–5,		160, 161,	
8.6-7	130		94, 98,		163, 165–	
8.6	104		100, 111,		7, 171,	
8.7	104		115, 139,		177, 179,	
8.9	4		141, 167,		182	
8.10-11	104, 105,		169, 172,	10.1–11.13	51, 52	
	114		174, 179,	10.1-5	39, 49,	
8.10	105		182, 183		51–5, 63,	
8.11	105	10–30	141		67–9, 71,	
8.12	105	10–29	1–4, 7, 14,		72	
8.13	148		15, 18,	10.1-3	52, 71	
8.14-16	105		20–2, 24,	10.1	5, 16,	
8.15-16	56		26, 30–4,		51–3, 68,	
8.15	105		36, 38, 41,		76	
8.18-21	105		43, 44, 47,	10.2	39, 40,	
8.18	105		48, 75, 83,		51–4,	
8.19	105		88–92, 96,			

		67–70, 72, 76, 96	11.4	76, 93	12.18	76
			11.5-11	76	12.20	56, 76
10.3		52, 53, 56, 68, 74, 76, 174, 79, 143, 144	11.6	74	12.21	76
			11.9	56	12.22	76, 143, 144
			11.11	73		
			11.12	76, 79	12.23	54, 76, 79
10.4-5		49, 52, 53, 71	11.13	76, 87	12.24	76
			11.14	76	12.25	76
10.4		39, 40, 51–5, 67, 69–72, 76, 96	11.15	76	12.26	75, 76
			11.16	76	12.27	76
			11.17	76	12.28	76, 79
			11.18	76, 54	13.1	76, 79
10.5		49, 52, 76	11.19	76	13.2	76
10.6		76, 79	11.20	56, 76, 143, 144	13.3	76, 54
10.7		76, 98			13.4-6	76
10.8		24, 76, 83	11.21	76	13.5	174
10.9		62, 76	11.22	76, 133	13.6	170, 180
10.10-19		69	11.23	74, 76	13.7	54, 76
10.10		76	11.24-27	76	13.8	54, 76
10.11		76	11.28-31	76	13.9	76
10.12		76	11.30	19	13.10	76
10.13		76, 83	11.31	180	13.11	76
10.16		71, 170, 180	12.1-4	53	13.12	19
			12.1	76, 174	13.13-14	24
10.18		76, 79	12.2	2, 44, 56, 76, 99, 143, 144, 146	13.13	76
10.19		76, 83			13.14	76
10.20		76, 78, 79			13.15	76, 96
10.21		71, 76			13.16	76, 79
10.22		76, 143, 144	12.3-4	64	13.17	76
			12.3	76	13.18	54, 76
10.23-27		53	12.4	76	13.19-22	76
10.23		76, 79, 133	12.5	76, 79	13.19	133
			12.6	76	13.21-22	180
10.24		71, 76, 74	12.7	76	13.23	76
10.25		76	12.8	76, 56	13.24	76
10.26		76, 79	12.9-14	7	13.25	52, 76
10.27		76, 143, 144	12.9	76	14-115	47
			12.10	76, 79	14	137
10.29-31		76	12.11	76	14.1-4	53
10.29		143–6, 151	12.12	76, 174	14.1	62, 76
			12.13	76	14.2	76, 78, 137, 141, 143, 144
10.31		83	12.14	76		
10.32		76, 79, 91	12.15-17	76		
11.1		76, 143, 144	12.15-16	79	14.3	76
			12.15	133, 137, 169	14.4	76
11.2		76			14.5	76
11.3		76	12.16	88	14.6	76

Proverbs (cont.)		15.1	76, 77, 78, 85, 86	15.31–16.8	170
14.7-9	76			15.31-33	170
14.7-8	79	15.2-7	53	15.31	76
14.7	78	15.2	40, 76–9, 82–6, 88, 90, 91	15.32	54, 76
14.8	4, 132, 133, 137, 140			15.33–16.9	43, 145, 149, 151, 160, 161, 168
		15.3	76, 79, 143, 144, 169		
14.9	78, 79				
14.10	54, 76			15.33–16.7	145
14.11-12	138	15.4	19, 76, 85–7	15.33	76, 143, 144
14.11	76				
14.12-13	133	15.5	76, 78, 79	16.1–22.16	51
14.12	43, 76, 129, 133, 134, 137–40, 170	15.6	76, 69	16.1-7	143
		15.7	76, 83	16.1	2, 44, 76, 144, 146, 160, 171
		15.8-9	79		
		15.8	76, 143, 144	16.2-5	146, 148
14.13	76				
14.14	56, 76	15.9	73-76, 143, 144	16.2	45, 76, 144–6, 168–70, 172, 176–82
14.15	76, 79, 133, 137, 140				
		15.10	76		
		15.11	76, 143, 144		
14.16-18	76				
14.17	56	15.12	76, 79	16.3	2, 44, 45, 76, 144–8, 150, 151, 160, 161, 163, 165–7, 170, 179
14.19	76, 79	15.13	76, 87		
14.20	54, 76	15.14	76, 79		
14.21	76, 78, 180	15.15	56, 76		
		15.16	69, 76, 143, 144		
14.22	76				
14.23	76	15.17	76		
14.24	76	15.18	56, 76, 89	16.4-5	146
14.25-27	76	15.19	76, 79	16.4	78, 76, 79, 144, 146, 148
14.26	96, 143, 144	15.20	76		
		15.21	76, 79, 132–4	16.5-7	76
14.27	143, 144				
14.28	76	15.22	76	16.5	2, 44, 144, 146, 148, 167, 170
14.29	76, 78, 87, 89, 90	15.23	76		
		15.24	76		
14.30	76, 172	15.25	71, 76, 137, 143, 144	16.6-7	170
14.31	76, 143, 144			16.6	144, 146, 150, 170, 181
14.32	76	15.26	76, 78, 143, 144		
14.33	76, 79			16.7	144
14.34	73, 76, 170, 180	15.27	76	16.8	76, 145, 170
		15.28	76, 79, 83		
14.35	76	15.29	76, 143, 144	16.9	2, 44, 45, 76, 143–6, 160, 166,
15.1-7	86				
15.1-4	86	15.30	76		

Index of References

	167, 170, 178, 179, 182	17.6	76	18.17	76	
		17.7	76, 78, 79	18.18-22	76	
		17.8	76, 133	18.22	34, 143, 144	
16.10	76	17.9	76			
16.11	76, 143, 144	17.10	76, 79	18.23	54	
		17.11	76	18.24	76, 133	
16.12	76	17.12	76, 79	19.1	76, 79	
16.13	76	17.13	76	19.2	76, 180	
16.14	76	17.14	76	19.3	76, 143, 144	
16.15	76	17.15	76, 143, 144	19.4-7	76	
16.16	41, 42, 76, 94–7, 112–16, 127, 128, 141	17.16	76	19.5	56	
		17.17	54, 76	19.6	99	
		17.18	76, 79	19.8	76	
		17.19	76	19.9	76	
16.17	54, 76	17.20	56, 76	19.10	76, 78, 79	
16.18	76, 87	17.21	76	19.11	76, 176	
16.19	76, 87	17.22	76	19.12	76	
16.20	76, 143, 144, 151	17.23	76	19.13	76	
		17.24	76, 79, 133	19.14	76, 143, 144	
16.21	76, 133, 135, 136, 140	17.25	76	19.15	56, 76	
		17.26	76, 78, 79	19.16	24, 76	
16.22	76	17.27-28	54	19.17	143, 144	
16.23-24	135, 140	17.27	76, 78, 89	19.21	76, 143, 144	
16.23	76, 79	17.28	133			
16.24-25	133	18.2	40, 76, 78, 79, 82–5, 88, 90, 91, 174	19.22	76	
16.24	76, 52			19.23	143, 144	
16.25	76			19.24	48, 60, 76, 79	
16.26	76					
16.27-30	76	18.3	76	19.25	76	
16.27-28	54	18.4	76	19.28	76, 79	
16.27	76	18.5	76, 78, 79	19.29	76, 135	
16.28	76, 135	18.6-8	76	20–22	76	
16.31	76	18.7	135	20.1	76	
16.32	56, 76, 78, 87	18.8	43, 129, 134–41	20.2	76, 180	
				20.3-5	76	
16.33	76, 143, 144	18.9	76, 78, 79	20.6	76, 133	
		18.10	76, 98, 143–6, 151	20.7	76	
17.1	76			20.8	76	
17.2	76			20.9	76, 170, 180	
17.3	76, 143, 144	18.11	76			
		18.12	76	20.10	76, 143, 144	
17.4	56, 76, 79, 133	18.13	83			
		18.14	87	20.11	76, 168	
17.5	76, 143, 144	18.15	76	20.12	76, 143, 144	
		18.16	76, 133			

Proverbs (cont.)		21.19	76	22.17–29.27	87, 116, 161, 163, 165
20.13	76, 77	21.20	76		
20.14-16	76	21.21	76		
20.15	113	21.22	76	22.17–23.11	163–6
20.17	76, 132, 133	21.23	76	22.17-21	10, 161, 164, 165, 179
20.18	76	21.24	76, 79, 98, 135		
20.19	56, 76	21.25	76	22.17-18	10, 165
20.22-24	143	21.26-27	79	22.17	5, 32, 162, 165, 166
20.22	44, 144–6, 151	21.26	76		
		21.27	76, 78	22.18	162, 164
20.23	76, 144	21.28	76	22.19	3, 145, 161–7
20.24	76, 144	21.29	76		
20.25	76	21.30	76, 95, 96, 143, 144	22.20	162
20.26	76, 79			22.21	162
20.27	76, 135, 143, 144	21.31	76, 143, 144	22.23	161, 164
				22.28	71
20.28	76	22.1	41, 42, 76, 94, 95, 97–100, 102, 111–13, 115, 116, 127, 128, 141	23.4	166
20.29	76			23.10	10
20.30	76, 135			23.17-18	163
21.1-3	143			23.17	161, 166, 172, 174, 180
21.1	144				
21.2	76, 144, 168				
				24–29	32
21.3	2, 44, 76, 144, 146	22.2	54, 76, 95, 96, 143, 144	24.1	172, 174
				24.8	151
21.4	76, 79, 170, 180, 181			24.9	135, 170, 180, 181
		22.3	76		
		22.4	76, 95, 96, 143, 144	24.12	169
21.5	76			24.13-14	174
21.6	19, 69, 76	22.5	76	24.18	89, 161
21.7	76	22.6	76	24.19	174
21.8	76, 137, 168	22.7	54, 76	24.21	161
		22.8	76	24.23-34	32
21.9	76	22.9	76	24.23-131.31	32
21.10-12	76	22.10	76	24.23	32
21.10	74	22.11	76	24.30-34	71
21.11	76	22.12	76, 143, 144, 169	25–29	19
21.12	143			25.1–29.27	32
21.13	76, 144	22.13	48, 60, 78, 79	25.2	161
21.14	76, 133			25.12	52
21.15	74, 76, 174	22.14-16	76	25.22	161
		22.14	56, 62, 89, 143, 144	25.25	52
21.16	76			26.5	169
21.17	76	22.17–31.31	3, 98	26.12	169
21.18	76, 79, 91			26.20	135
				26.22-26	133

26.22	135	30.4-9	118	*Jeremiah*	
27.5	82	30.4	118–21,	13.11	98
27.7	133		124	15.16	136
28	26	30.5-9	126	23.18	173
28.3	54	30.5	118, 122	23.22	173
28.4	24	30.6	118, 121	31	26
28.5	161	30.9	98		
28.6	54	30.10-17	117	*Lamentations*	
28.7	24	30.10	135	1.19	124
28.9	24	30.12	170		
28.11	4, 169	30.13	96	*Daniel*	
28.24	176	30.15-33	32	1.4	123
28.25	161, 163	30.18-19	117	2.21	123
29	32	30.20-23	133	8.23	4, 5
29.1	3	30.20-21	96	8.27	4
29.5	133	30.20	117, 132	11.24	151
29.8	87	30.21-33	117		
29.9	88	31	18, 20, 28	*Hosea*	
29.11	40, 83,	31.1-9	24, 32	7.15	151
	87–90	31.1	32, 117		
29.13	161	31.10-31	32	*Nahum*	
29.20	87			1.9	151
29.22	87-89	*Ecclesiastes*			
29.23	87	1.1-11	8	*Habakkuk*	
29.25-26	161	1.3	8	2.6	5
29.25	163	1.12-18	8		
30–31	21	2.1-11	8	*Zechariah*	
30-131	32, 116,	2.11	8	3.19-20	98
	117, 126	4.13	52	9.3	96
30	26, 32, 42,	7.1	99, 115		
	116	8.8-10	138	Apocrypha	
30.1-14	32	9.2-6	138	*Ben Sira*	
30.1-9	3, 27, 32,	10.4	87	1.1-10	11
	42, 94,	12.10	162	1.11-30	11
	116, 117,			2.1–4.10	11
	119–27,			2.1	11
	141	*Isaiah*		3.12	11
30.1-6	138	1	12	4.1	11
30.1-4	124, 126	5.20-21	169	4.11-19	11
30.1-3	118	5.25	169	4.20	11
30.1	32, 117,	11.2	123	21.12-26	66
	126	28.9	4	22.7-15	66
30.2-3	122–4, 126	29.24	135	41.11-13	99
30.2	117, 123	38.18	124		
30.3	42, 117,	56–66	26		
	123, 125,				
	126, 128				

MISHNAH
Pirkei Avot
4.13   99

ANCIENT NEAR EASTERN
SOURCES
Amenemhet
i.2   10

Amenemope
III.9–IV.2   9, 10
III.17–IV.2   164
V.8-9   173
VII.7-10   164
IX.10–X.15   164
X.12-15   164
X.12-13   164
X.14-15   164
XIII.15–
  XIV.3   173
XIII.15-16   173
XIV.2-3   173
XV.20-21   173
XVIII.8–
  XIX.1   173
XX.3-6   171
XXVII.13-15   6

Ani
7.4-5   136
7.4   10
7.9-10   136

Ankhsheshonq
§1–4   10
5.10   64
6.3   64
6.13-15   64
13.3   64
13.9   64
14.8   64
16.5   64
26.9   64

Gilgamesh
124-136   12

Insinger
2.10   65
3.2-8   65
4.9   65
7.11   65
12.4   65
12.23   65
14.5   65
34.11-12   65
34.12-13   65
35.11-12   65

265   64
298-324   64
352   64
388   64
515   64
523-524   64
526   64
531-572   64
548-552   171
548   64
573-574   64
575-587   64

Merikare
115-116   65

Ptahhotep
i.51-60   10
1–50   9
37–42   9
39   65
55   64
68   64
115-116   171
140-144   64
167   64
250   64

Shuruppak
ll. 1-13   14
ll. 1-8   13, 14
ll. 1-3   14
ll. 7-8   14
ll. 8–13   10
ll. 9-13   14
ll. 78-87   13
ll. 148-157   13

The Teaching of a Man for his Son
1–3   10

Index of Authors

Adams, S. L. 16, 32, 33
Aitken, K. 50, 56, 75
Aletti, J.-N. 21, 22, 61, 129–31, 134, 139, 157
Alster, B. 2, 13
Ansberry, C. B. 10, 50, 117, 121, 165
Askin, L. 32

Balentine, S. 8
Bartholomew, C. G. 7, 8
Barucq, A. 118, 119
Bassoumboul, E.-N. 157, 172
Baumann, G. 157
Bertheau, E. 16
Bland, D. 101
Bleek, F. 16
Boda, M. 170, 175, 181
Boström. L. 157, 176
Bridges, C. 16
Brown, W. P. 20, 66, 107
Byargeon, R. 29

Camp, C. V. 18, 157
Carr, D. M. 30, 31
Cheung, S. 147
Clifford, R. 3, 60
Clines, D. 8
Cohen, A. 16
Cook, J. 32
Corley, T. J. J. 11
Cornill, C. 16
Crenshaw, J. 11

Davison, W. T. 5, 16
Delitzsch, F. 29, 84, 95, 117, 118, 124, 132, 146
Dell, K. 143, 157
Derousseaux, L. 150
Dick, M. 119
Douglas, G. C. M. 16

Estes, D. J. 101
Ewald, H. 16, 30, 99

Fleming, J. 101
Fox, M. V. 5–7, 18, 20, 21, 29, 30, 32, 47, 55, 58, 60, 61, 63, 81, 88, 99, 101, 105, 108, 111, 117, 121, 124, 135, 145, 155, 156, 158, 163, 164, 166, 178
Frahm, E. 2
Frankenberg, W. 46
Fredericks, D. 8
Freuling, G. 77
Fuhs, H. 53, 63

Gemser, B. 11
Gerstenberger, E. 66
Gese, H. 170
Gilberg, M. 101, 158
Gilchrist, M. O. 102
Goldingay, J. 52, 53, 147
Gramberg, K. 46, 144

Haar Romeny, R. B. ter 13
Habel, N. 8
Hammond, H. 15
Hausmann, J. 47, 48, 50, 65
Heim, K. M. 18, 29, 30, 47, 49, 53, 137, 143, 146
Henry, M. 15
Herbert, A. S. 5
Hermisson, H.-J. 46
Hitzig, F. 29, 30
Hoglund, K. 66
Hornung, E. 171, 173
Horst, F. 120

Jones, E. 17
Jones, S. C. 102

Kayatz, C. 11
Keefer, A. 6, 59, 79, 105, 133, 136, 148
Keil, C. F. 16
Kidner, D. 66
Kim, H. S. 20
King, P. J. 57
Kitchen, K. A. 11, 30
Koch, K. 181
Kovacs, B. W. 46
Kynes, W. 120

Laisney, V. P.-M. 164
Lang, B. 81, 102
Lelièvre, A. 144
Lichtheim, M. 10, 65
Loader, J. A. 4, 29, 62, 157
Longman III, T. 20, 53, 68, 119, 125, 162, 166
Lyu, S. M. 47, 50, 65, 73, 74, 101

Maier, C. 104, 176
Mäkipelto, V. 12
Martens, E. 152
McCreesh, T. P. 148
McKane, W. 5, 48, 59, 97, 143
Meinhold, W. 53, 97, 107, 109, 136, 140, 145, 153, 163, 171
Miles, J. E. 58
Miller, J. 144
Milstein, S. J. 12–14, 31
Mommer, P. 168, 178
Moore, R. D. 119
Müller, A. 29, 47
Müller, R. 13
Muntinghe, H. 16
Murphy, R. E. 16, 157

Negoiță, A. 170
Nel, P. J. 77
Newsom, C. A. 132

Owens, D. C. 66

Pakkala, J. 13
Parkinson, R. B. 9
Pemberton, G. D. 101
Perdue, L. G. 8, 30, 65
Plöger, O. 21, 29, 53, 58, 88, 89, 97, 124, 138, 158, 165, 170

Pola, T. 153
Poole, M. 15
Preuss, H. D. 18

Rad, G. von 153
Richter, H.-F. 126
Ringgren, H. 4, 16, 170
Römheld, D. 164

Sæbø, M. 17, 18, 29, 30, 33, 48, 87, 106, 108, 111, 121, 138, 155, 162
Sandoval, T. 5, 19, 105
Sasson, I. 15
Saur, M. 18
Schäfer, R. 29, 107, 109, 149, 156
Scherer, A. 29, 138, 145, 146, 148, 153
Schipper, B. 26, 27, 30, 37, 108–10, 121, 122, 125
Schroer, S. 16
Schultz, C. 169
Schwab, Z. 112
Scoralick, R. 47, 53
Seidl, T. 66
Seow, C.-L. 8
Shead, A. G. 8
Shields, M. A. 8
Shupak, N. 6, 47, 65, 135, 136, 163
Sinnott, A. M. 101
Sneed, M. 102
Stager, L. E. 57
Steinmann, A. E. 8
Stendeback, F. J. 169
Stewart, A. 107, 112, 174
Stuart, M. 16

Toy, C. H. 29, 30, 70, 97

Umbreit, F. W. C. 16

Van Leeuwen, R. C. 19, 29, 55, 57, 63, 119–21, 126
Vergote, J. 173
Viviers, H. 102

Waltke, B. K. 5, 18, 21, 29, 32, 52, 53, 55, 58–62, 68, 83, 86, 88, 92, 95, 97, 98, 106, 108, 138, 156, 157, 178
Weeks, S. 5, 10, 11, 21, 23–5, 29, 63, 102, 157, 158

Westermann, C. 113, 114, 153, 154
Whybray, R. N. 10, 11, 18, 19, 54, 57, 69, 101, 102, 135, 156, 165
Wilbanks, P. F. 102
Wildeboer, G. 17, 30, 138, 181

Yee, G. 102
Yoder, C. 18, 58, 59, 79, 81, 101

Zabán, B. K. 96, 101
Zimmerli, W. 19

www.ingramcontent.com/pod-product-compliance
Lightning Source LLC
Chambersburg PA
CBHW072236290426
44111CB00012B/2118